ne l

CHARLES FROHMAN

Charles Frohman:
Manager and Man
by *Isaac F. Marcosson*
and *Daniel Frohman*

With an Appreciation
by James M. Barrie

*Illustrated
with
Portraits*

New York and London
Harper & Brothers
M · C · M · X · V · I

To

The Theater
That Charles Frohman
Loved and Served

Nought I did in hate but all in honor!
HAMLET

Contents

Illustrations

ILLUSTRATIONS

Charles Frohman:

an

Appreciation

By James M. Barrie

*T*HE man who never broke his word. There was a great deal more to him, but every one in any land who has had dealings with Charles Frohman will sign that.

I would rather say a word of the qualities that to his friends were his great adornment than about his colossal enterprises or the energy with which he heaved them into being; his energy that was like a force of nature, so that if he had ever "retired" from the work he loved (a thing incredible) companies might have been formed, in the land so skilful at turning energy to practical account, for exploiting the vitality of this Niagara of a man. They could have lit a city with it.

He loved his schemes. They were a succession of many-colored romances to him, and were issued to the world not without the accompaniment of the drum, but you would never find him saying anything of himself. He pushed them in front of him, always taking

care that they were big enough to hide him. When
they were able to stand alone he stole out in the dark
to have a look at them, and then if unobserved his
bosom swelled. I have never known any one more
modest and no one quite so shy. Many actors have
played for him for years and never spoken to him, have
perhaps seen him dart up a side street because they
were approaching. They may not have known that it
was sheer shyness, but it was. I have seen him ordered
out of his own theater by subordinates who did not
know him, and he went cheerfully away. "Good men,
these; they know their business," was all his comment.
Afterward he was shy of going back lest they should
apologize.

At one time he had several theaters here and was
renting others, the while he had I know not how many
in America; he was not always sure how many himself.
Latterly the great competition at home left him no
time to look after more than one in London. But only
one anywhere seemed a little absurd to him. He once
contemplated having a few theaters in Paris, but on discovering that French law forbids your having more than
one he gave up the scheme in disgust.

A sense of humor sat with him through every vicissi-
tude like a faithful consort.

"How is it going?" a French author cabled to him on
the first night of a new play.

"It has gone," he genially cabled back.

Of a Scotch play of my own that he was about to
produce in New York, I asked him what the Scotch
would be like.

"You wouldn't know it was Scotch," he replied, "but
the American public will know."

AN APPRECIATION

He was very dogged. I had only one quarrel with him, but it lasted all the sixteen years I knew him. He wanted me to be a playwright and I wanted to be a novelist. All those years I fought him on that. He always won, but not because of his doggedness; only because he was so lovable that one had to do as he wanted. He also threatened, if I stopped, to reproduce the old plays and print my name in large electric letters over the entrance of the theater.

A VERY distinguished actress under his management wanted to produce a play of mine of which he had no high opinion. He was in despair, as he had something much better for her. She was obdurate. He came to me for help, said nothing could move her unless I could. Would not I tell her what a bad play it was and how poor her part was and how much better the other parts were and how absolutely it fell to pieces after the first act? Of course I did as I was bid, and I argued with the woman for hours, and finally got her round, the while he sat cross-legged, after his fashion, on a deep chair and implored me with his eyes to do my worst. It happened long ago, and I was so obsessed with the desire to please him that the humor of the situation strikes me only now.

For money he did not care at all; it was to him but pieces of paper with which he could make practical the enterprises that teemed in his brain. They were all enterprises of the theater. Having once seen a theater, he never afterward saw anything else except sites for theaters. This passion began when he was a poor boy staring wistfully at portals out of which he was kept by the want of a few pence. I think when he first saw a theater he clapped his hand to his heart, and certainly he was true to his first love. Up to the end it was still the same treat to him to go in; he still thrilled when the band struck up, as if that boy had hold of his hand.

*I*N a sense he had no illusions about the theater, knew its tawdriness as he knew the nails on his stages (he is said to have known every one). He would watch the performance of a play in some language of which he did not know a word and at the end tell you not only the whole story, but what the characters had been saying to one another; indeed, he could usually tell what was to happen in any act as soon as he saw the arrangement of the furniture. But this did not make him *blasé*—a strange word, indeed, to apply to one who seemed to be born afresh each morning. It was not so much that all the world was a stage to him as that his stage was a world, a world of the "artistic temperament"—that is to say, a very childish world of which he was occasionally the stern but usually indulgent father.

His innumerable companies were as children to him; he chided them as children, soothed them, forgave them, and certainly loved them as children. He exulted in those who became great names in that world and gave them beautiful toys to play with; but, great as was their devotion to him, it is not they who will miss him most, but rather the far greater number who never "made a hit," but set off like the rest to do it and fell by the way. He was of so sympathetic a nature, he understood so well the dismalness to them of being "failures," that he saw them as children with their knuckles to their eyes, and then he sat back cross-legged on his chair with his knuckles, as it were, to his

AN APPRECIATION

eyes, and life had lost its flavor for him until he invented a scheme for giving them another chance.

*A*UTHORS of to-day sometimes discuss with one another what great writer of the past they would like most to spend an evening with if the shades were willing to respond, and I believe (and hope) that the choice most often falls on Johnson or Charles Lamb. Lamb was fond of the theater, and I think, of all those connected with it that I have known, Mr. Frohman is the one with whom he would most have liked to spend an evening. Not because of Mr. Frohman's ability, though he had the biggest brain I have met with on the stage, but because of his humor and charity and gentle chivalry and his most romantic mind. One can conceive him as often, sitting at ease, far back in his chair, cross-legged, occasionally ringing for another ice, for he was so partial to sweets that he could never get them sweet enough, and sometimes he mixed two in the hope that this would make them sweeter.

I hear him telling stories of the stage as only he could tell them, rising now and roaming the floor as he shows how the lady of the play receives the declaration, and perhaps forgetting that you are the author of the play and telling you the whole story of it with superb gesture and gleaming eyes. Then back again cross-legged to the chair. What an essay Elia might have made of that night, none of it about the stories told, all about the man in the chair, the humorous, gentle, roughly educated, very fine American gentleman in the chair!

J. M. Barrie.

London, 1915.

Charles Frohman

Charles Frohman

I

A CHILD AMID THE THEATER

ONE evening, toward the close of the 'sixties, a plump, rosy-cheeked lad in his eighth year stood enthralled in the gallery of the old Niblo's Garden down on lower Broadway in New York. Far below him on the stage "The Black Crook"—the extravaganza that held all New York—unfolded itself in fascinating glitter and feminine loveliness. Deaf to his brother's entreaties to leave, and risking a parental scolding and worse, the boy remained transfixed until the final curtain. When he reached home he was not in the least disturbed by the uproar his absence had caused. Quite the contrary. His face beamed, his eyes shone. All he could say was:

"I have seen a play. It's wonderful!"

The boy was Charles Frohman, and such was his first actual experience in the theater—the institution that he was to dominate in later years with far-flung authority.

To write of the beginnings of his life is to become almost immediately the historian of some phase of amusement. He came from a family in whom the love of mimic art was as innate as the desire for sustenance.

About his parents was the glamour of a romance as tender as any he disclosed to delighted audiences in the world of make-believe. His father, Henry Frohman, was both idealist and dreamer. Born on the pleasant countryside that encircles the town of Darmstadt in Germany, he grew up amid an appreciation of the best in German literature. He was a buoyant and imaginative boy who preferred reading plays to poring over tiresome school-books.

One day he went for a walk in the woods. He passed a young girl of rare and appealing beauty. Their eyes met; they paused a moment, irresistibly drawn to each other. Then they went their separate ways. He inquired her name and found that she was Barbara Strauss and lived not far away. He sought an introduction, but before it could be brought about he left home to make his fortune in the New World.

He was eighteen when he stepped down the gangplank of a steamer in New York in 1845. He had mastered no trade; he was practically without friends, so he took to the task which so many of his co-religionists had found profitable. He invested his modest financial nest-egg in a supply of dry goods and notions and, shouldering a pack, started up the Hudson Valley to peddle his wares.

Henry Frohman had a magnetic and fascinating personality. A ready story was always on his lips; a smile shone constantly on his face. It was said of him that he could hypnotize the most unresponsive housewife into buying articles she never needed. Up and down the highways he trudged, unmindful of wind, rain, or hardship.

New York was his headquarters. There was his home and there he replenished his stocks. He made friends quickly. With them he often went to the German theater. On one of these occasions he heard of a family named Strauss that had just arrived from Germany. They had been shipwrecked near the Azores, had endured many trials, and had lost everything but their lives.

"Have they a daughter named Barbara?" asked Frohman.

"Yes," was the reply.

Henry Frohman's heart gave a leap. There came back to his mind the picture of that day in the German woods.

"Where do they come from?" he continued, eagerly.

On being told that it was Darmstadt, he cried, "I must meet her."

He gave his friend no peace until that end had been brought about. He found her the same lovely girl who had thrilled him at first sight; he wooed her with ardor and they were betrothed.

He now yearned for a stable business that would enable him to marry. Meanwhile his affairs had grown. The peddler's pack expanded to the proportion of a wagonload. Then, as always, the great West held a lure for the youthful. In some indescribable way he got the idea that Kentucky was the Promised Land of business. Telling his fiancée that he would send for her as soon as he had settled somewhere, he set out.

But Kentucky did not prove to be the golden country. He was advised to go to Ohio, and it was while driving across the country with his line of goods that he came upon Sandusky. The little town on the shores of a smiling lake appealed to him strongly. It reminded him of the home country, and he remained there.

He found himself at once in a congenial place. There was a considerable German population; his ready wit and engaging manner made him welcome everywhere. The road lost its charm; he turned about for an occupation that was permanent. Having picked up a knowledge of cigar-making, he established a small factory which was successful from the start.

This fact assured, his next act was to send to New York for Miss Strauss, who joined him at once, and they were married. These were the forebears of Charles Frohman —the exuberant, optimistic, pleasure-loving father; the serene, gentle-eyed, and spacious-hearted woman who was to have such a strong influence in the shaping of his character.

The Frohmans settled in a little frame house on Lawrence Street that stood apart from the dusty road. It did not even have a porch. Unpretentious as it was, it became a center of artistic life in Sandusky.

Henry Frohman had always aspired to be an actor. One of the first things he did after settling in Sandusky was to organize an amateur theatrical company, composed entirely of people of German birth or descent. The performances were given in the Turner Hall, in the German tongue, on a makeshift stage with improvised scenery. Frohman became the directing force in the production of Schiller's and other classic German plays, comic as well as tragic.

Nor was he half-hearted in his histrionic work. One night he died so realistically on the stage that his eldest son, who sat in the audience, became so terrified that he screamed out in terror, and would not be pacified until his parent appeared smilingly before the curtain and assured him that he was still very much alive.

Frohman's business prospered. He began to build up trade in the adjoining country. With a load of samples strapped behind his buggy, he traveled about. He usually took one of his older sons along. While he drove, the boy often held a prompt-book and the father would rehearse his parts. Out across those quiet Ohio fields would come the thrilling words of "The Robbers," "Ingomar," "Love and Intrigue," or any of the many plays that the amateur company performed in Sandusky.

He even mixed the drama with business. Frequently after selling a bill of goods he would be requested by a customer, who knew of his ability, to recite or declaim a speech from one of the well-known German plays.

It was on his return from one of these expeditions that Henry Frohman was greeted with the tidings that a third son had come to bear his name. When he entered that little frame house the infantile Charles had made his first entrance on the stage of life. It was June 17, 1860, a time fateful in the history of the country, for already the storm-clouds of the Civil War were brooding. It was pregnant with meaning for the American theater, too, because this lusty baby was to become its Napoleon.

Almost before Charles was able to walk his wise and far-seeing mother, with a pride and responsibility that maintained the best traditions of the mothers in Israel, began to realize the restrictions and limitations of the Sandusky life.

"These boys of ours," she said to the husband, "have no future here. They must be educated in New York. Their careers lie there."

Strong-willed and resolute, she sent the two older sons, one at a time, on to the great city to be educated and make their way. The eldest, Daniel, went first, soon followed by Gustave. In 1864, and largely due to her insistent urging, the remainder of the family, which included the youthful Charles, packed up their belongings and, with the proceeds of the sale of the cigar factory, started on their eventful journey to New York.

They first settled in one of the original tenement houses of New York, on Rivington Street, subsequently moving to Eighth Street and Avenue D. Before long they moved over to Third Street, while their fourth residence was almost within the shadow of some of the best-known city theaters.

Henry Frohman had, as was later developed in his son Charles, a peculiar disregard of money values. Generous to a fault, his resources were constantly at the call of the needy. His first business venture in New York—a small soap factory on East Broadway—failed. Later he became part owner of a distillery near Hoboken, which was destroyed by fire. With the usual Frohman financial heedlessness, he had failed to renew all his insurance policies, and the result was that he was left with but a small surplus. Adversity, however, seemed to trickle from him like water. Serene and smiling, he emerged from his misfortune.

The only business he knew was the cigar business. With the assistance of a few friends he was able to start a retail cigar-store at what was then 708 Broadway. It was below Eighth Street and, whether by accident or design, was located in the very heart of the famous theatrical district which gave the American stage some of its greatest traditions.

A CHILD AMID THE THEATER

To the north, and facing on Union Square, was the Rialto of the day, hedged in by the old Academy of Music and the Union Square Theater. Down Broadway, and commencing at Thirteenth Street with Wallack's Theater, was a succession of more or less historic playhouses. At Eighth Street was the Old New York Theater; a few doors away was Lina Edwins's; almost flanking the cigar-store and ranging toward the south were the Olympic, Niblo's Garden, and the San Francisco Minstrel Hall. Farther down was the Broadway Theater, while over on the Bowery Tony Pastor held forth.

Thus the little store stood in an atmosphere that thought, breathed, and talked of the theater. It became the rendezvous of the well-known theatrical figures of the period. The influence of the playhouses extended even to the shop next door, which happened to be the original book-store founded by August Brentano. It was the only clearing-house in New York for foreign theatrical papers, and to it came Augustin Daly, William Winter, Nym Crinkle, and all the other important managers and critics to get the news of the foreign stage.

It was amid an environment touching the theater at every point that Charles Frohman's boyhood was spent. He was an impulsive, erratic, restless child. His mother had great difficulty in keeping him at school. His whole instinct was for action.

Gustave, who had dabbled in the theatrical business almost before he was in his teens, naturally became his mentor. To Charles, Gustave was invested with a rare fascination because he had begun to sell books of the opera in the old Academy of Music on Fourteenth Street, the forerunner of the gilded Metropolitan Opera

House. Every night the chubby Charles saw him forge
forth with a mysterious bundle, and return with money
jingling in his pocket. One night, just before Gustave
started out, the lad said to him:

"Gus, how can I make money like you?"

"I'll show you some night if you can slip away from
mother," was the brother's reply.

Unrest immediately filled the heart of Charles. Gustave had no peace until he made good his promise. A
week later he stole away after supper with his little
brother. They walked to the Academy, where the old
Italian opera, "The Masked Ball," was being sung.
With wondering eyes and beating heart Charles saw
Gustave hawk his books in the lobby, and actually sell
a few. From the inside came the strains of music, and
through the door a glimpse of a fashionable audience.
But it was a forbidden land that he could not enter.

Fearful of the maternal scolding that he knew was in
store, Gustave hurried his brother home, even indulging
in the unwonted luxury of riding on the street-car, where
he found a five-dollar bill. The mother was up and
awake, and immediately began to upbraid him for
taking out his baby brother at night, whereupon Gustave
quieted the outburst by permitting Charles to hand over
the five-dollar bill as a peace offering.

From that hour life had a new meaning for Charles
Frohman. He had seen his brother earn money in the
theater; he wanted to go and do likewise. The opportunity was denied, and he chafed under the restraint.

In the afternoon, when he was through with the school
that he hated, the boy went down to his father's store
and took his turn behind the counter. Irksome as was
this work, it was not without a thrilling compensation,

because into the shop came many of the theatrical personages of the time to buy their cigars. They included Tony Pastor, whose name was then a household word, McKee Rankin, J. K. Mortimer, a popular Augustin Daly leading man, and the comedians and character actors of the near-by theaters.

Here the magnetic personality of the boy asserted itself. His ready smile and his quick tongue made him a favorite with the customers. More than one actor, on entering the shop, asked the question: "Where is Charley? I want him to wait on me."

In those days much of the theatrical advertising was done by posters displayed in shop-windows. To get these posters in the most conspicuous places passes were given to the shopkeepers, a custom which still holds. The Frohman store had a large window, and it was constantly plastered with play-bills, which meant that the family was abundantly supplied with free admission to most of the theaters in the district. The whole family shared in this dispensation, none more so than Henry Frohman himself, who could now gratify his desire for contact with the theater and its people to an almost unlimited extent. His greatest delight was to distribute these passes among his boys. They were offered as rewards for good conduct. Charles frequently accompanied his father to matinées at Tony Pastor's and the other theaters. Pastor and the elder Frohman were great pals. They called each other by their first names, and the famous old music-hall proprietor was a frequent visitor at the shop.

But Charles became quite discriminating. Every Saturday night he went down to the old Théâtre Comique, where Harrigan and Hart were serving their apprenticeship for the career which made them the most famous Irish team of their time. The next morning at break-fast he kept the family roaring with laughter with his imitations of what he had seen and heard. Curiously enough, Tony Hart later became the first star to be presented by Charles Frohman.

All the while the boy's burning desire was to earn money in the theater. He nagged at Gustave to give him a chance. One day Gustave saw some handsome souvenir books of "The Black Crook," which was then having its sensatioal run at Niblo's Garden. He found that he could buy them for thirty-three cents by the half-dozen, so he made a small investment, hoping to sell them for fifty cents in the lobby of the theater. That evening he showed his new purchases to Charles.

Immediately the boy's eyes sparkled. "Let me see if I can sell one of them!"

"All right," replied Gustave; "I will take you down to Niblo's to-night and give you a chance."

The boy could scarcely eat his supper, so eager was he to be off. Promptly at seven o'clock the two lads (Charles was only eight) took their stand in the lobby, but despite their eager cries each was able to sell only a single copy. Gustave consoled himself with the fact that the price was too high, while Charles, with an optimism that never forsook him, answered, "Well, we have each sold one, anyhow, and that is something."

Charles's profit on this venture was precisely seventeen cents, which may be regarded as the first money he ever earned out of the theater.

But this night promised a sensation even greater. As the crowd in the lobby thinned, the strains of the overture crashed out. Through the open door the little boy saw the curtain rise on a scene that to him represented the glitter and the glory of fairyland. Beautiful ladies danced and sang and the light flashed on brilliant costumes. With their unsold books in their hands, the two boys gazed wistfully inside. Charles, always the aggressor, fixed the doorkeeper with one of his winning smiles, and the doorkeeper succumbed. "You boys can slip in," he said, "but you've got to go up in the balcony." Up they rushed, and there Charles stood delighted, his eyes sparkling and his whole face transfigured.

During the middle of the second act Gustave tugged at his sleeve, saying: "We'll have to go now. You follow me down."

With this he disappeared and hurried home. When he arrived he found the home in an uproar because Charles had not come back. Gustave ran to the theater, but the play was over, the crowd had dispersed, and the building was deserted. With beating heart and fearful of disaster to his charge, he rushed back to see Charles, all animation and excitement, in the midst of the family group, regaling them with the story of his first play. He had remained to the end.

That thrilling night at "The Black Crook," his daily contact with the actors who came into the store, his frequent visits to the adjoining playhouses, fed the fire of his theatrical interest. The theater got into his very blood.

A great event was impending. Almost within stone's-throw of the little cigar-store where he sold stogies to Tony Pastor was the Old New York Theater, which, after the fashion of that time, had undergone the evolution of many names, beginning with the Athenæum, and continuing until it had come under the control of the three famous Worrell sisters, who tacked their name to it. Shortly after the New Year of 1869 they produced the extravaganza "The Field of the Cloth of Gold," in which two of them, Sophie and Jane, together with Pauline Markham, one of the classic beauties of the time, appeared. Charles had witnessed part of this extravaganza one afternoon. It kindled his memories of "The Black Crook," for it was full of sparkle and color. Charles and Gustave had made the acquaintance of Owen, the doorkeeper. One afternoon they walked over to the theater and stood in the lobby listening to a rehearsal.

Owen, who knew the boys' intense love of the theater, spoke up, saying: "We need an extra page to-night. How would you like to go on?"

Both youngsters stood expectant. They loved each other dearly, yet here was one moment where self-interest must prevail. Charles fixed the doorkeeper with his hypnotic smile, and he was chosen. Almost without hearing the injunction to report at seven o'clock, Charles ran back to the store, well-nigh breathless with expectancy over the coming event. With that family feeling which has marked the Frohmans throughout their whole life, Gustave hurried down-town to notify their eldest brother to be on hand for the grand occasion.

Charles ate no supper, and was at the stage-door long before seven. Rigged up in a faded costume, he carried a banner during the performance. His two elder brothers sat in the gallery. All they saw in the entire brilliant spectacle was the little Charles and his faded flag.

Charles got twenty-five cents for his evening's work, and brought it home bubbling with pride. To his great consternation he received a rebuke from his mother and the strong injunction never to appear on the stage again.

This was Charles Frohman's first and only appearance on any stage. In the years to come, although he controlled and directed hundreds of productions, gave employment to thousands of actors in this country, England, and France, and ruled the destinies of scores of theaters, he never appeared in a single performance. Nor had he a desire to appear.

It will be recalled that in one way or another a great many passes for the theater found their way into the hands of the elder Frohman, who, in his great generosity of heart, frequently took many of the neighboring children along. He was the type of man who loves to bestow pleasure. But this made no difference with Charles. He was usually able to wring an extra pass from the bill-poster or some of the actors who frequented the store. Hence came about his first contract, and in this fashion: At that time Gustave Frohman was a famous cyclist. He was the first man to keep a wheel stationary, and he won prizes for doing so. He had purchased his bicycle with savings out of the theatrical earnings, and his bicycle and his riding became a source of great envy to Charles, who asked him one night if he would teach him how to ride.

"Yes," replied Gustave, "I'll teach you if you will make a contract with me to provide five dollars' worth of passes in return."

"Good!" said Charles, and the deal was closed.

Gustave kept his word, and down in Washington Place, in front of the residence of old Commodore Vanderbilt, Charles learned to ride. He kept his part of the contract, too, and delivered five dollars' worth of passes ahead of schedule time.

One of Gustave's cycling companions was the son of George Vandenhoff, the famous reader. Through him he met the father, who engaged him to post his placards for his series of lectures on Dickens. Charles accompanied Gustave on these expeditions, and got his first contact with theatrical advertising. Frequently he held the ladder while Gustave climbed up to hang a placard. Charles often employed his arts to induce an obdurate shopkeeper to permit a placard in his window. These cards were not as attractive as those of the regular theaters and it took much persuasion to secure their display. Charles sometimes sat in the box-office of Association Hall, where the Vandenhoff lectures were given and where Gustave sold tickets. It was here that Charles got his introduction to the finance of the theater.

These days in the early 'seventies were picturesque and carefree for Charles. The boy was growing up in an atmosphere that, unconsciously, was shaping his whole future life. In the afternoon he continued his service behind the counter, hearing the actors tell stories of their triumphs and hardships. Often he slipped next door to Brentano's, where he was a welcome visitor and where he pored over the illustrations in the theatrical journals.

Life at the store was not without incident. Among those who came in to buy cigars were the Guy brothers, famous minstrels of their time. They were particular chums of Gustave, and they likewise became great admirers of the little Charles. At the boys' request they would step into the little reception-room behind the store and practise their latest steps to a small but appreciative audience. This was Charles Frohman's first contact with minstrelsy, in which he was to have such an active part later on.

Strangely enough, music and moving color always fascinated Charles Frohman. At that time, for it was scarcely more than a decade after the Civil War, there were many parades in New York, and all of them passed the little Broadway cigar-store. To get a better view, Charles frequently climbed up on the roof and there beheld the marching hosts with all their tumult and blare. Here it was, as he often later admitted, that he got his first impressions of street-display and brass-band effects that he used to such good advantage.

A picturesque friendship of those early days was with the clock - painter Washburn, perhaps the foremost worker of that kind in this country. He painted the faces of all the clocks that hung in front of the jewelers' shops in the big city. He always painted the time at 8.17½ o'clock, and it became the precedent which most clock-painters have followed ever since.

Charles watched Washburn at work. One reason for his interest was that it dealt with gilt. The old painter took such a fancy to the lad that he wanted him to become his apprentice and succeed him as the first clock-face painter of his time. But this work seemed too slow for the future magnate.

Now came the first business contact of a Frohman with the theater, and here one encounters an example of that team-work among the Frohman brothers by which one of them invariably assisted another whenever opportunity arose. Frequently they created this opportunity themselves. To Gustave came the distinction of being the first in the business, and also the privilege of bringing into it both of his brothers. Having hovered so faithfully and persistently about the edges of theatricals, Gustave now landed inside.

It was at the time of the high-tide of minstrelsy in this country—1870 to 1880. Dozens of minstrel companies, ranging from bands of real negroes recruited in the South to aggregations of white men who blacked their faces, traveled about the country. The minstrel was the direct product of the slave-time singer and entertainer. His fame was recognized the world over. The best audiences at home, and royalty abroad, paid tribute to his talents. Out of the minstrel ranks of those days emerged some of the best known of our modern stars—men like Francis Wilson, Nat Goodwin, Henry E. Dixey, Montgomery and Stone, William H. Crane, and scores of others.

One of the most famous organizations of the time was Charles Callender's Original Georgia Minstrels, hailing from Macon, Georgia, composed entirely of negroes and headed by the famous Billy Kersands. Ahead of this show was a mulatto advance-agent, Charles Hicks. He did very well in the North, but when he got down South he faced the inevitable prejudice against doing business with a negro. Callender needed some one to succeed him. A man whom Gustave Frohman had once befriended, knowing of his intense desire to enter the profession, recommended him for the position, and he got it.

All was excitement in the Frohman family. At last the fortunes of one member were definitely committed to the theater, and although it was a negro minstrel show, it meant a definite connection with public entertainment.

No one, not even Gustave himself, felt the enthusiasm

so keenly as did little Charles, then twelve years old. He buzzed about the fortunate brother.

"Do you think you can get me a job as programmer with your show?" he asked.

"No," answered the new advance-agent. "Don't start in the business until you can be an agent or manager."

On August 2, 1872, Gustave Frohman started to Buffalo to go ahead of the Callender Minstrels. Charles followed his brother's career with eager interest, and he longed for the time when he would have some connection with the business that held such thrall for him.

Life now lagged more than ever for Charles. He chafed at the service in the store; he detested school; his one great desire was to earn money and share in the support of the family. His father urged him to prepare for the law.

"No," he said, "I won't be a lawyer. I want to deal with lots of people."

Charles frequently referred to Tony Pastor. "He's a big man," he would often say. "I would like to do what he is doing."

A seething but unformed aspiration seemed to stir his youthful breast. Once he heard his eldest brother recite some stanzas of Alexander Pope, in which the following line occurs:

The whole, the boundless continent is ours.

This line impressed the lad immensely. It became his favorite motto; he wrote it in his sister's autograph-album; he spouted it on every occasion; it is still to be found in his first scrap-book framed in round, boyish hand.

Now the singular thing about this sentiment is that

17

he never quoted it correctly. It was a life-long failing. His version—and it was strangely prophetic of his coming career—was:

The whole—the boundless earth—is mine.

Meanwhile, Daniel Frohman had gone from *The Tribune* to work in the office of *The New York Graphic*, down in Park Place near Church Street. *The Graphic* was the aristocrat of newspapers—the first illustrated daily ever published anywhere. With the usual family team-work, Daniel got Charles a position with him in 1874. He was put in the circulation department at a salary of ten dollars a week, his first regular wage. It was a position with which personality had much to do, for one of the boy's chief tasks was to select a high type of newsboy equipped to sell a five-cent daily. His genial manner won the boys to him and they became his loyal co-workers.

With amazing facility he mastered his task. Among other things, he had to count newspapers. It was before the day of the machine enumerator, and the work had to be done by hand. Charles developed such extraordinary swiftness that patrons in the office often stopped to watch him. In throwing papers over the counter it was necessary to be accurate and positive, and here came the first manifestation of his dogged determination. He never lost his cunning in counting papers, and sometimes, when he was rich and famous, he would take a bundle of newspapers, to help a newsboy in the street, and run through them with all his old skill and speed.

Though his fingers were in the newspapers, his heart yearned for the theater. This ambition was heightened by the fact that his brother Daniel, having heeded the lure of Gustave, joined the Callender Minstrels as advance-agent, while Gustave remained back with the show. Slowly but surely the theater was annexing the Frohman boys. In the summer of 1874 Charles was drawn into its charmed circle, and in a picturesque fashion.

It was the custom for minstrel companies and other theatrical combinations to rent theaters outright during the dull summer months. The playhouses were glad to get the rental, and the organizations could remain intact during what would otherwise be a period of disorganization and loss. Gustave, therefore, took Hooley's Theater in Brooklyn for summer minstrel headquarters, and on a memorable morning in July Charles was electrified to receive the following letter from him:

> *You can begin your theatrical career in the box-office of Hooley's Theater in Brooklyn. Take a ferry and look at the theater. Hooley is going to rent it to us for the summer. Your work will begin as ticket-seller. You will have to sell 25, 50, and 75 cent tickets, and they will all be hard tickets, that is, no reserved seats. Get some pasteboard slips or a pack of cards and practise handling them. Your success will lie in the swiftness with which you can hand them out. With these rehearsals you will be able to do your work well and look like a professional.*

Charles immediately bought a pack of the thickest playing-cards he could find and began to practise with them. Soon he became an expert shuffler. Often he used his father's cigar counter for a make-believe box-office sill, and across it he handed out the pasteboards to imaginary patrons. A dozen times he went over to Brooklyn and gazed with eager expectancy at the old theater, destined, by reason of his association with it, to be a historic landmark in the annals of American amusement.

He wrote Gustave almost immediately:

I will be ready when the time comes.

That great moment arrived the first Monday in August, 1874. Charles could scarcely contain his impatience. So well had the publicity work for the performance been done by the new advance-agent that when the boy (he was just fourteen) raised the window of the box-office at seven o'clock there was a long line waiting to buy tickets. The final word of injunction from Gustave was:

"Remember, Charley, you must be careful, because you will be personally responsible for any shortage in cash when you balance up."

The house was sold out. When Gustave asked him, after the count-up, if he was short, the eager-faced lad replied:

"I am not short—I am fifty cents over!"

"Then you can keep that as a reward for your good work," said Gustave.

Callender was on hand the opening night. He watched the boy in the box-office with an amused and lively interest. When Charles had finished selling tickets, Callender stepped up to him with a smile on his face and said:

"Young fellow, I like your looks and your ways. You and I will be doing business some day."

A CHILD AMID THE THEATER

During this engagement, and with the customary spirit of family co-operation, Gustave said to Charles: "You can give your sister Rachel all the pennies that come in at the Wednesday matinée." At this engagement very little was expected in the way of receipts at a midweek matinée.

But Gustave did not reckon with Charles. With an almost uncanny sense of exploitation which afterward enabled him to attract millions of theater-goers, the boy kept the brass-band playing outside the theater half an hour longer than usual. This drew many children just home from school, and they paid their way in pennies. The receipts, therefore, were unexpectedly large. When sister Rachel came over that day her beaming brother filled her bag with coppers.

The summer of 1874 was a strenuous one for Charles Frohman. By day he worked in *The Graphic* office, only getting off for the matinées; at night he was in the box-office at Hooley's in Brooklyn, his smiling face beaming like a moon through the window. He was in his element at last and supremely happy. When the season ended the Callender Minstrels resumed their tour on the road and Charles went back to the routine of *The Graphic* undisturbed by the thrill of the theater.

He was developing rapidly. Daily he became more efficient. The following year he was put in charge of a branch office established by *The Graphic* in Philadelphia. Now came his second business contact with the theater. Callender's Minstrels played an engagement at Wood's Museum, and Daniel came on ahead to bill the show. Charles immediately offered his services. His advice about the location of favorite "stands" was of great service in getting posters displayed to the best advantage. It was the initial expression of what later amounted to a positive genius in the art of well-directed bill-board posting.

While prowling around Philadelphia in search of amusement novelty—a desire that remained with him all his life—Charles encountered a unique form of public entertainment which had considerable vogue. It was Pepper's "Ghost Show," and was being shown in a small hall in Chestnut Street.

The "Ghost Show" was an illusion. The actors seemed to be on the stage. In reality, they were under the stage, and their reflection was sent up by refracting mirrors. This enabled them (in the sight of the audience) to appear and disappear in the most extraordinary fashion. People apparently walked through one another, had their heads cut off, were shown with daggers plunged in their breasts. The whole effect was weird and thrilling.

This show impressed Charles greatly, as the unusual invariably did. It gave him an idea. When Charles Callender joined his minstrel show at Philadelphia, young Frohman went to him with this proposition:

"I believe," he said with great earnestness, "that there is money in the 'Ghost Show.' The trouble with it now is that it is not being properly advertised. If you will let me have a hundred dollars, I will take charge of it and I think we can make some money out of it. It won't interfere with my work with *The Graphic*."

Charles, who seldom left anything to chance, had already made an arrangement with the manager of the show to become his advertising agent.

Callender, who liked the boy immensely, readily consented and gave him the required money, thus embarking Charles on his first venture with any sort of capital.

Unfortunately, the show failed. Charles maintained that the Philadelphians lacked imagination, but with his usual optimism he was certain that it would succeed on the road. When he approached Callender again and offered to take it out on the road the minstrel magnate slapped him on the shoulder and said:

"All right, my boy. If you say so, I believe you. You can take the show out and I'll back you."

Charles counseled with Gustave, who continued as his theatrical monitor. Eagerly he said:

"I've got a great chance. Callender is going to back me on the road with the 'Ghost Show.'"

"No," said Gustave, firmly, "your time has not come. Wait, as I told you before, until you can go out ahead of a show as agent."

Bitter as was the ordeal, Charles took his brother's advice, and the "Ghost Show" was abandoned to its fate.

II

EARLY HARDSHIPS ON THE ROAD

THE Christmas of 1876 was not a particularly merry one for Charles Frohman. The ardent boy, whose brief experience in Hooley's box-office had fastened the germ of the theater in his system, chafed at the restraint that kept him at a routine task. But his deliverance was at hand.

Shortly before the close of the old year Gustave quit the Callender Minstrels. With a capital of fifty-seven dollars he remained in Chicago, waiting for something to turn up. One day as he sat in the lobby of the old Sherman House he was accosted by J. H. Wallick, an actor-manager who had just landed in town with a theatrical combination headed by John Dillon, a well-known Western comedian of the time. They were stranded and looking for a backer.

"Will you take charge of the company?" asked Wallick.

"I've only got fifty-seven dollars," said Gustave, "but I'll take a chance."

Between them they raised a little capital and started on a tour of the Middle West that was destined to play a significant part in shaping the career of Charles. In the company besides John Dillon were his wife, Louise Dillon (afterward the ingénue of Daniel Frohman's Lyceum Company); George W. Stoddart, brother of

HARDSHIPS ON THE ROAD

J. H. Stoddart of A. M. Palmer's Company, his wife and his daughter, Polly Stoddart, who married Neil Burgess; John F. Germon; Mrs. E. M. Post, and Wesley Sisson. Their repertory consisted of two well-worn but always amusing plays, "Our Boys" and "Married Life."

Gustave was to remain with the company until they reached Clinton, Iowa. After that he was to go ahead while Wallick was to remain with the company. When Gustave was about to leave, the company protested. He had won their confidence, and they threatened to strike. What to do with Wallick was the problem.

"Why not make him stage-manager?" suggested Dillon.

"All right," said Gustave, "but who is to go ahead of the show?"

The company was gathered on the stage of the Davis Opera House. Gustave scratched his head. Then he turned quickly on the group of stage folk and said:

"I've got some one for you. I'll wire my brother Charles to come on and be advance-agent."

Thus it came about that from a little Iowa town there flashed back to New York on a memorable morning in January, 1877, the following telegram from Gustave to Charles Frohman:

> *Your time has come at last. Am wiring money for ticket to St. Paul, where you begin as agent for John Dillon. Will meet you 2 A.M. at Winona, where you change cars and where I will instruct.*

Charles happened to be at home when this telegram came. It was the first he had ever received. With trembling hands he tore it open, his rosy face broke into a seraphic smile, and the tears came into his eyes. He

3

rushed to his mother, threw his arms around her, and gasped:

"At last I'm in the business!"

He lost no time in starting. With a single grip-sack, which contained his modest wardrobe, the eager boy started on his first railroad journey of any length into the great West. It was the initial step of what, from this time on, was to be a continuous march of ever-widening importance.

Begrimed but radiant, the boy stepped from a day-coach at two o'clock in the morning at Winona. No scene could have been more desolate. Save for the station-master and a solitary brakeman there was only one other person on hand, and that individual was the faithful Gustave, who advanced swiftly through the gloom and greeted his brother enthusiastically.

Charles was all excitement. He had not slept a wink. It was perhaps the longest and most irksome journey he ever took. He was bubbling with the desire to get to work.

The two brothers went to a hotel where Gustave had a room, and there they sat for four hours. It is a picture well worth keeping in mind: the pleased older boy, eager to get his brother started right; the younger lad all ears, and his eyes big with wonder and anticipation. There was no thought of food or rest. Gustave was enthusiastic about the company. He said to his brother:

"Why, Charley, we've got real New York actors, and our leading lady, Louise Dillon, has a genuine sealskin coat. That coat will get us out of any town. You've got no 'Ghost Show' amateurs to handle now, but real actors and actresses."

Then came an announcement that startled the boy, for Gustave continued:

"Your salary is to be twenty-five dollars a week and hotel bills, but you must not spend more than one dollar and a half a day for meals and room."

In this dingy room of an obscure hotel in a country town Charles Frohman got his first instructions in practical theatrical work. Perhaps the most important of this related to bill-posting. In those days it was a tradition in theatrical advertising that whoever did the most effective bill-posting in a town got the audience. Most of the publicity was done with posters. An advance-agent had to be a practical bill-poster himself. To get the most conspicuous sites for bills and to keep those bills up until the attraction played became the chief task of the advance-agent. The provincial bill-posters were fickle and easily swayed. The agent with the most persuasive personality, sometimes with the greatest drinking capacity, won the day.

All this advice, and much more, was poured by Gustave into the willing ears of the youthful Charles. No injunction laid on that keen-eyed boy in the gray dawn of that historic morning back in the 'seventies was more significant than these words from his elder brother:

"Your success in handling the bill-poster does not lie through a barroom door. Give him all the passes he wants, but never buy him a drink."

That those words sank deeply into Charles Frohman is shown by the fact that he seldom drank liquor. His chief tipple through all the coming crowded years was never stronger than sarsaparilla, soda-water, or lemonade.

The task ahead of Charles would have staggered

any but the most dauntless enthusiasm. Among other things, as Gustave discovered, there was no route for the company after St. Paul, which was to be played the following week.

"You must discover new towns and bill them," he said. "Get what printing you want. The printers have been instructed to fill orders from you."

The hours sped on. Charles asked a thousand questions, and Gustave filled him with facts as dawn broke and day came. It was nearly seven o'clock, time for his train for St. Paul to leave. Charles would not hear of having breakfast. He was too full of desire to get to work.

Among other things, Charles carried a letter from Gustave to Wallick, who was temporarily ahead of the show, which said:

> *This is my brother Charles, who will take the advance in your place.*

The first word that came from the young advance-agent announced action, for he wired:

> *All right with Wallick. Have discovered River Falls.*

River Falls, it happened, had been "discovered" before and abandoned, but Charles thought he was making route history.

Charles immediately set to work with the extraordinary energy that always characterized him. The chief bill-poster in St. Paul was named Haines. Charles captured him with his engaging smile, and he became a willing slave. It was Haines who taught him how to post bills.

Later on when Gustave arrived with the show, he spoke of the boy with intense pride. He said:

"I have taught your brother Charley how to post bills. He took to it like a duck to water. He didn't mind how much paste he spattered over himself. His one desire was to know how to do the job thoroughly. I am going to make him the greatest theatrical agent in the world."

Curiously enough, Haines lived to be a very old man, and in the later years of his life he was able to stick up the twenty-eight-sheet stands that bore in large type the name of the little chubby protégé he had introduced to the art of bill-posting back in the long ago.

At St. Paul Charles had opposition—a big musical event at Ingersoll Hall—and this immediately tested his resource. He got his printing posted in the best places, went around to the newspaper offices and got such good notices that John Dillon was inspired to remark that he had never had such efficient advance work. It is interesting to remember that at this time Charles Frohman was not yet eighteen years old.

Now came the first evidence of that initiative which was such a conspicuous trait in the young man. He had come back to see the performances of his company, and had watched them with swelling pride. Several times he said, and with pardonable importance:

"What *we* need is a new play. *We* must have something fresh to advertise."

The net result of this suggestion was that his brother obtained the manuscript of "Lemons," a comedy that, under the title of "Wedlock for Seven," had been first produced at Augustin Daly's New Fifth Avenue Theater in New York. A copy of the play was sent on to

Charles to enable him to prepare the presswork for it, and it was the first play manuscript he ever read. "Lemons" vindicated Charles's suggestion, because it added to the strength of the repertory and brought considerable new business.

Charles took an infinite pride in his work. He was eager for suggestions, he worked early and late, and when the season closed at the end of June he was a full-fledged and experienced advance-agent. With his brother he reached Chicago July 4th. In the lobby of Hooley's Theater he was introduced to R. M. Hooley, who, after various hardships, again controlled the theater which bore his name, now Powers' Theater. Out of that chance meeting came a long friendship and a connection that helped in later years to give Charles Frohman his first spectacular success, for it was Mr. Hooley who helped to back "Shenandoah."

On July 5th, six months after he had left the East for his first start, Charles appeared at his mother's home in New York, none the worse for his first experience on the road.

Charles was soon eager for the next season. Gustave had signed a contract with John Dillon to take him out again, this time as part owner of the company. He and George Stoddart agreed to put up two hundred and fifty dollars each to launch the tour of the Stoddart Comedy Company with John Dillon as star. Charles was to continue as advance-agent.

It was a long summer for the boy. When August arrived and the time came to start west there was a financial council of war. Gustave counted on getting his capital from members of the family, but no money was forthcoming. Daniel had received no salary from Callender, and the great road project seemed on the verge of failure. Charles was disconsolate. But the mother of the boys, ever mindful of their interest, said, in her serene way:

"I can get enough money to send you to Chicago and I will put up some lunches for you."

Charles was eagerly impatient to start. He nagged at his brother:

"Gus, when do we start for Chicago? Do we walk?"

He was sent down-town to find out the cheapest route, and he returned in great excitement, saying:

"The cheapest way is over the Baltimore & Ohio, second class, but it is the longest ride. We can ride in the day-coach, and even if we have no place to wash we will get to Chicago, and that is the main thing."

When they reached Chicago the first of the long chain of disasters that was to attend them on this enterprise developed.

Stoddart was penniless. The two hundred and fifty dollars that he expected to contribute to the capital of the new combination was swept away in the failure of the Fidelity Bank. He had looked forward to Gustave for help, and all the while Gustave, on that long, toilsome journey west, was hoping that his partner would provide the first railroad fares. So they sat down and pooled their woes, wondering how they could start their tour, with Charles as an interested listener.

Every now and then he would chirp up with the question:

"How do I get out of town?"

Finally Gustave, always resourceful, said:

"You don't need any money, Charley. I've got railroad passes for you, and you can give the hotels orders on me for your board and lodging."

It was a custom in those days for advance-agents to give orders for their obligations—hotel, rent of hall, bill-posting, and baggage—upon the company that followed. Hotels in particular were willing to accept orders on the treasurer of a theatrical company about to play a date, because, in the event of complete failure, there was always baggage to seize and hold.

So, armed with passes and with the optimism of youth and anticipation, Charles set forth on what became in many respects the most memorable road experience in his life. The first town he billed was Streator, Illinois. Then he hurried on to Ottawa and Peoria, where they were to play during fair week, which was the big week of the year. Misfortune descended at Streator, for despite the lavish display of posters and the ample advance notice that Charles lured the local editors into publishing, the total receipts on the first night were seventy-seven dollars. This, and more, had already been pledged before the curtain went up, and Gustave was not even able to pay John Dillon his seven dollars and seventy cents, which represented his ten per cent. of the gross receipts.

By "traveling on their baggage," which was one of the expedients of the time and a custom which has not entirely passed out of use, the company got to Ottawa, where Charles joined them. Here, in a comic circumstance, he first developed the amazing influence that he was able to exert on people.

Although an admirable actor with a large following and the most delightful and companionable of men, John Dillon had one unfortunate failing. He was addicted to drink, and, regardless of consequences, he would periodically succumb to this weakness. At Ottawa, the town crowded with visitors for the annual fair, Dillon fell from grace. The bill for the evening was "Lemons," and there was every indication that the house would be sold out. The receipts were badly needed, too.

Late in the afternoon came the terrifying news that Dillon lay stupefied from liquor in his room. Everybody save Charles was in despair. Dillon had conceived a great fancy for Charles, and he was deputized to take the actor in hand, get him to the theater, and coerce him through the play.

Charles responded nobly. He aroused the star, took him to the theater in a carriage, and stood in the wings throughout the whole performance, coaching and inspiring his intoxicated star. By an amusing circumstance, Dillon was required to play a drunken scene in "Lemons." He performed this part with so much realism that the audience gave him a great ovation. The real savior of that performance was the chubby lad who stood in the wings with beating heart, fearful every moment that Dillon would succumb.

New and heavier responsibilities now faced Charles Frohman. The company was booked to play a week in Memphis, Tennessee, the longest and most important stand of the tour. In those days the printers who supplied the traveling companies with advertising matter were powers to be reckoned with. When the supply of printing was cut off the company was helpless.

Charles H. McConnell, of the National Printing Company, who supplied the Stoddart Company with paper, was none too confident of the success of that organization. When he heard of the Memphis engagement he insisted that Gustave, who was older and more experienced, be sent ahead to pave the way. Charles was sent back to manage the company, and now came his first attempt at handling actors. He rose to the emergency with all his characteristic ingenuity.

He began at Champaign, Illinois. The first test of his resource came at a one-night stand—Waupaca, Iowa—where "Lemons" was billed as a feature. The prospects for a big house were good. Board and railroad fare seemed assured, when just before supper-time John F. Germon, one of the company, approached Charles in great perturbation.

"We can't play to-night. Mrs. Post is sick."

Mrs. Post played the part of the old woman in the play, and it was a very important rôle.

Charles Frohman only smiled, as he always did in an emergency. Then he said to Germon:

"You're a member of the well-known Germon family, aren't you? Then live up to its reputation and play the part yourself."

"But how about my mustache?" asked Germon.

"I will pay for having it shaved off," replied Frohman. The net result was that Germon sacrificed his mustache, played the part acceptably without any one in the audience discovering that he was a man masquerading as an old woman. Charles put Wallick, who was acting as stage-manager, in Germon's part. Thus the house was saved and the company was able to proceed.

With his attractive ways and eternal thoughtfulness Charles captivated the company. He supplied the women with candy and bought peanuts for the men. On that trip he developed his fondness for peanuts that never forsook him. He almost invariably carried a bag in his pocket. When he could not get peanuts he took to candy.

A great friendship struck up between Frohman and Stoddart, who, in a way, was a character. He played the violin, and when business was bad and the company got in the dumps Stoddart added to their misfortunes by playing doleful tunes on his fiddle. But that fiddle had a virtue not to be despised, because it was Stoddart's bank. In its hollow box he secreted his modest savings, and in more than one emergency they were drawn on for company bed and board. When the organization reached Memphis Charles had so completely won the affections of the company that they urged him to stay on with them. But business was business, and he had to go on in advance.

Charles now went ahead to "bill" Texas. The reason for the expedition was this:

In Memphis business was so bad that the manager of the theater there advised Gustave to send the company through Texas, where, he assured them, there would be no opposition, and they would have the state to themselves. This advice proved to be only too true, for the company not only had the state to itself, but the state for a time held the company fast—in the unwilling bonds of financial misfortune.

The plan was to play the best towns in Texas and then go back through the Middle West, where John Dillon had a strong following, and where it was hoped the season could close with full pockets. Up to this time the company had received salaries with some degree of regularity. But from this time on they were to have a constantly diminishing acquaintance with money, for hard luck descended upon them the moment they crossed the frontiers of the Lone Star State.

It was about this time that Charles Callender, at the solicitation of Gustave, purchased an interest in the Stoddart Comedy Company for a hundred-dollar bill. This bill was given to Charles as a "prop." In those days the financial integrity of the legitimate theatrical combination was sometimes questioned by hard-hearted hotel-keepers. The less esthetic "variety" troupes, minstrel shows, and circuses enjoyed a much higher credit. An advance-agent like Charles sometimes found difficulty in persuading the hotel people to accept orders on the company's treasurer.

With characteristic enterprise Charles used the hundred-dollar bill as a symbol of solvency. He flashed it on hotel-keepers and railway agents in the careless way that inspired confidence, and, what was more to the point, credit. He carried this hundred-dollar bill for nearly a month. Often when asked to pay his board bill he would produce the note and ask for change. Before the startled clerk could draw his breath he would add:

"Perhaps it might be best if I gave you an order on the treasurer."

This always served to get him out of town without spending cash for hotel bills.

Texas was still a rough country, and Charles's reckless display of the hundred-dollar bill once gave him a narrow escape from possible death. He had made the usual careless display of wealth at a small hotel in Calvert. The bad man of the town witnessed the performance and immediately began to shadow the young advance-agent. When Charles retired to his room he found, to his dismay, that there was no lock on the door. He had a distinct feeling that a robbery would be attempted, so he quietly left the hotel and spent the night riding back and forth on the train between Calvert and Dallas. This cost him nothing, for he had a pass.

At Galveston occurred an unexpected meeting. Daniel Frohman, who was ahead of Callender's Minstrels, had arrived in town by boat from New Orleans (there being no railway connection then) to book his show for the next week. On arriving at the Tremont Opera House he was surprised to see Charles writing press notices in the box-office.

"What are you doing here?" he asked. "I thought you were in Tennessee."

Charles walked to the window and said, with great pride, "We play here all next week."

"Have you got the whole week?" asked Daniel.

"Yes," was the reply.

"But can't you give me Monday or Tuesday night?" asked Daniel.

"Impossible," replied Charles, haughtily.

"All right," said Daniel, in friendly rivalry, "then I will have to hire Turner Hall and knock you out for two nights with our brass-band parade."

Charles then came out into the lobby and confessed that his company was up against it, and that it meant bread and butter and possibly the whole future of the company if he could only play Galveston.

"We are coming here on our trunks," he said, "and we've got to get some money."

Daniel immediately relented. He arranged with the railroad to delay the train and thus make a connection which would carry his company on through to the interior. He booked Galveston for the second week following. This left the week in question free to Charles, who breathed easier.

Charles now went on and billed Sherman, Houston, and Dallas. At Dallas the hard luck that had gripped the company the moment it left Memphis descended more vigorously than before. Dillon not only fell from grace again, but disappeared. Gustave Frohman had vowed that he would discharge him if he went on another spree, and he kept his word. They were in a real predicament, with star gone, business bad, and practically stranded a thousand miles from home.

Charles, who frequently came back to join the company, was the one bright spot of those precarious days, for he never lost his optimism or his smile.

"What we need," he said at a council of war in Dallas, "is a new play. I have been reading in the *New York Clipper* about one called 'Pink Dominoes.' I think it is just the thing for us to do. In fact, I have already sent for a copy of it."

The play arrived the next day, and when George Stoddart read it to him the young agent bubbled with laughter and said:

"It's bound to be a big success."

It was decided to put on "Pink Dominoes" at Houston. Charles remained behind and watched the rehearsals, the first of the kind he had ever seen. Contrary to all expectations, Houston was shocked by the play. The audience literally "walked out" and the run of one night ended.

Misfortunes now crowded thick and fast. Salaries had ceased entirely, and it was with the utmost difficulty that the company proceeded on its way. As a crowning hardship, Callender repented of his bargain and withdrew the much-used and treasured hundred-dollar bill.

When Charles met Gustave in Seguin he said: "We're up against a hard proposition. The people want John Dillon. It's hard to book an attraction without a star."

In this statement Charles Frohman expressed a truth that he afterward made one of his theatrical axioms, for he became the leading exponent of the star system, and developed, in fact, into the king of the star-makers.

Charles rose supreme over the hardships that filled his colleagues with gloom. Many a night, in order to save hotel bills, he slept on a train as it shunted back and forth between small towns. He always turned up in the morning smiling and serene, with cheer for his now discouraged and almost disgruntled colleagues.

Louise Dillon's sealskin sack rendered heroic service during these precarious days. It was almost literally worn out as collateral. As Gustave had predicted, it got the company out of town on more than one occasion. A little incident will indicate some of the ordeals of that stage of the tour. At Hempstead a "norther" struck the town and the temperature dropped. Wesley Sisson caught a hard cold and concluded to get what he called "a good sweat." He had scarcely made his preparations and settled himself in bed when he heard a rap at the door and a voice said, "Open up."

'Who's that?" asked Sisson.

"Charley," was the reply. "Let me in. There isn't a spare bed in this house and I am freezing to death."

"All right," said Sisson, "but you don't want to come in here, because I am trying to sweat to death."

"Great Scott!" yelled Frohman, "that's what I want to do."

Sisson let him in and he remained all night.

Everywhere Charles Frohman drew people to him. The first time he booked Houston he made friends with Colonel McPherson, who owned the Perkins Opera House and the inevitable saloon alongside. The old manager—a rather rough customer who had killed his man—was a great casino-player, and Charles beguiled several hours with him one night at a game while waiting for a train.

In one of the company's darkest hours he said to Stoddart:

"I've got an idea. Let's play Houston."

"But we've just been there," said Stoddart.

"Never mind," said Charles. "I'll fix it."

The next day he turned up at Houston and went to Colonel McPherson.

"What, you here again?" he asked.

"We've come back," replied Charles with ready resource, "to play a special benefit for your School Teachers' Association."

The old man chuckled. "Well, if you can get 'em in the house you are all right."

Charles was already planning a series of benefits for volunteer firemen and widows and orphans in future towns. It was a case of "anything to get a crowd." He hesitated a moment, then faced the old man with his winning smile and said:

"Colonel, I wish you would let me have fifty dollars to send back to the company."

"All right, my boy; there's the safe. Help yourself. Hurry up. Let us have a game of casino."

Charles wired the much-needed money to his brother,

then came back and dutifully played the game. But neither trumped-up benefits for the most worthy of causes nor the unfailing good-humor of the boyish advance-agent could stem the tide of adversity. Things went from bad to worse. Louise Dillon, all hope of salary gone, gave her little remaining capital to Gustave, saving only enough for her railway fare, and went back to her home in Cincinnati. Stoddart now played more dolefully than ever on his violin, ransacked its recesses, and turned over his last cent for the common good.

"We've got to get back North," said Gustave.

With the utmost effort, and by pawning jewelry and clothes, the company gladly saw the last trace of Texas disappear over the horizon.

It was a hard journey back. At Pine Bluff, Arkansas, Charles had to wait for the company because he did not have enough cash to go on ahead. Here the whole company was stranded until several of the members succeeded in getting enough money from home by wire to send them on.

Memphis proved to be a life-saver. Here the company took a steamboat down the Arkansas. It is notable because thus early Charles showed that eagerness to take a chance which eventually caused his death, for, on this trip, as on the *Lusitania*, he had been warned not to sail.

The river was low and the pilot was reckless. Whenever the boat groaned over a bar Charles would say, "That's great," although the other members of the company shivered with apprehension.

By using every device and resource known to the traveling company of those days, the Stoddart Comedy Company finally reached Richmond, Kentucky. It had left a trail of baggage behind; there was not a watch in the whole aggregation. Charles went on ahead to Cincinnati to book and bill the adjacent towns.

At Richmond Gustave had an inspiration. Then, as always, "Uncle Tom's Cabin" was the great life-saver of the harassed and needy theatrical organization. The play was always accessible and it almost invariably drew an audience.

"Why not have a real negro play Uncle Tom?" said Gustave.

So he wired Charles as follows:

> *Get me an Eva and send her down with Sam Lucas. Be sure to tell Sam to bring his diamonds.*

Sam Lucas was a famous negro minstrel who had been with the Callender company. He sported a collection of diamonds that made him the envy and admiration of his colleagues. Gustave knew that these jewels, like Louise Dillon's sealskin sack, meant a meal ticket for the company and transportation in an emergency.

Charles engaged Sallie Cohen (now Mrs. John C. Rice), and sent her down with Lucas, who, by the way, provided the money for the trip. Charles then proceeded to cover his "Lemons" posters with "Uncle Tom's Cabin" printing which he hastily acquired, and awaited results.

"Uncle Tom's Cabin" was played to a packed house at Richmond, and the company was able to get out of Kentucky. Gustave now had visions of big business in Ohio, and especially at Wilmington, which was Sam Lucas's home town. But the result was the usual experience with home patronage of home talent, and only a handful of people came to see the play. Sallie

Cohen, despairing of getting her salary, had quit the company, and on this night Polly Stoddart, who was a tall, well-developed woman, had to play Little Eva. When she sat on the lap of Wesley Sisson, who played her father, she not only hid him from sight, but almost crushed him to earth.

Wilmington proved to be the last despairing gasp of the Stoddart Comedy Company, for the trouble-studded tour now ended. Some of Lucas's diamonds were pawned to get the company back to Cincinnati.

The sad news was telegraphed to Charles, who was billing Newport, Kentucky, which is just across the Ohio River from Cincinnati. He received the message while standing on a step-ladder with a paste-brush in his hand. Now came an early evidence of his humor and equanimity. He calmly went on posting the bill for the show that he knew would never appear. Afterward in reciting the incident he made this explanation:

"I didn't want to tell the bill-poster that the company was closed, because he had just made a fresh bucket of paste and I didn't want him to waste it. Besides, he had become enthusiastic at the prospect of seeing a real negro Uncle Tom, and I had just given him some passes for the show. I didn't want all his disappointments to come at one time."

After all the hardships of the previous months, and with salaries unpaid, the company now found itself stranded in the spring of 1878 at the Walnut Street Hotel in Cincinnati. Gustave's problem was to get his people home. Fortunately, most of them lived in the Middle West. By pawning some of his clothes and making other sacrifices he was able to get them off. Only Frank Hartwell and Charles were left behind.

Gustave got a pass to Baltimore, where he borrowed enough money from Callender, then in his decline, to take care of Hartwell. Charles was left behind as security for the whole Frohman bill at the Walnut Street Hotel. Although Charles was amiable and smiling, the hotel thought that his cheerful demeanor was an unsatisfactory return for board and lodging, so he was asked to vacate his room after a few days. He now spent his time walking about the streets and eating one meal a day. At night he sat in the summer-gardens "across the Rhine," listening to the music, and then seeking out a place where he could get a bed for a quarter.

By giving an I O U to the same Pennsylvania ticket-agent who had staked Gustave, and with five dollars telegraphed by the indefatigable brother back in New York, he got as far as Philadelphia. He landed there without a cent in his pocket.

"I must get home," he said.

He got on a day-coach of a New York train without the vestige of a ticket and still penniless. In those days the cars were heated by stoves, and near each stove was a large coal-box.

When Charles heard the conductor's cry, "Tickets, please!" he hid himself in the coal-box and remained there until the awful personage passed by. Being small, he could pull the lid of the box down and be completely hidden from sight. After the conductor passed, he scrambled out and resumed his seat. He had to repeat this performance several times on the trip. Afterward in speaking of it he said:

"I wasn't a bit frightened for myself. I knew I would suffer no harm. My chief concern was for a kind-hearted old man who sat in the seat next to the coal-box. He was much more agitated than I was."

On a bright May afternoon Charles turned up, sooty but smiling, at 250 East Seventy-eighth Street, where the Frohman family then lived. He had walked all the way up-town from the ferry. His first greeting to Gustave was:

"Well, when do we start again?"

III

*I*NSTEAD of discouraging him, Charles Frohman's baptism of hardship with the John Dillon companies only filled him with a renewed ardor for the theatrical business. The hunger for the road was strong in him. Again it was Gustave who proved to be the good angel, and who now led him to a picturesque experience.

During the summer of 1878 J. H. (Jack) Haverly acquired the Callender Original Georgia Minstrels, and Gustave, who had an important hand in the negotiation, was retained as manager. He started for the Pacific coast with his dusky aggregation, and in Chicago fell in with his new employer.

Haverly was then at the high tide of his extraordinary career. He was in many respects the amusement dictator of his time. Beginning as owner of a small variety theater in Toledo, Ohio, he had risen to be the manager of half a dozen important theaters in New York, Chicago, and Philadelphia. Not less than ten traveling companies bore his name.

By instinct a plunger, his daring deals became the theatrical talk of the country. He was a dashing and conspicuous figure; his spacious shirt-front shone with diamonds, and he wore a large flat-crowned stiff hat in which he carried all his correspondence and private papers.

46

Haverly specialized in minstrels, for he was a genius at capitalizing the enthusiasm of the theater-going public. Just at this time he was launching the greatest of all his traveling enterprises. To meet the competition of the newly formed Barlow, Wilson, Primrose and West minstrels he decided to merge all his white minstrel companies into the Haverly Mastodons. It was to include forty star performers, more than had ever before been assembled in a minstrel organization. So proud was Haverly of this total that the advertising slogan of the company, which was echoed from coast to coast, and which became a popular theatrical phrase everywhere, was "Forty—Count 'Em—Forty."

Gustave found Haverly in the throes of Mastodon-making. Always solicitous of the family interest, he asked him if he had engaged a treasurer. When Haverly replied that he had not, Gustave immediately spoke up:

"Why don't you hire my brother Charley? He has had experience on the road."

"All right, Gus," he replied. "I've got two Frohmans with me now. If Charley is as good as they are, he is all right."

Thus it came about that for the first time the three Frohman brothers were associated under the same employer.

Gustave wired the good news and transportation to the eager and impatient Charles, who had irked under the inactivity of a hot summer in New York. Gustave added ten dollars and instructed his brother to buy a new suit, for the Frohman family funds were in a more or less sad way.

Henry Frohman's generosity and his absolute inability to press the payment of debts due him had brought the father to a state of financial embarrassment, and the burden of the family support fell upon the sons.

In a few days Charles showed up smiling in Chicago, but he had suffered disaster on the way. The ten-dollar "hand-me-down" suit had faded overnight, and when Charles appeared it was a sad sight.

"You can't meet Jack Haverly in that suit," said Gustave.

"All right," said Charley, "I will go to a tailor and have it fixed in some way."

The tailor, apparently, worked a miracle with the clothes, for Charles became presentable and was introduced to the great man, who, like most other people, readily succumbed to the boy's winning manner.

"You and I will work the public, all right," he said to Charles. What was more important, Haverly informed him that he was to act as treasurer of the Mastodons at a salary of ten dollars a week, with an allowance of one dollar and a half a day for board and lodging.

A serious complication now faced the boy. It was in the middle of July; the company was not to start until August, and he could draw no salary until the engagement began. With the assistance of Gustave he rented a two-dollar-a-week room and existed on a meal-ticket good for twenty-two fifteen-cent meals that he had bought for three dollars.

Charles sat at rehearsals with Haverly. He had a genius for stage effects and made many practical suggestions. The big brass-band, an all-important adjunct of the minstrel show, fascinated him. When the season opened with a flourish the receipts amazed him.

For the first time he came in contact with real money. The gross income of the Dillon company had never exceeded a thousand dollars a week; now he was handling more than that sum every night.

After a brief engagement at the Adelphi Theater in Chicago, which Haverly owned, the "Forty—Count 'Em—Forty" started on their long tour which rounded out the amusement apprenticeship of Charles Frohman.

Charles now made his first real appearance before the public, and in spectacular fashion. It was the custom of a minstrel company to parade each day. With their record-breaking organization the Mastodons gave this feature of minstrelsy perhaps its greatest traditions. Wearing shining silk hats, frock-coats, and lavender trousers, and headed by "the world's greatest minstrel band," the "Forty—Count 'Em—Forty" swayed the heart and moved the imagination of admiring multitudes wherever they went.

Charles, who to the end of his days despised a silk hat, now wore one for the first time, but under protest. However, he manfully took his place in the front set of fours with the ranking officers of the organization, and marched many a weary mile. So great was his dislike for a silk hat even then that he invariably carried a cap in his pocket and the moment the parade was over the abhorred headpiece was removed.

The first stop of the Mastodons was at Toledo, Ohio. A great crowd assembled around the theater, and the treasurer, a weak little man, seemed afraid to raise the window. "They'll run over me," he whined.

"All right," said Charles. "I'll take the window and sell the tickets."

Up to this time his only box-office experience had been as a mere lad at Hooley's Theater in Brooklyn, but he handled that big crowd with such skill and speed that even "Big Bill" Foote, who was the manager of the company, patted him on the back and said a kind word.

Foote, who was Charles's superior officer on this trip, was a type of the big, loud, blustering theatrical man of the time. He was six feet tall, and he towered over his youthful assistant, who was his exact opposite in manner and speech. Yet between these two men of strange contrast there developed a close kinship. The little, plump, rosy-cheeked treasurer could handle the big, bluff, noisy manager at will. Such was Charles Frohman's experience with men always.

The first tour was replete with stirring incident. When the company reached Bradford, Pennsylvania, they found the town in the throes of oil excitement. Oil was on everybody's tongue and ankle-deep in some of the streets. A great multitude collected at the theater. After the first part of the show the gallery, which was full of people, creaked and settled a few inches, creating a near panic. While this was being subdued an oil-warehouse on the outskirts of the town burst into flames. Most of the volunteer firemen were in the theater watching the minstrels. When an agitated individual out on the sidewalk yelled "Fire!" a real panic started inside the theater and there was a mad rush for the door.

Charles had just finished taking the tickets and stood with the ticket-box in his hand, trying to calm the crowd, but he was as a straw in the wind. The maddened people ran over him. When the excitement cleared away he was found almost buried in mud, mire, and oil outside, his clothes torn to shreds, but he still grasped the precious box in his hand.

MINSTREL DAYS

Now began a comradeship that was unique in the history of theatricals. The Mastodons, destined for long and continuous association, became a sort of traveling club. It was really a fine group of men, and the favorite of the organization was the rosy little treasurer who day by day fastened himself more firmly in the hearts of his colleagues.

Nor was this due to the fact that he was "Haverly's pocket-book," as the men affectionately called him, and their first aid in all financial need. He was the friend, confidant, and repository of all their troubles. With characteristic humor he gave each member of the company a day on which he could relate his hardships. He had a willing ear and an open hand.

When he could not give them the relief they sought he invariably said with that constant smile, "Well, I sympathize with you, anyhow."

Frohman was custodian of the company funds. One day in Denver four members of the company found themselves without a cent. Charles had tided them over so many difficulties that they hesitated to ask him again. As they talked their troubles over they saw him coming down the street. Instantly all four went down on their knees and held up their hands in supplication. When Charles saw them he said, "How much do you want?" And they got it.

He was always playing some practical joke. With half a dozen members of the company he formed a little club which often had supper after the play. This club was the fountain-head of a thousand jests and pranks. On one occasion Charles suggested that for the sake of the novelty of the thing every member of the club have his head shaved. The group went to a barber-shop.

Only one chair was vacant, however, and Charles Cushman got that chair. While his dome was being shorn of every vestige of hair Charles nudged the others and they crept away. When Cushman emerged, bald as a babe, he found himself alone. The joke was on him.

In his joke Charles was usually aided and abetted by Johnnie Rice, one of the many famous minstrels of that name. Rice could never resist the temptation to stroke long whiskers. Whenever the house was unusually big Charles took Rice out of the company for the first part and got him to assist him with the ticket-taking. Any spectator with a long facial hirsute growth was sure to have it caressed to the accompaniment of "Ticket, please."

Sometimes the men in the company, knowing of Rice's eccentricity, often watched the gallery for such a performance, and it invariably made them laugh. Once while the Mastodons were playing an engagement at the Olympic in St. Louis they were surprised to find Rice sitting in a front orchestra seat, wearing a long pair of Dundreary whiskers. He looked so solemn that every one on the stage burst into laughter. It almost broke up the performance. Charles had provided the whiskers.

It was on this minstrel tour that Charles Frohman gave the first real expression to his talents for publicity. Everything about a minstrel company was showy and flashy. So Charles originated a unique idea of establishing a reputation for solvency. He bought a small iron safe about three feet high. On it were painted in large gilt letters, "Treasurer, Haverly's Mastodon Minstrels."

In reality there was very little need for this safe, because "Jack" Haverly's constant and insistent demands for cash kept the company coffers stripped of surplus.

Charles saw in this safe a spectacular means of advertising. It was put conspicuously on the top of the first load of baggage that went to the hotel. He always engaged at least four men to unload it from the truck. It was then placed in a conspicuous position in the hotel lobby and invariably drew a comment like this:

"Gee whiz! That Haverly show has got so much money that it is carrying a safe to hold it."

This was precisely the response that Charles desired. No sooner was the safe unloaded in the lobby than Charles approached it with great ceremony, holding a bunch of one-dollar bills in his hand. This immediately attracted a crowd. With an admiring gallery, he would stow away the money. Just as soon as the crowd dispersed he would be back on the job removing this "prop" capital to where it was needed.

He was always alert to publicity possibilities. Among other things he organized a drum corps composed of volunteers who were only too glad to serve him. He inspired this corps to such proficiency that its marching and counter-marching became a feature of the parades. By diverting the drum corps to one part of the town and the parade to another, having them unite later on, he was able to attract two big street crowds and then bring them together at a common point.

All the while the boy was growing in responsibility. Without a murmur he assumed practically all the duties of manager. He arranged the parades, visited the newspaper offices, devised new numbers for the company, handled the money, and always remained serene, undisturbed, smiling, and optimistic.

Now came evidence of his initiative. While his first desire was to build up the attractiveness of his bill, he combined with it a genuine desire to develop his associates. Frequently he would say to men like the three Gorman brothers—George, James, and John—who were among his prime pals in the company:

"Why don't you rehearse some new steps? I'll go on and watch you at rehearsals and we can put it in the bill."

Out of such incidents as this came a dozen new features.

During this tour Charles displayed on many occasions what amounted to a reckless disregard of danger. He had proved on the Dillon tour that he was always willing to take a chance.

Once while climbing a steep incline on the way to Grass Valley in California their special train stopped. When he asked what the trouble was he was told that they would have to wait on a switch while another train came down the single track. He was afraid he would miss the evening's performance, so he asked the engineer if he could beat the down train to the double track. On being told that there was a chance, he said:

"Take it and go as fast as you can." He made his town in time.

Again in Colorado his train was stopped by a slight fire on a bridge. He urged the conductor to go across, and was so insistent that the man yielded, and the train got over just before the flames leaped up and the structure began to crackle.

What would have been an ordinary theatrical season waned. A minstrel company, however, seldom closed for the summer, so the tour continued. For the first time Charles Frohman crossed the continent. Despite its high-sounding name and the glitter and splash that marked its spectacular progress from place to place, the long trip of the Mastodons was not without its hardships, for business was often bad. Nor did it lack interesting episodes.

Once while making an over-Sunday jump from St. Paul to Omaha the train broke down somewhere in Iowa, and at seven o'clock the company was four hours from its destination. The house had been sold out. Charles immediately began to send optimistic and encouraging telegrams.

"Hold the crowd," he wired. "We are on the way. Tell them we will give them a double show."

From every station he sent on some cheering message. When the train was half an hour from Omaha he sought out Sam Devere, the prize banjoist of the company and a great fun-maker.

"Go into the baggage-car and black up," he said to Sam. "I want to rush you on to the theater as soon as we get to town."

They reached Omaha at eleven-fifteen o'clock. Charles hustled Devere up to the opera-house in a hack. The comedian went before the curtain and entertained the audience until midnight. When the company arrived not twenty people had left. The final curtain dropped at two-thirty o'clock before a delighted but weary crowd. The telegrams from the treasurer which were read to the audience had saved the day—and the receipts.

In the early stages of this long journey of the Mastodons came an episode that made an indelible impress upon the memory of young Charles. In view of the later history of the two actors in it, it is both picturesque and historic.

It was in Cleveland, and the day was hot. The Mastodons had just finished their parade, and Charles, weary, perspiring, and wearing the abhorred silk hat, entered the box-office of the Opera House on Cleveland Avenue. Sitting in the treasurer's seat at the window he saw a sturdy lad fingering a pile of silver dollars. He slipped them in and out with an amazing dexterity. Hearing a noise, he looked up and beheld young Frohman with the tile tilted back on his head.

The boys' eyes met. Into each came a wistful look.

"I wish I had that silk hat of yours," said the boy at the window.

"I wish I could do what you are doing with that money," was the response from the envied one.

Such was the first meeting between Charles Frohman and A. L. Erlanger.

Here is another episode of those early days that resulted in a lifelong and significant friendship. In a Philadelphia newspaper office Charles met a rangy, keen-eyed young man named Alf Hayman, who was advance-agent for Mr. and Mrs. W. J. Florence. When Hayman and Charles had concluded their business they started out for a walk. The Colonnade Hotel, at the corner of Fifteenth and Chestnut streets, was then the fashionable hotel of the city. In the course of this walk the two boys (they were each scarcely twenty) stopped in front of the hostelry, and Charles said:

"Some day I hope to have enough money to stop at the Colonnade."

He never forgot this, and whenever he met Hayman in Philadelphia he would always insist upon walking over to the hotel and recalling the conversation. Hayman afterward became general manager of all the Charles Frohman forces and remained until the end perhaps the closest of all the business associates of the manager.

Thus passed the years 1878 and 1879. Charles was growing in authority and experience until he was really doing all of "Big Bill" Foote's work and his own. Now came a great and thrilling experience.

Haverly sent the Mastodons on their first trip to England, and Charles naturally went along. It was the first of the many trips he was to make to the country which in time he was to annex to his own amusement kingdom.

In July, 1880, the company sailed on the *Canada*, and their arrival in London created a sensation. The men, headed by "Big Bill" Foote and Charles Frohman— "The Long and the Short of It," as they were called— marched with their hat-boxes to the old Helvetia Hotel in Soho.

Overnight their printing—the first colored paper ever used on an English bill-board—was posted, and it startled the staid Londoners. It made them realize that a wide-awake aggregation was in town. Charles knew that a real opportunity confronted him, and he rose to the occasion.

The engagement opened on July 30th at Her Majesty's Theater. The sacred precincts that Patti, Neilson, Gerster, and Campanini had adorned now resounded with the jokes and rang with the old-time plantation melodies of the American negro. The début was an enormous success and the prosperity of the engagement was insured.

Before long came a request from the royal household to make ready the royal box. The fun-loving Prince of Wales, afterward King Edward VII., wanted to see an American minstrel show.

But it was the wide-awake Charles who had started the machinery that led to this royal dictate. He realized soon after his arrival how important a royal visit would be. He got in touch with the right people, and the net result was that on a certain night in December the red canopy and carpet that betoken the royal visit were spread before Her Majesty's Theater.

By virtue of his rank "Big Bill" Foote should have received the royal party on behalf of the company. But Foote fled from the responsibility, and Charles, wearing his much-hated evening clothes and the equally despised silk hat, did the honors. The royal party included Edward, his wife, Alexandra (now the Queen Mother), his brother Clarence (now dead), and a troop of royal children old enough to stay up late at nights.

With his usual foresight Frohman had prepared himself for all the formalities that attended a royal visit to the theater. Among other things he found out that precedent decreed that the entire performance must be directed toward the royal box. With much effort he carefully impressed this fact upon the company. He even had a rehearsal the morning of the royal night and all eyes were ordered to be "dressed" toward the big, canopied box.

But these well-laid plans miscarried, for this is what happened:

The curtain had risen on the assembled fun-makers; their swinging opening chorus had given the show a rousing start, and the interlocutor had said those well-known introductory minstrel words, "Gentlemen, be seated." The royal party was well bestowed in its place and every gleaming eyeball on the stage was centered on the glittering representatives of the reigning house of Britain. Just at that moment a flutter ran through the theater. The only remaining vacant box, and opposite to the one used by the royal family, was suddenly occupied by the most entrancing and radiant feminine vision that these American minstrels had ever seen. It was Lily Langtry, then in the full tide of her marvelous beauty, and wearing an extremely low-cut evening gown.

The Mastodons were only human. They had never beheld such loveliness, to say nothing of a gown cut so low. They forgot all the careful coaching of Frohman and fixed their eyes on the beauty-show in the box.

Charles stood anxiously in the back of the house, fearing that the royal displeasure would be aroused. But his fears were groundless. The hypnotized minstrels on the stage were only part of an admiring host that had for its most distinguished head the Prince of Wales himself.

The "Forty—Count 'Em—Forty" now became the vogue in London. Royalty had set the stamp of its approval, and aristocracy flocked. One night in the momentary absence of the chief usher, Charles, who was always on the job, escorted a distinguished group of nobility to a box. After bowing them in a member of the party slipped a shilling into his hand, which Frohman, of course, refused.

"Take it, you beggar," said the peer, with some irritation, throwing the coin at him.

"Thank you, sir," responded Frohman, picking it up

and slipping it into his pocket. He kept it as a lucky-piece for twenty years, often telling the story of how he got it.

On Christmas Day, 1880, came a concrete evidence of the affection in which Charles was held by his minstrel colleagues. They assembled on the stage of Her Majesty's Theater and presented him with a gold watch and chain. The charm was a tiny reproduction of the famous safe that Charles had introduced into the company, and which was his inseparable companion. Charles never carried a watch, and this timepiece, together with many other similar gifts, was put away among his treasures.

One day, accompanied by Robert Filkins, the advance-agent, Charles had occasion to see Col. M. B. Leavitt, who was a notable theatrical figure of the time, with extensive interests in this country and abroad. After Leavitt had regaled the younger men with an account of his varied activities, Charles suddenly exclaimed to him:

"Gee! But you've got London by the neck, haven't you?"

Many years later Leavitt again met Charles Frohman in London. The encounter this time took place on the Strand, in front of the Savoy, where Frohman was installed in his usual luxurious suite. He now controlled half a dozen theaters in the British metropolis and he was a world theatrical figure. Leavitt, whose memory is one of the wonders of the amusement business, clapped the magnate on the shoulder and repeated the words spoken to him so long ago:

"Gee! Frohman, *you*'ve got London by the neck, haven't you?"

After a tour of the provinces the company returned home and opened in Brooklyn.

With the return to America came the first realization of one of Charles Frohman's earlier dreams. "Big Bill" Foote, fascinated by the lure of English life, bought a small hotel near London and settled down. This left the managership of the company vacant. Although Charles had practically done all the work for nearly a year, he was, so far as title was concerned, treasurer.

Immediately there was a scramble for the position of manager. Among those who sought it were Robert Filkins, William S. Strickland, and a number of other mature and experienced men.

But when the company heard that an outsider sought the position to which Charles was entitled there was great indignation. A meeting of protest, instigated by the Gorman brothers and Eddie Quinn, was held on the stage in Brooklyn, and a round-robin, signed by every member of the company, was despatched to Jack Haverly, insisting that Charles Frohman be made the manager.

A little later Charles walked back on the stage after the night's performance and quietly remarked:

"Boys, I am your new manager."

A great shout of delight went up. The rosy, boyish youth (for he had scarcely entered his twenties) was lifted to the shoulders of half a dozen men and to the words of a favorite minstrel song, "Hear Those Bells," a triumphant march was made around the stage. None of the many honors that came to him in his later years touched him quite so deeply as that affectionate demonstration.

It was now 1881, and once more the "Forty—Count 'Em—Forty" set forth to rediscover America, with Charles Frohman as manager. His name now appeared at the head of the bill, and to celebrate the great event Eddy Brooke wrote a "Frohman March," which had a conspicuous place on the program.

Strangely prophetic of the circumstances which brought about his untimely death was an incident which occurred while the company was going by boat from New York to New London. It was a bitter cold night when the aggregation boarded the old *John B. Starin.* The decks were piled with waste, cord, and jute for the New England mills.

"What a fine night for a fire on board!" remarked Frohman as he led his "soldiers," as he always called the Mastodons, aboard. Everybody retired early. At two o'clock in the morning there was great excitement. Men rushed frantically about; there were calls for hose, and the Mastodons, most of them clad in their night-clothes and trousers, rushed, frightened, on deck. They found a fire raging aft.

Immediately panic reigned. The coolest man aboard was the smallest. Here, there, and everywhere went Charles, urging everybody to be quiet.

"There is no danger," he said. "Let us all go in the cabin and wait."

Under his direction the passengers assembled in the water-soaked saloon and there waited until the flames were subdued. Here was evidence of the equanimity with which he faced disaster and which marked him on that ill-starred day when he was plunged to his death in the Irish Sea.

On through the summer of 1881 the Mastodons went

their way. Charles was now able to watch the minstrel parade from the sidewalk, but he was still the friend, philosopher, and guide of the company to which he was now bound by nearly three years of constant association.

They played Washington during the Garfield inaugural week. Charles realized that here was a great opportunity for spectacular publicity. First of all he took his now famous band down to the Willard Hotel and serenaded the new executive. A vast crowd gathered; the President-elect appeared at the window, smiled and bowed, and then sent for the little manager, to whom he expressed his personal thanks. Then a heaven-born opportunity literally fell into his hands.

To the same hotel came the Massachusetts Phalanx, of Lowell, which had secured a conspicuous place in the inaugural parade. Their arrangement committee had seen the Haverly parade, and the members were so greatly impressed with the band that they asked if its services could be secured.

"Certainly," said Frohman. "You can have not only the band, but the whole company will escort you in the parade."

Thus it came about that the Haverly Mastodon Minstrels headed the third division of the Garfield inaugural parade. Ever mindful and proud of his men, Frohman, at his personal expense, bought a buttonhole bouquet for every member for the occasion and fastened it on their coats himself. On the sidewalk he followed with admiring eye and flushed face the progress of his company.

By a curious coincidence the Haverly Mastodons played Washington during the week of the Garfield funeral, and the band marched in the funeral parade to the station, playing "Nearer, My God, to Thee."

A happier sequel of the inaugural episode came when the minstrels next played Lowell, where they were received by the Phalanx in full uniform, paraded through the town, with Charles marching proudly at the head. The Phalanx was host at a banquet given at the armory after the performance.

The Mastodons were now making their way to the Pacific coast. At the same time Gustave Frohman was in San Francisco with the Number One "Hazel Kirke" Company, direct from the Madison Square Theater in New York, which was playing at the California Theater.

One morning in May, 1881, he received the following telegram from Charles, dated Salt Lake City:

> *Am stranded here with the "Big Forty." So is Frank Sanger with "A Bunch of Keys." Theater management has failed to send railroad fares. Wire me what you can. Will return amount out of receipts Bush Street Theater.*

The manager of the Bush Street Theater, in San Francisco, had agreed to provide railroad transportation for the company from Salt Lake City to San Francisco and had not kept his agreement. The receipts in the former city did not leave a sufficient surplus to negotiate this jump.

Gustave wired the needed cash, and Charles showed up on time in San Francisco. For the second and only other time in his theatrical career Charles was somewhat downcast. Despite his effective services during the preceding years, Haverly had only raised his salary to twenty-five dollars a week. The boy had handled hundreds of thousands of dollars and had helped in no small way to give to the organization its prestige and its *esprit de corps*. He was now, in the phraseology of his associates, "the whole show." His word was law with the company, and the men adored him.

He met Gustave at the Palace Hotel and said to him, "I suppose the time has come for me to quit Haverly."

"All right," said Gustave, still the good angel. "I'll put you out ahead of our Number Two 'Hazel Kirke' Company at a salary of seventy-five dollars a week. You can start out right away. What do you say?"

Charles thought a moment, and then said: "Well, Gus, it's pretty tough to go ahead of a Number Two company even at seventy-five dollars a week when you have been manager of Haverly's Mastodons. The money doesn't mean anything to me. I like the minstrel boys and they like me."

He still hesitated and walked up and down the room two or three times, as was his habit. Finally he came over to his brother and said, decisively:

"I'll take it."

During this memorable visit to San Francisco occurred another event that had large influence on the whole future life of the young man. One night in a famous ratheskeller on Kearney Street he saw an artistic-looking youth with curly hair and dreamy eyes sitting in the midst of a group of actors. This youth was David Belasco, who had passed from actor to author-stage-manager and whose melodrama, "American Born," was running at the Baldwin Theater. Frohman had seen this play and was much impressed with it. Thrillers had interested him from the start.

Gustave, who was with Belasco, said to him: "There's my brother Charley. You ought to know him."

Simultaneously Belasco was pointed out to Charles. They glanced up at the same time, nodded smilingly across the space between, and later on when they were introduced Charles expressed his great admiration for "American Born." Belasco had just received the offer from Daniel Frohman to come to the Madison Square Theater in New York as stage-manager.

Out of this contact came the association between Charles Frohman and David Belasco that added much to their achievements.

Charles gave Haverly notice, and at Indianapolis he left the Mastodons. He slipped away without farewells, and when his absence became known a gloom settled down on the company. Unconsciously the rosy-cheeked boy had become its inspiration. For weeks the performances lacked their customary zip and enthusiasm.

His minstrel days over, save for two brief intervals, Charles was now about to begin his connection with the Madison Square Theater. It was to mark, because of the men with whom he now became associated and the revolution in theatrical methods which he brought about, the first really significant epoch in his crowded career.

IV

IN THE NEW YORK THEATRICAL WHIRLPOOL

*W*HEN Charles Frohman went to the Madison Square Theater in 1881 the three Frohman brothers were literally installed for the first time under the same managerial roof. From this hour on the affairs of Charles were bound up in large theatrical conduct.

Since the Madison Square Theater thus becomes the background of his real activities, the shell out of which he emerged as a full-fledged manager, the institution, and its significance in dramatic history, are well worth recording here.

The little Madison Square Theater, located back of the old Fifth Avenue Hotel, on Twenty-fourth Street near Broadway, was established at a time when a new force was hovering over the New York stage. This playhouse, destined to figure so prominently in the fortunes of all the Frohmans, and especially Charles, grew out of the somewhat radical convictions of Steele Mackaye, one of the most brilliant and erratic characters of his time. He was actor, lecturer, and playwright, and he taught the art of acting on lines laid down by Delsarte. Dr. George Mallory, editor of *The Churchman*, became interested in his views and regarded Mackaye as a man with a distinct mission. He induced his brother, Marshall Mallory, to build the Madison Square Theater.

Steele Mackaye was the first director, and, with the active co-operation of the Mallorys, launched its career. Dr. Mallory believed that the drama needed reform; that the way to reform it was to play reformed drama. So the place was dedicated to healthy plays. "A wholesome place for wholesome amusement" became the slogan. Contracts for plays were made only with American authors. Here were produced the earlier triumphs of Steele Mackaye, Bronson Howard, William Gillette, H. H. Boyessen, and Mrs. Frances Hodgson Burnett. In this house, in "May Blossom," De Wolf Hopper first appeared in a stock company, afterward going into musical comedy. Among the actors seen on its boards during the Frohman régime were Agnes Booth, Viola Allen, Effie Ellsler, Georgia Cayvan, Mrs. Whiffen, Marie Burroughs, Annie Russell, George Clarke, Jeffreys Lewis, C. W. Couldock, Thomas Whiffen, Dominick Murray, and Eben Plympton. Rose Coghlan was also a member of the company, but had no opportunity of playing.

The house had certain unique and attractive qualities. It had been charmingly decorated by Louis C. Tiffany, and one of its principal features was a double stage, which enabled the scenery for one act to be set while another was being played before the audience. Thus long waits were avoided.

The name of Frohman was associated with this theater from the very start, because its first manager was Daniel Frohman. It opened in February, 1880, with Steele Mackaye's play "Hazel Kirke," which was an instantaneous success. The little theater, with its novel stage, intimate atmosphere, admirable company, and a policy that was definite and original, became one of the most popular in America. "Hazel Kirke" ran four hundred and eighty-six nights in New York City without interruption, which was a record run up to that time. In the original cast were Effie Ellsler, Eben Plympton, Mr. and Mrs. Whiffen, and Charles W. Couldock.

The Madison Square Theater was also an important factor in New York dramatic life and began to rival the prestige of the Wallack, Palmer, and Daly institutions. Its fame, due to the record-breaking "Hazel Kirke" success, became nation-wide.

Now began an activity under its auspices that established a whole new era in the conduct of the theater. It was the dawn of a "big business" development that sent the Madison Square successes throughout the country, and Charles Frohman was one of its sponsors.

Gustave Frohman had been engaged as director of the traveling companies. He engaged Charles as an associate. The work of the Frohmans was carefully mapped out. It was Daniel's business to select the casts, organize and rehearse the companies in New York; Gustave took general charge of the road equipment; while Charles arranged and booked the road tours.

It was after the phenomenal first season's run of "Hazel Kirke" that Charles Frohman hung up his hat in the little "back office" of the Madison Square Theater to begin the work that was to project his name and his talents prominently for the first time. New York sizzled through the hottest summer it had ever known; Garfield lay dying, and the whole country was in a state of unrest. Charles sweltered in his little cubbyhole, but he was enthusiastic and optimistic about his new job.

Gustave and Charles had complete charge of all the traveling companies that developed out of the series of "runs" at the theater. They inaugurated a whole new and brilliant theatrical activity in towns and cities removed from theatrical centers, regarding which the other big managers in New York were ignorant.

With the organization of these Madison Square companies the "Number Two Company" idea was born. It was a distinct innovation. A play like "Hazel Kirke," for example, was played by as many as five companies at one time, each company being adjusted financially to the type of town to which it was sent. "Hazel Kirke" appeared simultaneously in New York City at three different theaters, each with a separate and distinct type of audience.

Under the direction of Gustave and Charles, the outside business of the Madison Square Theater spread so rapidly that in a short time fourteen road companies carried the name of the establishment to all parts of the United States. Despite their youth, the three Frohmans had had a very extensive experience over the whole country.

In those days the booking of road attractions was not made through syndicates. Applications for time had to be made individually to every manager direct, even in the case of the most obscure one-night stand. The big New York managers only concerned themselves with the larger cities in which their companies made annual appearances. The smaller towns had to trust to chance to get attractions outside the standard "road shows."

Charles realized this lack of booking facilities, and dedicated his talents and experience to remedying it. His seasons on the road with John Dillon and the

Haverly Minstrels had equipped him admirably. He not only displayed remarkable judgment in routing companies, but he was now able to express his genius for publicity. He always believed in the value of big printing.

"Give them pictures," he said.

He urged a liberal policy in this respect, and the Madison Square Theater backed his judgment to the extent of more than one hundred thousand dollars a year for picture posters and elaborate printing of all kinds. The gospel of Madison Square Theater art and its enterprises was thus spread broadcast, not with ordinary cheap-picture advertising, but with artistic lithographs. In fact, here began the whole process of expensive and elaborate bill-posting, and Charles Frohman was really the father of it.

Under his direction the first "flashlights" ever taken of a theatrical company for advertising purposes were made at the Madison Square Theater.

Charles was now director of nearly a score of agents who traveled about with the various companies. He vitalized them with his enthusiasm. In order to expedite their work, Charles and his brothers rented and furnished a large house on Twenty-fourth Street near the theater. It was in reality a sort of club, for a dining-room was maintained, and there were a number of bedrooms. When the agents came to town they lodged here. Charles, Gustave, and Daniel also had rooms in this house. A dressmaking department was established on the premises where many of the costumes for the road companies were made.

During these days Charles gave frequent evidence of

his tact and persuasiveness. Often when matters of policy had to be fixed and discussed, the managers of out-of-town theaters would be called to New York. It was Charles's business to take them in hand and straighten out their troubles. They would leave, feeling that they had got the best "time" for their theaters and that they had made a friend in the optimistic little man who was then giving evidence of that uncanny instinct for road management that stood him in such good stead later on.

With his usual energy Charles was interested in every phase of the Madison Square Theater. Frequently, accompanied by Wesley Sisson, who succeeded Daniel Frohman during the latter's occasional absences from the theater, he would slip into the balcony and watch rehearsals. He sat with one leg curled under him, following the scenes with keenest interest. More than once his sharp, swift criticism helped to smooth away a rough spot.

He impressed his personality and capacity upon all who came in contact with him. It was said of him then, as it was said later on, that he could sit in his little office and make out a forty weeks' tour for a company without recourse to a map. In fact, he carried the whole theatrical map of the country under his hat.

In the strenuous life of those Madison Square days came some of Charles Frohman's closest and longest friendships.

The first was with Marc Klaw. It grew out of play piracy, the inevitable result of the theater's successes. Throughout the country local managers began to steal the Madison Square plays and put them on with "fly-by-night" companies. Since they were unable to get manuscripts of the play, the pirates sent stenographers to the theater to copy the parts. These stenographers had to sit in the dark and write surreptitiously. In many instances, in order to keep the lines of their notes straight, they stretched strings across their note-books.

Gustave Frohman happened to be in Louisville with the Number One "Hazel Kirke" Company. He was looking about for a lawyer who could investigate and prosecute the piracy of the Madison Square plays. He made inquiry of John T. Macauley, manager of Macauley's Theater, who said:

"There's a young lawyer here named Marc Klaw who is itching to get into the theatrical business. Why don't you give him a chance?"

Frohman immediately engaged Klaw to do some legal work for the Madison Square Theater, and he successfully combated the play pirates in the South. The copyright laws then were inadequate, however, and Klaw was ordered to New York, where, after a short preliminary training, he was sent out as manager of the Number Two "Hazel Kirke" Company of which Charles Frohman was advance-agent. In this way the meeting between the two men, each destined to wield far-flung theatrical authority, came about.

Charles resented going out with a "Number Two" Company, so to placate his pride and to give distinction to the enterprise, Daniel put Georgia Cayvan, leading lady of the Madison Square Theater, at the head of the cast.

There was good business method in putting out Miss Cayvan on this tour, because she was a New-Englander, born at Bath, Maine, and Bath was included in this tour.

When Charles reached Bath ahead of the show he rode on the front seat of the stage to the hotel. He told the driver that he was coming with a big New York show, and said:

"I've got a big sensation for Bath."

"What's that?" said the driver.

"We have Miss Cayvan as the leading lady," answered Frohman.

"Miss Who?" asked the driver.

"Miss Cayvan—Miss Georgia Cayvan, leading woman of the Madison Square Theater," answered Frohman, with a great flourish.

"Oh," replied the driver, "you mean our little Georgie. We heard tell that she was acting on the stage, and now I guess some folks will be right smart glad to see her."

Charles was so much interested in Miss Cayvan's appearance in her home town that he came back and joined the company on its arrival and was present at the station when Marc Klaw brought the company in.

Quite a delegation of home people were on hand to meet Miss Cayvan, and she immediately assumed the haughty airs of a prima donna.

Charles was much amused, and decided to "take her down" in an amiable way. So he stepped up to her with great solemnity, removed his hat, and said, after the manner of his old minstrel days:

"Miss Cayvan, we parade at eleven."

Miss Cayvan saw the humor of the situation, took the hint, and got down off her high horse. In the company with Miss Cayvan at that time were Maude Stuart, Charles Wheatleigh, Frank Burbeck, W. H. Crompton, and Mrs. E. L. Davenport, the mother of Fanny Davenport.

While Charles was impressing his personality and talents at the Madison Square Theater and really finding himself for the first time, Gustave Frohman met Jack Haverly on the street one day. The old magnate said, with emphasis:

"Gus, I've got to have Charles back."

"You can't have him," said Gustave.

"But I must," said Haverly.

"Well, if you pay him one hundred and forty-six dollars a week (one hundred and twenty-five dollars salary and twenty-one dollars for hotel bills) you can have him for a limited time."

"All right," said Haverly.

Charles went back to the Mastodons, where he received a royal welcome. But his heart had become attuned to the real theater—to the hum of its shifting life, to the swift tumult of its tears and laughter. The excitement of the drama, and all the speculation that it involved (and he was a born speculator), were in his blood. He heeded the call and went back to the Madison Square Theater.

But the minstrel field was to claim him again and for the last time. Gustave conceived a plan to send the Callender Minstrels on a spectacular tour across the continent. The nucleus of the old organization, headed by the famous Billy Kersands, was playing in England under the name of Haverly's European Minstrels, Haverly having acquired the company some years before. Charles was sent over to get the pick of the Europeans for the new aggregation. Accompanied by

Howard Spear, he sailed on June 7, 1882, on the *Wyoming*.

He encountered some difficulty in getting the leading members, so with characteristic enterprise he bought the whole company from Haverly and brought it back to the United States, where it was put on the road as Callender's Consolidated Spectacular Colored Minstrels. On all the bills appeared the inscription "Gustave and Charles Frohman, Proprietors." As a matter of fact, Charles had very little to do with the company, although he made a number of its contracts. His financial interest was trivial. Gustave used his name because Charles had been prominently associated with the Mastodons and he had achieved some eminence as a minstrel promoter.

Having launched the Callender aggregation, he went on to Chicago, where Gustave was putting on David Belasco's play "American Born," with the author himself as producer. Charles joined his brother in promoting the enterprise.

Now began the real friendship between Charles Frohman and David Belasco. The chance contact in San Francisco a few years before was now succeeded by a genuine introduction. The men took to each other instinctively and with a profound understanding. They shared the same room and had most of their meals together. Then, as throughout his whole life, Charles consumed large portions of pie (principally apple, lemon meringue, and pumpkin) and drank large quantities of lemonade or sarsaparilla. One day while they were having lunch together Frohman said to Belasco:

"You and I must do things together. I mean to have

my own theater in Broadway and you will write the plays for it."

"Very well," replied the ever-ready Belasco. "I will make a contract with you now."

"There will never be need of a contract between us," replied Frohman, who expressed then the conviction that guided him all the rest of his life when he engaged the greatest stars in the world and spent millions on productions without a scrap of paper to show for the negotiation.

Charles worked manfully for "American Born." It was in reality his first intimate connection with a big production. At the outset his ingenuity saved the enterprise from threatened destruction. Harry Petit, a local manager, announced a rival melodrama called "Taken From Life" at McVicker's Theater, and had set his opening date one night before the inaugural of "American Born."

Charles scratched his head and said, "We must beat them to it."

He announced the "American Born" opening for a certain night and then opened three nights earlier, which beat the opposition by one night.

Belasco's play was spectacular in character and included, among other things, a realistic fire scene. When the time came for rehearsal the manager of the theater said that it could not be done, because the fire laws would be violated.

"I'll fix that," said Charles.

He went down to the City Hall, had a personal interview with the mayor, and not only got permission for the scene, but a detail of real firemen to act in it.

While in Chicago, Belasco accepted Daniel Frohman's

offer to come to New York as stage-manager of the Madison Square Theater. Charles and Belasco came east together, and the intimacy of this trip tightened the bond between them. The train that carried them was speeding each to a great career.

With Belasco installed as stage-manager there began a daily contact between the two. Belasco went to Frohman with all his troubles. In Frohman's bedroom he wrote part of "May Blossom," in which he scored his first original success at the Madison Square. Charles was enormously interested in this play, and after it was finished carried a copy about in his pocket, reading it or having it read wherever he thought it could find a friendly ear.

So great was Belasco's gratitude that he gave Charles a half-interest in it, which was probably the first ownership that Charles Frohman ever had in a play.

During those days at the Madison Square, when both Frohman and Belasco were seeing the vision of coming things, they often went at night to O'Neil's Oyster House on Sixth Avenue near Twenty-second Street. The day's work over, they had a bite of supper, in Frohman's case mostly pie and sarsaparilla, and talked about the things they were going to do.

Charles Frohman's ambition for a New York theater obsessed him. One night as they were walking up Broadway they passed the Fifth Avenue Hotel. A big man in his shirt-sleeves sat tilted back in his chair in front of the hotel. The two young men were just across the street from him. Frohman stopped Belasco, pointed to the man, and said:

"David, there is John Stetson, manager of the Fifth Avenue Theater. Well, some day I am going to be as

big a man as he is and have my own theater on Broadway."

Those were crowded days. Charles not only picked
and "routed" the companies, but he kept a watchful eye
on them. This meant frequent traveling. For months
he lived in a suit-case. At noon he would say to his
stenographer, "We leave for Chicago this afternoon,"
and he was off in a few hours. At that time "Hazel
Kirke," "The Professor," "Esmeralda," "Young Mrs.
Winthrop," and "May Blossom" were all being played
by road companies in various parts of the United States,
and it was a tremendous task to keep a watchful eye on
them. It was his habit to go to a town where a company
was playing and not appear at the theater until the
curtain had risen. The company had no warning of
his coming, and he could make a good appraisal of their
average work.

On one of the many trips that he made about this time
he gave evidence of his constant humor.

He went out to Columbus, Ohio, to see a "Hazel
Kirke" company. He arrived at the theater just before
matinée, and as he started across the stage he was met
by a newly appointed stage-manager who was full of
authority.

"Where are you going?" asked the man.

"To Mr. Hagan's dressing-room."

"I'll take the message," said the stage-director.

"No, I want to see him personally."

"But you can't. I am in charge behind the curtain."

Frohman left without a word, went out to the box-
office and wrote a letter, discharging the stage-director.
Then he sat through the performance. Directly the

curtain fell the man came to him in a great state of mind.

"Why did you discharge me, Mr. Frohman?"

Frohman smiled and said: "Well, it was the only way that I could get back to see my actors. If you will promise to be good I will re-engage you." And he did.

It was on a trip of this same kind that Charles had one of his many narrow escapes from death. During the spring of 1883 he went out to Ohio with Daniel to visit some of the road companies. Daniel left him at Cleveland to go over and see a performance of "The Professor" at Newcastle, while Charles went on to join Gustave at Cincinnati.

Charles was accompanied by Frank Guthrie, who was a sort of confidential secretary to all the Frohmans at the theater. Shortly before the train reached Galion, Charles, who sat at the aisle, asked his companion to change places. Ten minutes later the train was wrecked. Guthrie, who sat on the aisle seat, was hurled through the window and instantly killed, while Charles escaped unhurt.

Daniel heard of the wreck, rushed to the scene on a relief train, expecting to find his brother dead, for there had been a report that he was killed. Instead he found Charles bemoaning the death of his secretary.

A month afterward Charles and Marc Klaw were riding in the elevator at the Monongahela House in Pittsburg when the cable broke and the car dropped four stories. It had just been equipped with an air cushion, and the men escaped without a scratch.

Along toward the middle of 1883 there were signs of a break at the Madison Square Theater. Steele Mackaye had quarreled with the Mallorys and had left, taking Gustave with him to launch the new Lyceum Theater on Fourth Avenue and Twenty-third Street. Daniel was becoming ambitious to strike out for himself, while Charles was chafing under the necessity of being a subordinate. He yearned to be his own master. "I must have a New York production," he said. The wish in his case meant the deed, for he now set about to produce his first play.

Naturally, he turned to Belasco for advice and co-operation. Both were still identified with the Madison Square Theater, which made their negotiations easy.

In San Francisco Charles had seen a vivid melodrama called "The Stranglers of Paris," which Belasco had written from Adolphe Belot's story and produced with some success. Osmond Tearle, then leading man for Lester Wallack and New York's leading matinée idol, had played in the West the part of Jagon, who was physically one of the ugliest characters in the play.

"'The Stranglers of Paris' is the play for me," said Frohman to Belasco.

"All right," said David; "you shall have it."

The original dramatization was a melodrama without a spark of humor. In rewriting it for New York, Belasco injected considerable comedy here and there.

Frohman, whose vision and ideas were always big, said:

"We've got to get a great cast. I will not be satisfied with anybody but Tearle."

To secure Tearle, Frohman went to see Lester Wallack for the first time. Wallack was then the enthroned theatrical king and one of the most inaccessible of men. Frohman finally contrived to see him and made the proposition for the release of Tearle. Ordinarily Wal-

lack would have treated such an offer with scorn.
Frohman's convincing manner, however, led him to
explain, for he said:

"Mr. Tearle is the handsomest man in New York,
and if I loaned him to you to play the ugliest man ever
put on the stage he would lose his drawing power for
me. I am sorry I can't accommodate you, Mr. Frohman. Come and see me again."

Out of that meeting came a friendship with Lester
Wallack that developed large activities for Charles, as
will be seen later on.

Unable to get Tearle, Belasco and Frohman secured
Henry Lee, a brilliant and dashing leading actor who
had succeeded Eben Plympton in the cast of "Hazel
Kirke." The leading woman was Agnes Booth, a well-
known stage figure. She was the sister-in-law of Edwin
Booth, and an actress of splendid quality.

Unfortunately for him, the leading theaters were all
occupied. There were only a few playhouses in New
York then, a mere handful compared with the enormous
number to-day. But a little thing like that did not
disturb Charles Frohman.

Up at the northwest corner of Thirty-fifth Street and
Broadway was an old barnlike structure that had been
successively aquarium, menagerie, and skating-rink. It
had a roof and four walls and at one end there was a
rude stage.

One night at midnight Charles, accompanied by
Belasco, went up to look at the sorry spectacle. As
a theater it was about the most unpromising structure
in New York.

"This is all I can get, David," said Charles, "and it
must do."

"But, Charley, it is not a theater," said Belasco.

"Never mind," said Frohman. "I will have it made into one."

The old building was under the control of Hyde & Behman, who were planning to convert it into a vaudeville house. Frohman went to see them and persuaded them to turn it into a legitimate theater. Just about this time the Booth Theater at Twenty-third Street and Sixth Avenue was about to be torn down. Under Charles's prompting Hyde & Behman bought the inside of that historic structure, proscenium arch, stage, boxes, and all, and transported them to the Thirty-fifth Street barn. What had been a bare hall became the New Park Theater, destined to go down in history as the playhouse that witnessed many important productions, as well as the first that Charles Frohman made on any stage. Years afterward this theater was renamed the Herald Square.

Charles Frohman now had a play, a theater, and a cast. With characteristic lavishness he said to Belasco: "We must have the finest scenic production ever made in New York."

He had no capital, but he had no trouble in getting credit. Every one seemed willing to help him. He got out handsome printing and advertised extensively. He spared nothing in scenic effects, which were elaborate. He devoted every spare moment to attending rehearsals.

Among the supernumeraries was a fat boy with a comical face. At one of the rehearsals he sat in a boat and reached out for something. In doing this he fell overboard. He fell so comically that Belasco made his fall a part of the regular business. His ability got him a few lines, which were taken from another actor. This fat-faced, comical boy was John Bunny, who became the best-known moving-picture star in the United States, and who to the end of his days never forgot that he appeared in Charles Frohman's first production. He often spoke of it with pride.

The autumn of 1883 was a strenuous one, for Charles had staked a good deal on "The Stranglers of Paris." Yet when the curtain rose on the evening of November 10, 1883, he was the same smiling, eager, but imperturbable boy who years before had uttered the wish that some day he would put on a play himself in the great city. He now saw that dream come true. He was just twenty-three.

"The Stranglers of Paris" made quite a sensation. The scenic effects were highly praised, and especially the ship scene, which showed convicts in their cages, their revolt, the sinking of the vessel, Jagon's struggle in the water, his escape from death, and his dramatic appeal to Heaven. Lee scored a great success and dated his popularity from this appearance.

Many of the lines in the piece were widely quoted, one of them in particular. It was in substance, "Money has power to open prison gates, and no questions asked."

It was the time of sensational graft revelations, and theater-goers thought that it fitted the New York situation.

"The Stranglers of Paris" ran at the New Park Theater until December 9, when it was taken on the road. It continued on tour for a considerable period, playing most of the principal cities of the East, but the production was so expensive that it made no money. In fact, Charles lost on the enterprise, but it did not in

VIOLA ALLEN

the least dash his spirits. He was supremely content because at last he had produced a play.

"The Stranglers of Paris" filled the budding manager with a renewed zeal to be a producer. He was still enthusiastic about the melodrama, so he secured a vivid piece by R. G. Morris, a New York newspaper man, called "The Pulse of New York," which he produced at the Star Theater, Thirteenth Street and Broadway, which had been originally Wallack's Theater.

In the cast was a handsome, painstaking young woman named Viola Allen, whom Charles had singled out because of her admirable work in a play that he had seen, and who was headed for a big place in the annals of the American theater. The youthful manager encouraged her and did much to aid her progress.

Others in the cast were Caroline Hill, A. S. Lipman, Edward S. Coleman, L. F. Massen, Frank Lane, Henry Tarbon, W. L. Denison, George Clarke, H. D. Clifton, Ada Deaves, Max Freeman, Edward Pancoast, Frank Green, Gerald Eyre, Nick Long, Frederick Barry, Oscar Todd, John March, Charles Frew, Richard Fox, James Maxwell, J. C. Arnold, Stanley Macy, Lida Lacy, George Mathews, and William Rose.

"The Pulse of New York" was produced May 10, 1884, but ran only three weeks. Once more Charles faced a loss, but he met this as he met the misfortunes of later years, with smiling equanimity.

Now came a characteristic act. He was still in the employ of the Madison Square Theater and had a guarantee of one hundred dollars a week. Although he had devoted considerable time to his two previous productions, he was an invaluable asset to the establishment.

He now felt that the time had come for him to choose between remaining at the Madison Square under a guarantee and striking out for himself on the precarious sea of independent theatrical management. He chose the latter, and launched a third enterprise.

In his wanderings about New York theaters Charles saw a serious-eyed young actress named Minnie Maddern. He said to Daniel:

"I have great confidence in that young woman. Will you help me put her out in a piece?"

"All right," replied his brother.

The net result was Miss Maddern in "Caprice."

In view of subsequent stage history this company was somewhat historic. Miss Maddern's salary was seventy-five dollars a week. Her leading man, who had been a general-utility actor at the Lyceum, and who also received seventy-five dollars a week, was Henry Miller. A handsome young lad named Cyril Scott played a very small part and got fifteen dollars a week. The total week's salary of the company amounted to only six hundred and ninety dollars.

"Caprice" opened at Indianapolis November 6, 1884, and subsequently played Chicago, St. Louis, Evansville, Dayton, and Baltimore, with a week at the Grand Opera House in New York, where its season closed. It made no money, but it did a great deal toward advancing the career of Miss Maddern, who afterward became known to millions of theater-goers as Mrs. Fiske.

Charles had now made three productions on his own hook and began to impress his courage and his personality on the theatrical world. He had definitely committed himself to a career of independent management, and from this time on he went it alone.

V

BOOKING-AGENT AND BROADWAY PRODUCER

*T*HE season of 1883–84 had seen Charles Frohman launched as independent manager. He had at its conclusion cut his managerial teeth on the last of three productions which, while not financially successful, had shown the remarkable quality of his ability. People now began to talk about the nervy, energetic young man who could go from failure to failure with a smile on his face. It is a tradition in theatrical management that successful starts almost invariably mean disastrous finishes. An auspicious beginning usually leads to extravagance and lack of balance. Failure at the outset provokes caution. Charles, therefore, had enough early hard jolts to make him careful.

He always admired big names. Thus it came about that his next venture was associated with a name and a prestige that meant much and, later on, cost much. Just about that time he met a handsome young English actor named E. H. Sothern, who had come to this country with his sister and who had appeared for a short time with John McCullough, the tragedian. Sothern had returned to New York and was looking for an engagement.

In those days actors usually secured engagements by running down rumors of productions that were afloat on the Rialto. In this way Sothern heard that Charles

Frohman was about to send out an English play called "Nita's First," which had been produced at Wallack's Theater. Sothern called on Frohman and asked to be engaged.

"What salary do you want?" asked Frohman.

Sothern said he wanted fifty dollars.

"All right," said Frohman. "The part is worth seventy-five dollars, and I'll pay it."

Twenty years later the manager paid this same actor a salary of one hundred thousand dollars for a season of forty weeks in Shakespearian rôles.

"Nita's First," however, ran for only two weeks on the road, and Charles ended the engagement. The reason was that he had conceived what he considered a brilliant idea.

Lester Wallack and the Wallack Theater Company almost dominated the New York dramatic situation. The company, headed by Wallack himself, included Rose Coghlan, Osmond Tearle, John Gilbert, and a whole galaxy of brilliant people. The Wallack Theater plays were the talk of the town. Frohman had an inspiration which he communicated one day to Lester Wallack's son, Arthur, whom he knew. To Arthur he said:

"What do you think about my taking the Wallack successes out on the road? It is a shame not to capitalize the popular interest in them while it is hot. Look at what the Madison Square Theater has been doing. Will you speak to your father about it?"

Arthur spoke to his father, who was not averse to the idea, and Charles was bidden to the great presence. He had met Lester Wallack before when he tried to engage Osmond Tearle for "The Stranglers of Paris." Now came the real meeting. After Frohman had stated his case with all his persuasion, he added:

"I am sure I can make you rich. You have over-looked a great chance to make money."

Lester Wallack said, "It is a good idea, Mr. Frohman, but your company must reflect credit upon the theater, and your leading woman must be of the same type as my leading woman, Rose Coghlan."

Charles immediately said, "The company shall be worthy of you and the name it bears."

Lester Wallack agreed to rehearse the company and to permit his name to be used in connection with it. After Charles left, Lester Wallack said to his son:

"Watch that young man, Arthur. He is going to make his mark."

Arthur Wallack was about to take a trip to England, and Charles commissioned him to engage the leading people. He therefore engaged Sophie Eyre, who had been leading woman at the Drury Lane Theater, and W. H. Denny.

Charles himself selected the remaining members of the company, who were Newton Gotthold; C. B. Wells; Charles Wheatleigh; Max Freeman; Rowland Buckstone; Henry Talbot; Sam Dubois; George Clarke; Fred Corbett; Louise Dillon, who had been with him in the precarious Stoddart Comedy days; Kate Denin Wilson; Agnes Elliot; and Grace Wilson.

At the time he engaged the Wallack Theater Company Charles had no office. He was then living at the Coleman House on Broadway, just opposite the then celebrated Gilsey House. Most of the engagements were made as he sat in a big leather chair in the lobby, with one foot thrown over an arm of it.

The principal capital that Charles had for this venture was five thousand dollars put up by Daniel J.

Bernstein, who became treasurer of the company. Alf Hayman, whom Frohman had met in Philadelphia, was engaged as advance-agent.

It was a courageous undertaking even for a seasoned and well-financed theatrical veteran. Although Lester Wallack was well known, his theater and its successes were not familiar to the great mass of people outside New York. In those days theatrical publicity was not as widespread as now. No wonder, then, that the daring of a young manager of twenty-five in taking out a company whose weekly salary list was nearly thirteen hundred dollars was commented on.

Charles called his aggregation the Wallack Theater Company. The repertoire consisted mainly of "Victor Durand," a play by Henry Guy Carleton which had been produced at Wallack's on December 13, 1884. Subsequently the company also played "Moths," "Lady Clare," "Diplomacy," and Belasco's "La Belle Russe."

This tour, which was to write itself indelibly on the career of Charles Frohman, began in Chicago and was continued through the South to New Orleans, where a stay of six weeks was made at the St. Charles Theater. Belasco joined them here for a week to put on "The World," which had been produced at Wallack's a short time before.

In New Orleans occurred one of those encounters in Charles Frohman's life that led to lifelong friendship. Two years before, while playing a Madison Square company at one of the theaters in St. Louis, he had met a bright young man in the box-office named Augustus Thomas. Thomas was then a newspaper man and was beginning to write plays. He told Charles that he had just made a short play out of Frances Hodgson Burnett's story, "Editha's Burglar."

In New Orleans Charles discovered that young Thomas was playing in his own play at a near-by theater and went over to see him. After the performance he visited him in his dressing-room, renewed his acquaintance, and said to him with the optimism of youth:

"Mr. Thomas, I hope that some day you will write a play for me."

The company now made a tour of Texas, where the troubles began. Business declined, but Frohman succeeded in landing the company in Chicago after a series of misfortunes. Here Sophie Eyre retired and was succeeded by Louise Dillon as leading woman. Charles, of course, had no money with which to buy costumes, so she pawned her jewels and used the proceeds. Sadie Bigelow took her place as ingénue.

Charles now started his famous tour of the Northwest which rivaled the Stoddart days in hardship and in humor. The Northern Pacific Railroad had just been opened to the coast, and Charles followed the new route. A series of tragic, dramatic, and comic experiences began. The tour was through the heart of the old cow country. One night, when the train was stalled by the wrecking of a bridge near Miles City, Montana, a group of cowboys started to "shoot up" the train. Frohman, with ready resource, singled out the leader and said:

"We've got a theatrical company here and we will give you a performance."

He got Rowland Buckstone to stand out on the prairie and recite "The Smuggler's Life," "The Execution," and "The Sanguinary Pirate" by the light of a big bonfire which was built while the show was going on. This tickled the cowboys and brought salvos of shots and shouts of laughter.

At Miles City occurred what might have been a serious episode. When the company reached the hotel at about eleven in the morning Charles Wheatleigh, the "first old man," asked the hotel-keeper what time breakfast was served. When he replied "Eight-thirty o'clock," Wheatleigh pounded the desk and said:

"That is for farmers. When do artists eat?"

The clerk was a typical Westerner, and thought this was an insult. He made a lunge for Wheatleigh, when Frohman stepped in and settled the difficulty in his usual suave and smiling way.

At Butte came another characteristic example of the Frohman enterprise and resource. It was necessary at all hazards to get an audience. When Charles got there he found that the wife of the leading gambler had died. He expressed so much sympathy for the bereaved man that he was made a pall-bearer, and this act created such an impression on the townspeople that they flocked to the theater at night.

At Missoula, Montana, Charles went out ahead of the show for a week. Approaching the treasurer at the box-office, he said:

"Will you please let me have a hundred dollars on account of the show?"

"I can't," replied the man. "We haven't sold a single seat for any of your performances."

Frohman thought a moment and walked out of the lobby. All afternoon orders for seats began to come in to the box-office. Late in the afternoon, when Frohman got back, the agent smiled and said:

"Mr. Frohman, I can let you have that hundred dollars now. We are beginning to have quite an advance sale."

Frohman had gone down-town and sent in the orders for the seats himself. He used fictitious names.

Now began a summer of hardships. With the utmost difficulty the company got to Portland, Oregon, where Charles established a sort of headquarters. From this point he sent the company on short tours. But business continued to be bad.

He started a series of "farewell" performances, as he did in Texas, and placarded the city with the bills announcing "positively" closing performances. These bills were typical of the publicity talents of Charles Frohman. He headed them "Good-by Engagements," and added the words, "A Long, Lingering Farewell." Under "Favorites' Farewell" he printed the names of the members of the company with the titles or parts in which they were known. "Good-by, Louise Dillon, our Esmeralda"; "Good-by, Kate Denin Wilson, Pretty Lady Dolly"; "Good-by, Charles B. Wells, Faithful Dave Hardy"; "Good-by, Rowland Buckstone, Some Other Man"—were typical illustrations of his attempt to make a strong appeal for business.

Actual money in the company was a novelty. Bernstein's five thousand dollars had long since vanished. When a member of the company wanted some cash it had to be extracted from the treasurer in one-dollar instalments.

Despite the hardships, the utmost good humor and feeling prevailed. Most of the members of the company were young; there was no bickering. They knew that Frohman's struggle was with and for them. They called him "The Governor," and he always referred to them as his "nice little company." All looked forward confidently to better days, and in this belief they were supported and inspired by the cheery philosophy of the manager.

Charles's resource was tested daily. He had booked a near-by town for fair week, which always meant good business. At last he had money in sight. The local manager, however, insisted upon a great display of fancy printing. Charles was in a dilemma because he owed his printer a big bill and he had no more lithographs on hand. A friend who was in advance of William Gillette's play, "The Private Secretary," came along with a lot of his own paper. Charles borrowed a quantity of it and also from the "Whose Baby Are You?" company, covered over these two titles with slips containing the words "Lady Clare," the piece he was going to present. He billed the town with great success and was able to keep going.

During the Portland sojourn Charles sent the company on to Salem, Oregon. While there, six members had their photographs taken with a disconsolate look on their faces and with Buckstone holding a dollar in his hand. They sent the picture to Frohman with the inscription:

"From your nice little company waiting for its salary."

At Portland, Oregon, A. D. Charlton, who was passenger agent of the Northern Pacific Railroad, and who had been of great service to Charles in extricating him from various financial difficulties, said to him one day:

"Frohman, I want you to meet a very promising little actress who is out here with her mother."

Frohman said he would be glad, and, accompanying Charlton to his office, was introduced to Annie Adams, a well-known actress from Salt Lake City, and her wistful-eyed little daughter, Maude. They were both members of the John McGuire Company. This was Charles Frohman's first meeting with Maude Adams.

At Portland Frohman added "Two Orphans" and "Esmeralda" to the company's repertoire. But it barely got them out of town at the really and truly "farewell."

Now began a return journey from Portland that was even more precarious than the trip out. Baggage had to be sacrificed; there was scarcely any scenery. One "back drop" showing the interior of a cathedral was used for every kind of scene, from a gambling-house to a ball-room. To the financial hardship of the homeward trip was added real physical trial. Frohman showed in towns wherever there was the least prospect of any kind of a house. The company therefore played in skating-rinks, school-houses, even barns. In some places the members of the company had to take the oil-lamps that served as footlights back in the makeshift dressing-rooms while they dressed.

At Bozeman, Montana, occurred an incident which showed both the humor and the precariousness of the situation. Frohman assembled the company in the waiting-room of the station and, stepping up to the ticket-office, laid down one hundred and thirty dollars in cash.

"Where do you want to go?" asked the agent.

Shoving the money at him, Frohman said, "How far will this take us?"

The agent looked out of the window, counted up the company, and said, "To Billings."

Turning to the company, Frohman said, with a smile, "Ladies and gentlemen, we play Billings next."

Just then he received a telegram from Alf Hayman, who was on ahead of the company:

> *What town shall I bill?*

Frohman wired back:

> *Bill Billings.*

Hayman again wired:

> *Have no printing and can get no credit. What shall I do?*

Frohman's resource came into stead, for he telegraphed:

> *Notify theaters that we are a high-class company from Wallack's Theater in New York and use no ordinary printing. We employ only newspapers and dodgers.*

At Missoula, Montana, on their way back, a member of the company became dissatisfied and stood with his associates at the station where two trains met, one for the east and one for the west. As the train for the east slowed up the actor rushed toward it and, calling to the members of the company, said:

"I am leaving you for good. You'll never get anywhere with Frohman."

The company, however, elected to stay with Frohman. In later years this actor fell into hardship. Frohman singled him out, and from that time on until Frohman's death he had a good engagement every year in a Frohman company.

At Bismarck, North Dakota, the company gave "Moths." In this play the spurned hero, a singer, has a line which reads, "There are many marquises, but very few *tenors.*"

Money had been so scarce for months that this remark was the last straw, so the company burst into laughter, and the performance was nearly broken up. Frohman, who stood in the back of the house, enjoyed it as much as the rest.

Through all these hardships Frohman remained serene and smiling. His unfailing optimism tided over the dark days. The end came at Winona, Minnesota. The company had sacrificed everything it could possibly sacrifice. Frohman borrowed a considerable sum from the railroad agent to go to Chicago, where he obtained six hundred dollars from Frank Sanger. With this he paid the friendly agent and brought the company back to New York.

Even the last lap of this disastrous journey was not without its humor. The men were all assembled in the smoking-car on the way from Albany to New York. Frohman for once sat silent. When somebody asked him why he looked so glum, he said, "I'm thinking of what I have got to face to-morrow."

Up spoke Wheatleigh, whose marital troubles were well known. He slapped Frohman on the back and said:

"Charley, your troubles are slight. Think of me. I've got to face my wife to-morrow."

It was characteristic of Frohman's high sense of integrity that he gave his personal note to each member of the company for back salary in full, and before five years passed had discharged every debt.

On arriving in New York Charles had less than a dollar in his pocket, his clothes were worn, and he looked generally much the worse for wear. On the street he met Belasco. They pooled their finances and went to "Beefsteak John's," where they had a supper of kidney stew, pie, and tea. They renewed the old experiences at O'Neil's restaurant and talked about what they were going to do.

The next day Frohman was standing speculatively in front of the Coleman House when he met Jack Rickaby, a noted theatrical figure of the time. Rickaby slapped the young man on the back and said:

"Frohman, I am glad you have had a good season. You're going to be a big man in this profession."

He shook Frohman's hand warmly and walked away.

It was the first cheering word that Frohman had heard. The news of his disastrous trip had not become known. Always proud, he was glad of it. After Rickaby had shaken his hand he felt something in it, and on looking he saw that the big-hearted manager had placed a hundred-dollar bill there. Rickaby had known all along the story of the Wallack tour hardships, and it was his way of expressing sympathy. Frohman afterward said it was the most touching moment in his life. Speaking of this once, he said:

"That hundred-dollar bill looked bigger than any sum of money I have ever had since."

It was late in 1885 when Charles returned from the disastrous Wallack's Theater tour, bankrupt in finance, but almost over-capitalized in courage and plans for the future. Up to that time he had no regular office. Like many of the managers of the day, his office was in his hat. Now, for the first time, he set up an establishment of his own. It required no capital to embark in the booking business in those days. Nerve and resiliency were the two principal requisites.

The first Frohman offices were at 1215 Broadway, in the same building that housed Daly's Theater. In two small rooms on the second floor Charles Frohman laid the corner-stone of what in later years became a chain of offices and interests that reached wherever the English language was spoken on the stage. The interesting contrast here was that while Augustin Daly, then in the heyday of his great success, was creating theatrical history on the stage below him, Charles Frohman was beginning his real managerial career up-stairs.

Frohman's first associate was W. W. Randall, a San Francisco newspaper man whom he had met in the Haverly's Minstrel days, in the mean time manager of "The Private Secretary" and several of the Madison Square companies on the road. He was alert and aggressive and knew the technique of the theatrical business.

Charles Frohman's policy was always pretentious, so he set up two distinct firms. One was the "Randall's Theatrical Bureau, Charles Frohman and W. W. Randall, Managers," which was under Randall's direction and which booked attractions for theaters throughout the country on a fee basis. The other was called "Frohman & Randall, General Theatrical Managers." Its function was to produce plays and was directly under Charles's supervision. The two firm names were emblazoned on the door and business was started. Their first employee was Julius Cahn.

These offices have an historic interest aside from the fact that they were the first to be occupied by Charles Frohman. Out of them grew really the whole modern system of booking attractions. Up to that era theatrical booking methods were different from those of the present time; there were no great centralized agencies to book attractions for strings of theaters covering the entire country. Union Square was the Rialto, the heart and center of the booking business. The out-of-town manager came there to fill his time for the season. Much of the booking was done in a haphazard way on the sidewalk, and whole seasons were booked on the curb, merely noted in pocket note-books. Two methods of booking were then in vogue: one by the manager of a company who wrote from New York to the towns for time; the other through an agent of out-of-town house managers located in New York. It was this latter system that Frohman and Randall began to develop in a scientific fashion. Charles's extensive experience on the road and his knowledge of the theatrical status of the different towns made him a valuable agent.

Frohman and Randall at that time practically had the field to themselves. Brooks & Dickson, an older firm which included the well-known Joseph Brooks of later managerial fame, had conducted the first booking-office of any consequence, but had now retired. H. S. Taylor had just established on Fourteenth Street Taylor's Theatrical Exchange, destined to figure in theatrical history as the forerunner of the Klaw & Erlanger business.

Despite the high-sounding titles on the door, the

Frohman offices were unpretentious. Frohman and Randall had a desk apiece, and there was a second-hand iron safe in the corner. When Frohman was asked, one day soon after the shingle had been hung out, what the safe was for, he replied, with his characteristic humor:

"We keep the coal-scuttle in it."

As a matter of fact there was more truth than poetry in this remark, because the office assets were so low that during the winter the firm had to burn gas all day to keep warm. When asked the reason for this, Frohman said, jocularly:

"We can get more credit if we use gas, because the gas bill has to be paid only once a month. Coal is cash."

Indeed, the office was so cold during that season that it came to be known in the profession as the "Cave of the Winds," and this title was no reflection on the vocal qualities of the proprietors.

It was during those early and precarious days when Frohman was still saddled with the debts of the Wallack's tour that one of the most amusing incidents of his life happened. One morning he was served with the notice of a supplementary proceeding which had been instituted against him. He was always afraid of the courts, and he was much alarmed. He rushed across the street to the Gilsey House and consulted Henry E. Dixey, the actor, who was living there. Dixey's advice was to get a lawyer. Together they returned to the Daly's Theater Building, where Frohman knew a lawyer was installed on the top floor. They found the lawyer blacking that portion of his white socks that appeared through the holes in his shoes.

Frohman stated his case, which the lawyer accepted. He then demanded a two-dollar fee. Frohman had only one dollar in his pocket and borrowed the other dollar from Dixey.

"This money," said the lawyer, "is to be paid into the court. How about my fee?"

Frohman fumbled in his pocket and produced a ten-cent piece. He handed it to the lawyer, saying: "I will pay you later on. Here is your car-fare. Be sure to get to court before it opens."

Frohman and Dixey left. Frohman was much agitated. They walked around the block several times. When he heard the clock strike ten he said to Dixey:

"Now the lawyer is in the court-room and the matter is being settled." In his expansive relief he said: "I have credit at Browne's Chop House. Let us go over and have breakfast."

At the restaurant they ordered a modest meal. As Frohman looked up from his table he saw a man sitting directly opposite whose face was hid behind a newspaper. In front of him was a pile of wheat-cakes about a foot high.

"Gee whiz!" said Frohman. "I wish I had enough money to buy a stack of wheat-cakes that high."

As he said this to Dixey the man opposite happened to lower his paper and revealed himself to be the lawyer Frohman had just engaged. He was having a breakfast spree himself with the two dollars extracted from his two recent clients.

Business began to pick up with the new year. The first, and what afterward proved to be the most profitable, clients of the booking-office were the Baldwin and California theaters in San Francisco. They were dominated by Al Hayman, brother of Alf, a man who now came intimately into Charles Frohman's life and remained so until the end. He was a Philadelphian who had conducted various traveling theatrical enterprises in Australia and had met Frohman for the first time in London when the latter went over with the Haverly Mastodons. Hayman admired Frohman very much and soon made him general Eastern representative of all his extensive Pacific coast interests.

Hayman was developing into a magnate of importance. With his assistance Charles was able to book a company all the way from New York to San Francisco. Charles made himself responsible for the time between New York and Kansas City, while Hayman would guarantee the company's time from Kansas City or Omaha to the coast.

Frohman and Randall made a good team, and they soon acquired a chain of more than three hundred theaters, ranging from music-halls in small towns that booked the ten-twenty-thirty-cent dramas up to the palatial houses like Hooley's in Chicago, the Hollis in Boston, and the Baldwin in San Francisco.

It was a happy-go-lucky time. If Frohman had ten dollars in his pocket to spare he considered himself rich. Money then, as always, meant very little to him. It came and went easily.

While the booking business waxed in volume the production end of the establishment did not fare so well. Charles had this activity of the office as his particular domain, and with the instinct of the plunger now began to put on plays right and left.

Just before the association with Randall, Frohman had become manager of Neil Burgess, the actor, and had booked him for a tour in a play called "Vim." A disagreement followed, and Frohman turned him over to George W. Lederer, who took the play out to the coast.

A year after this episode came the first of the many opportunities for fortune that Charles Frohman turned down in the course of his eventful life. This is the way it happened:

Burgess, who was quite an inventive person, had patented the treadmill mechanism to represent horse-racing on the stage, a device which was afterward used with such great effect in "Ben-Hur." He was so much impressed with it that he had a play written around it called "The County Fair."

Burgess, who liked Frohman immensely, tried to get him to take charge of this piece, but Frohman would not listen to the proposition about the mechanical device. He was unhappy over his experience about "Vim," and whenever Burgess tried to talk "The County Fair" and its machine Frohman would put him off.

Burgess finally went elsewhere, and, as most people know, "The County Fair" almost rivaled "The Old Homestead" in money-making ability. The horse-racing scene became the most-talked-of episode on the stage at the time, and Burgess cleared more than a quarter of a million dollars out of the enterprise. Charles Frohman afterward admitted that his prejudice against Burgess and his machine had cost his office at least one hundred thousand dollars.

Frohman and Randall now launched an important venture. McKee Rankin, who was one of the best-known players of the time, induced them to become his managers in a piece called "The Golden Giant," by

Clay M. Greene. Charles, however, agreed to the proposition on the condition that Rankin would put his wife, Kitty Blanchard, in the cast. They had been estranged, and Frohman, with his natural shrewdness, believed that the stage reunion of Mr. and Mrs. McKee Rankin would be a great drawing-card for the play. Rankin made the arrangements, and the Fifth Avenue Theater was booked for two weeks, commencing Easter Monday, 1886.

The theater was then under the management of John Stetson, of Boston, and both Frohman and Rankin looked forward to doing a great business. In this cast Robert Hilliard, who had been a clever amateur actor in Brooklyn, made his first professional appearance. Charles supervised the rehearsals and had rosy visions of a big success. At four o'clock, however, on the afternoon of the opening night, Charles went to the box-office and discovered the advance sale had been only one hundred dollars.

"I tell you what to do, Randall," quickly thought out Frohman, "if Stetson will stand for it we will paper the house to the doors. We must open to a capacity audience."

When Frohman put the matter before Stetson he said he did not believe in "second-hand reconciliations," but assented to the plan. Frohman gave Randall six hundred seats, and the latter put them into good hands. The *première* of "The Golden Giant," to all intents and purposes, took place before a crowded and paying house. In reality there was exactly two hundred and eighty-eight dollars in the box-office. Business picked up, however, and the two weeks' engagement proved prosperous. The play failed on the road, however, and the

Frohman offices lost over five thousand dollars on the venture. Rankin had agreed to pay Frohman forty per cent. of the losses. That agreement remained in force all his life, for it was never paid.

In Charles's next venture he launched his first star. Curiously enough, the star was Tony Hart, a member of the famous Irish team of Harrigan and Hart, who had delighted the boyhood of Frohman when he used to slip away on Saturday nights and revel in a show.

Tony Hart, during the interim, had separated from Harrigan, and in some way Charles obtained the manuscript of a farce-comedy by William Gill called "A Toy Pistol."

Charles had never lost his admiration for Hart, and when he saw that the leading character had to impersonate an Italian, a young Hebrew, an Irishwoman, and a Chinaman, Frohman said, "Tony Hart is the very person."

Accordingly, he engaged Hart and a company which included J. B. Mackey, F. R. Jackson, T. J. Cronin, D. G. Longworth, Annie Adams, Annie Alliston, Mattie Ferguson, Bertie Amberg, Eva Grenville, Vera Wilson, Minnie Williams, and Lena Merville.

This production had an influence on Charles Frohman's life far greater than the association with his first star, for Annie Adams now began a more or less continuous connection with Charles Frohman's companies. Her daughter, the little girl whom Charles had met casually years before, was now about to make her first New York appearance as member of a traveling company in "The Paymaster." Already the energetic mother was importuning Charles to engage the daughter. His answer was, "I'll give her a chance as soon as I can."

He little dreamed that this wisp of a girl was to become in later years his most profitable and best-known star.

Charles was, of course, keenly interested in "A Toy Pistol." He conducted the rehearsals, and on February 20, 1886, produced it at what was then called the New York Comedy Theater. It failed, however. The New York Comedy Theater was originally a large billiard-hall in the Gilsey Building, on Broadway between Twenty-eighth and Twenty-ninth streets, and had been first named the San Francisco Minstrel Hall. It became successively Haverly's Comedy Theater and the New York Comedy Theater. Subsequently, it was known as Hermann's Theater, and was the scene of many of the earlier Charles Frohman productions.

Charles now became immersed in productions. About this time Archibald Clavering Gunter, who had scored a sensational success with his books, especially "Mr. Barnes of New York," had written a play called "A Wall Street Bandit," which had been produced with great success in San Francisco. Frohman booked it for four weeks at the old Standard Theater, afterward the Manhattan, on a very generous royalty basis, and plunged in his usual lavish style. He got together a magnificent cast, which included Georgia Cayvan, W. J. Ferguson, Robert McWade, Charles Bowser, Charles Wheatleigh, and Sadie Bigelow. The play opened to capacity and the indications were that the engagement would be a success; but it suddenly fizzled out. On Sunday morning, when Charles read the papers with their reviews of the week, he said to Randall, with his usual philosophy:

"We've got a magnificent frost, but it was worth doing."

This production cost the youthful manager ten thousand dollars.

Frohman still had control of "time" at the Standard, so he now put on a play, translated by Henri Rochefort, called "A Daughter of Ireland," in which Georgia Cayvan had the title rôle. Here he scored another failure, but his ardor remained undampened and he went on to what looked at that moment to be the biggest thing he had yet tried.

Dion Boucicault was one of the great stage figures of his period. He was both actor and author, and wrote or adapted several hundred plays, including such phenomenal successes as "Colleen Bawn," "Shaughraun," which ran for a year simultaneously in London, New York, and Melbourne, and "London Assurance." There was much talk of his latest comedy, "The Jilt." Frohman, who always wanted to be associated with big names, now arranged by cable to produce this play at the Standard. Once more he plunged on an expensive company which included, among others, Fritz Williams, Louise Thorndyke, and Helen Bancroft.

For four weeks he cleared a thousand a week. Then he put the company on the road, where it did absolutely nothing. Charles, who had an uncanny sense of analysis of play failures, now declared that the reason for the failure was that theater-goers resented Boucicault's treatment of his first wife, Agnes Robertson. Boucicault had declared that he was not the father of her child, and when she sued him in England the courts gave her the verdict. Meanwhile Boucicault married, and in the eyes of the world he was a bigamist. This experience, it is interesting to add, taught Charles Frohman never to engage stars on whom there was the slightest smirch of scandal or disrepute.

At Montreal Boucicault refused to continue the tour, and this engagement, like so many of its predecessors, left Charles in a financial hole. Despite all these reverses he was able to make a livelihood out of the booking end of the office, which thrived and grew with each month. Nor was he without his sense of humor in those days.

One day he met a certain manager who had lost a great deal of money in comic opera. Frohman said to him that he heard that there was much money in the comic-opera end of the business.

"So there is," replied the manager.

"You ought to know," responded Frohman, "for you have put enough into it."

This remark, often attributed to others, is said to have originated here.

Frohman was now an established producer, and although the tide of fortune had not gone altogether happily with him, he had a Micawber-like conviction that the big thing would eventually turn up. Now came his first contact with Bronson Howard, who, a few years later, was to be the first mile-stone in his journey to fame and fortune.

Howard's name was one to conjure with. He had produced "Young Mrs. Winthrop," "The Banker's Daughter," "Saratoga," and other great successes. Charles Frohman, yielding, as usual, to the lure of big names, now put on Howard's play, "Baron Rudolph," for which George Knight had paid the author three thousand dollars to rewrite. Knight gave Frohman a free hand in the matter of casting the production, and it was put on at the Fourteenth Street Theater in an elaborate fashion. The company included various people who later on were to become widely known. Among them were George Knight and his wife, George Fawcett, Charles Bowser, and a very prepossessing young man named Henry Woodruff.

"Baron Rudolph" proved to be a failure, and it broke Knight's heart, for shortly afterward he was committed to an insane asylum from which he never emerged alive. It was found that while the play was well written there was no sympathy for a ragged tramp.

Whether he thought it would change his luck or not, Charles now turned to a different sort of enterprise. He had read in the newspapers about the astonishing mind-reading feats in England of Washington Irving Bishop. Always on the lookout for something novel, he started a correspondence with Bishop which ended in a contract by which he agreed to present Bishop in the United States in 1887.

Bishop came over and Frohman sponsored his first appearance in New York on February 27, 1887, at Wallack's Theater. With his genius for publicity, Frohman got an extraordinary amount of advertising out of this engagement. Among other things he got Bishop to drive around New York blindfolded. He invited well-known men to come and witness his marvelous gift in private. All of which attracted a great deal of attention, but very little money to the box-office. Frohman and Bishop differed about the conduct of the tour that was to follow, and M. B. Leavitt assumed the management.

BOOKING-AGENT; PRODUCER

While at 1215 Broadway Charles Frohman established another of his many innovations by getting out
what was probably the first stylographic press sheet.
This sheet, which contained news of the various attractions that Frohman booked, was sent to the leading
newspapers throughout the country and was the forerunner of the avalanche of press matter that to-day is
hurled at dramatic editors everywhere.

The booking business had now grown so extensively
that the office force was increased. First came Julius
Cahn, who assisted Randall with the booking. Al
Hayman took a desk in Frohman's office, which, because
of Hayman's extensive California enterprises, had a
virtual monopoly on all Western booking.

Now developed a curious episode. Charles, with his
devotion to big names, used the words "Daly's Theater
Building" on his letter-heads. This so infuriated Daly
that he sent a peremptory message to the landlord insisting that Frohman vacate the building. Frohman
and Randall thereupon moved their offices up the block
to 1267 Broadway.

Charles Frohman made every possible capitalization
of this change. Among other things he issued a broad-
side, announcing the removal to new offices, and making
the following characteristic statement:

> *Our agency, we are pleased to state, has been
> an established success from the very start. We
> now represent every important theater in the
> United States and Canada, as an inspection of
> our list will show, and we will always keep up
> the high standard of attractions that have been*

booked through this office, and we want the busi-
ness of no others. Mr. E. E. Rice, the well-known
manager and author, will have adjoining offices
with us, and his attractions will be booked through
our offices. We transact a general theatrical
business (excepting that pertaining to a dramatic
or actor's agency), and are in competition with
no other exchange, booking agency, or dramatic
concern. Neither do we have any desk-room to
let, reserving all the space of our office for our
own use.

Attached to this announcement was a list of theaters
that he represented, which was a foot long. He was
also representing Archibald Clavering Gunter, who had
followed up "A Wall Street Bandit" with "Prince
Karl," and Robert Buchanan, author of "Lady Clare"
and "Alone in London."

Frohman and Randall stayed at 1267 Broadway for a
year. Shortly before the next change Randall, who had
become extensively interested in outside enterprises,
retired from the firm. His successor as close associate
with Charles Frohman was Harry Rockwood, ablest of
the early Frohman lieutenants.

Rockwood was a distinguished-looking man and a
tireless worker. The way he came to be associated with
Charles Frohman was interesting. His real name was
H. Rockwood Hewitt, and he was related to ex-Mayor
Abram S. Hewitt of New York. He had had some
experience in Wall Street, but became infected with the
theatrical virus.

One day in 1888 a well-groomed young man approached Gustave Frohman at the Fourteenth Street

Theater. He introduced himself as Harry Hewitt. He said to Frohman:

"My name is Hewitt. I would like to get into the theatrical business."

Gustave invited him to come around to the Madison Square Theater the next day, and asked him what he would like to do.

"Oh, I should like to do anything."

Frohman then gave him an imaginary house to "count up."

Rockwood, who was an expert accountant, did the job with amazing swiftness. Whereupon Gustave Frohman telephoned to Charles Frohman as follows:

"I've got the greatest treasurer in the world for you. Send for him."

Charles engaged him for a Madison Square Company, and in this way Rockwood's theatrical career started. It was the fashion of many people of that time interested in the theatrical business to change their names, so he became Harry Rockwood. In the same way Harry Hayman, brother of Al and Alf Hayman, changed his name to Harry Mann.

In 1889 came the separation between Randall and Frohman. Randall set up an establishment of his own at 1145 Broadway, while Charles, who was now an accredited and established personage in the theatrical world, took a suite at 1127 Broadway, adjoining the old St. James Hotel. In making this change he reached a crucial point in his career, for in these offices he conceived and put into execution the spectacular enterprises that linked his name for the first time with brilliant success.

VI

WITH his installation in the new offices at 1127 Broadway there began an important epoch in the life of Charles Frohman. The Nemesis which had seemed to pursue his productions now took flight. The plump little man, not yet thirty, who had already lived a lifetime of strenuous and varied endeavor, sat at a desk in a big room on the second floor, dreaming and planning great things that were soon to be realized.

Although staggering under a burden of debt that would have discouraged most people, Frohman, with his optimistic philosophy, felt that the hour had come at last when the tide would turn. And it did. At this time his financial complications were at their worst. Some of them dated back to the disastrous Wallack Company tour; others resulted from his impulsive generosity in indorsing his friends' notes. He was so involved that he could not do business under his own name, and for a period the firm went on as Al Hayman & Company.

One of the very first enterprises in the new offices cemented the friendship of Charles Frohman and William Gillette. While at the Madison Square Theater he had booked Gillette's plays, "The Professor" and "The Private Secretary." Frohman, with Al Hayman as partner, induced Gillette to make a dramatization of

114

WILLIAM GILLETTE

Rider Haggard's "She," which was put on at Niblo's
Garden in New York with considerable success. Wilton
Lackaye and Loie Fuller were in the cast.

Gillette now tried his hand at a war play called
"Held by the Enemy," which Frohman booked on the
road. Frohman was strangely interested in "Held by
the Enemy." It had all the thrill and tumult of war
and it lent itself to more or less spectacular production.
When the road tour ended, Frohman, on his own hook,
took the piece and the company, which was headed by
Gillette, for an engagement at the Baldwin Theater in
San Francisco. He transported all the original scenery,
which included, among other things, some massive
wooden cannon.

The San Francisco critics, however, slated the piece
unmercifully. The morning after the opening Gillette
stood in the lobby of the Palace Hotel with the newspapers in his hand and feeling very disconsolate. Up
bustled Frohman in his usual cheery fashion.

"Look what the critics have done to us," said Gillette,
gloomily.

"But we've got all the best of it," replied Frohman,
with animation.

"How's that?" asked Gillette, somewhat puzzled.

"*They've* got to stay here."

This little episode shows the buoyant way in which
Frohman always met misfortune. His irresistible humor was the oil that he invariably spread upon the
troubled waters of discord and discouragement.

It was while selecting one of the casts of "Held by
the Enemy," which was revived many times, that
Charles Frohman made two more lifelong connections.

At the same boarding-house with Julius Cahn lived

an ambitious young man who had had some experience as an actor. He was out of a position, so Cahn said to him one day:

"Come over to our offices and Charles Frohman will give you a job."

The young man came over, and Cahn introduced him to Frohman. Soon he came out, apparently very indignant. When Cahn asked him what was the matter he said:

"That man Frohman offered me the part of a nigger, *Uncle Rufus*, in that play. I was born in the South, and I will not play a nigger. I would rather starve."

Cahn said, "You will play it, and your salary will be forty dollars a week."

The young man reluctantly accepted the engagement and proved to be not only a satisfactory actor, but a man gifted with a marvelous instinct as stage-director. His name was Joseph Humphreys, and he became in a few years the general stage-director for Charles Frohman, the most distinguished position of its kind in the country, which he held until his death.

About this time Charles Frohman renewed his acquaintance with Augustus Thomas. Thomas walked into the office one day and Rockwood said to him:

"You are the very man we want to play in 'Held by the Enemy.'"

Thomas immediately went in to see Frohman, who offered him the position of *General Stamburg*, but Thomas had an engagement in his own play, "The Burglar," which was the expanded "Editha's Burglar," and could not accept. Before he left, however, Frohman, whose mind was always full of projects for the future, renewed the offer made in New Orleans, for he said:

"Thomas, I still want you to write that play for me."

With "Held by the Enemy" Charles Frohman seemed to have found a magic touchstone. It was both patriotic and profitable, for it was nothing less than the American flag. Having raised it in one production, he now turned to the enterprise which unfurled his success to the winds in brilliant and stirring fashion.

Early in 1889 R. M. Field put on a new military play called "Shenandoah," by Bronson Howard, at the Boston Museum. Howard was then the most important writer in the dramatic profession. He had three big successes, "Young Mrs. Winthrop," "Saratoga," and "The Banker's Daughter," to his credit, and he had put an immense amount of work and hope into the stirring military drama that was to have such an important bearing on the career of Charles Frohman. The story of Frohman's connection with this play is one of the most picturesque and romantic in the whole history of modern theatrical successes. He found it a Cinderella of the stage; he proved to be its Prince Charming.

Oddly enough, "Shenandoah" was a failure in Boston. Three eminent managers, A. M. Palmer, T. Henry French, and Henry E. Abbey, in succession had had options on the play, and they were a unit in believing that it would not go.

Daniel Frohman had seen the piece at Boston with a view to considering it for the Lyceum. He told his brother Charles of the play, and advised him to go up and see it, adding that it was too big and melodramatic for the somewhat intimate scope of the small Lyceum stage.

So Charles went to Boston. On the day of the night

on which he started he met Joseph Brooks on Broadway and told him he was going to Boston to try to get "Shenandoah."

"Why, Charley, you are crazy! It is a failure! Why throw away your money on it? Nobody wants it."

"I may be crazy," replied Frohman, "but I am going to try my best to get 'Shenandoah.'"

Before going to Boston he arranged with Al Hayman to take a half-interest in the play. When he reached Boston he went out to the house of Isaac B. Rich, who was then associated with William Harris in the conduct of the Howard Athenæum and the Hollis Street Theater. Rich was a character in his way. He had been a printer in Bangor, Maine, had sold tickets in a New Orleans theater, and had already amassed a fortune in his Boston enterprises. He was an ardent spiritualist, and financed and gave much time to a spiritualistic publication of Boston called *The Banner of Light*. One of his theatrical associates at that time, John Stetson, owned *The Police Gazette*.

Rich conceived a great admiration for Frohman, whom he had met with Harris in booking plays for his Boston houses. He always maintained that Frohman was the counterpart of Napoleon, and called him Napoleon.

On this memorable day in Boston Frohman dined with Rich at his house and took him to see "Shenandoah." When it was over Frohman asked him what he thought of it.

"I'll take any part of it that you say," replied Rich.

"If I were alone," answered Frohman, "I would take you in, but I have already given Al Hayman half of it."

Frohman was very much impressed with "Shenandoah," although he did not believe the play was yet in shape for success. After the performance he asked Mr. Field if he could get the rights. Field replied:

"Abbey, French, and Palmer have options on it. If they don't want it you can have it."

Frohman returned to New York the next day, and even before he had seen Bronson Howard he looked up his friend Charles Burnham, then manager of the Star Theater, and asked him to save him some time.

Frohman now went to see Howard, who then lived at Stamford. He expressed his great desire for the play and then went on to say:

"You are a very great dramatist, Mr. Howard, and I am only a theatrical manager, but I think I can see where a possible improvement might be made in the play. For one thing, I think two acts should be merged into one, and I don't think you have made enough out of Sheridan's ride."

When he had finished, Howard spoke up warmly and said, "Mr. Frohman, you are right, and I shall be very glad to adopt your suggestions."

The very changes that Howard made in the play were the ones that helped to make it a great success, as he was afterward frank enough to admit.

Frohman now made a contract for the play and went to Burnham to book time. Burnham, meanwhile, had been to Boston to see the play, and he said:

"I saved six weeks for you at the Star for 'Shenandoah.'"

From the very beginning of his association with "Shenandoah" Charles Frohman had an instinct that the play would be a success. He now dedicated himself to its production with characteristic energy.

Scarcely had he signed the contract for "Shenandoah" than occurred one of the many curious pranks of fate that were associated with this enterprise. Al Hayman, who had a half-interest in the piece, was stricken with typhoid fever in Chicago on his way to the coast. He thought he was going to die, and, not having an extraordinary amount of confidence in "Shenandoah," he sold half of his half-interest to R. M. Hooley, who owned theaters bearing his name in Chicago and Brooklyn.

With his usual determination to do things in splendid fashion, Frohman engaged a magnificent cast. Now came one of the many evidences of the integrity of his word. Years before, when he had first seen Henry Miller act in San Francisco he said to him:

"When I get a theater in New York and have a big Broadway production you will be my leading man."

He had not yet acquired the theater, but he did have the big Broadway production, so the first male character that he filled was that of *Colonel West*, and he did it with Miller.

This cast included not less than half a dozen people who were then making their way toward future stardom. He engaged Wilton Lackaye to play *General Haverill;* Viola Allen played *Gertrude Ellingham;* Nanette Comstock was the original *Madeline West;* Effie Shannon portrayed *Jennie Buckthorn;* while Dorothy Dorr played *Mrs. Haverill*. Other actors in the company who later became widely known were John E. Kellard, Harry Harwood, Morton Selten, and Harry Thorn.

Charles determined that the public should not lose sight of "Shenandoah." All his genius for publicity was concentrated to this end. Among the ingenious agencies

that he created for arousing suspense and interest was
a rumor that the manuscript of the third act had been
lost. He put forth the news that Mr. Howard's copy
was mislaid, and a city-wide search was instituted. All
the while that the company was rehearsing the other
acts the anxiety about the missing act grew. A week
before the production Frohman announced, with great
effect, that the missing manuscript had been found.

When the doors of the Star Theater were opened on
the evening of September 9, 1889, for the first performance of "Shenandoah," the outlook was not very
auspicious. Rain poured in torrents. It was almost
impossible to get a cab. Al Hayman, one of the owners
of the play, who lived at the Hotel Majestic, on West
Seventy-second Street, was rainbound and could not
even see the *première* of the piece.

However, a good audience swam through the deluge,
for the gross receipts of this opening night, despite the
inclement conditions outside, were nine hundred and
seventy-two dollars. This was considered a very good
house at the standard prices of the day, which ranged
from twenty-five cents to one dollar and a half.

The play was an immense success, for at no time during the rest of the engagement did the receipts at any
performance go below one thousand dollars. The
average gross receipts for each week were ten thousand
dollars.

Charles Frohman watched the *première* from the rear
of the house with a beating heart. The crash of applause after the first act made him feel that he had
scored at last. After the sensational ending of the
third act, which was Sheridan's famous ride, he rushed
back to the stage, shook Henry Miller warmly by the

hand, and said: "Henry, we've got it. The horse is yours!"

He meant the horse that the general rode in the play.

This horse, by the way, was named Black Bess. It got so accustomed to its cue that it knew when it had to gallop across the stage. One night during the third act this cue was given as usual. Its rider, however, was not ready, and the horse galloped riderless across the stage.

"Shenandoah" led to a picturesque friendship in Charles Frohman's life. On the opening night a grizzled, military-looking man sat in the audience. He watched the play with intense interest and applauded vigorously. On the way out he met a friend in the lobby. He stopped him and said, "This is the most interesting war play I have ever seen."

The friend knew Charles Frohman, who was standing with smiling face watching the crowd go out. He called the little manager over and said: "Mr. Frohman, I want you to meet a man who really knows something about the Civil War. This is General William T. Sherman."

Sherman and Frohman became great friends, and throughout the engagement of "Shenandoah" the old soldier was a frequent visitor at the theater. He then lived at the Fifth Avenue Hotel, and often he brought over his war-time comrades.

Not only did "Shenandoah" mark the epoch of the first real success in Frohman's life, but it raised his whole standard of living, as the following incident will show.

When "Shenandoah" opened, Frohman and Henry Miller, and sometimes other members of the company, went around to O'Neil's on Sixth Avenue, scene of the old foregatherings with Belasco, and had supper. As the piece grew in prosperity and success, the supper party gradually moved up-town to more expensive restaurants, until finally they were supping at Delmonico's. "We are going up in the world," said Frohman, with his usual humor. At their first suppers they smoked ten-cent cigars; now they regaled themselves with twenty-five-cent Perfectos.

Unfortunately the successful run of "Shenandoah" at the Star had to be terminated on October 12th because the Jefferson & Florence Company, which had a previous contract with the theater and could not be disposed of elsewhere, came to play their annual engagement in "The Rivals." Frohman transferred the play to Proctor's Twenty-third Street Theater, which was from this time on to figure extensively in his fortunes, and the successful run of the play continued there. Wilton Lackaye retired from the cast and was succeeded by Frank Burbeck, whose wife, Nanette Comstock, succeeded Miss Shannon in the rôle of *Jenny Buckthorn*.

Frohman was now able to capitalize his brilliant road-company experience. The success of the play now assured, he immediately organized a road company, in which appeared such prominent actors as Joseph Holland, Frank Carlyle, and Percy Haswell. He established an innovation on October 26th by having this company come over from Philadelphia, where it was playing, to act in the New York house.

The two-hundred-and-fiftieth performance occurred on April 19, 1890, when the run ended. It was a memorable night. Katherine Grey and Odette Tyler meanwhile had joined the company. The theater was draped in flags, and General Sherman made a speech in which he praised the accuracy of the production.

With his usual enterprise and resource, Charles Frohman introduced a distinct novelty on this occasion. He had double and triple relays of characters for the farewell performance. Both Lilla Vane and Odette Tyler, for example, acted the part of *Gertrude Ellingham;* Wilton Lackaye, Frank Burbeck, and George Osborne played *General Haverill;* Alice Haines and Nanette Comstock did *Jenny Buckthorn;* while Morton Selten and R. A. Roberts doubled as *Captain Heartsease.*

Frohman now put the original "Shenandoah" company on the road. Its first engagement was at McVicker's Theater in Chicago. Frohman went along and took Bronson Howard with him.

Most of the Chicago critics liked "Shenandoah." But there was one exception, a brilliant Irishman on *The Tribune.* Paul Potter, whose play, "The City Directory," was about to be produced in Chicago, was a close friend of Howard. He wanted to do something for the Howard play, so he got permission from Robert W. Patterson, editor in chief of *The Tribune,* to write a Sunday page article about "Shenandoah." Frohman was immensely pleased, and through this he met Potter, who became one of his intimates.

Then came the opening of Potter's play at the Chicago Opera House. Although Potter knew most of the critics, there was a feeling that they would forget all friendship and do their worst. Five minutes after the curtain went up the piece seemed doomed.

But an extraordinary thing happened. From a stage box suddenly came sounds of uncontrollable mirth. The audience, and especially the critics, looked to see

who was enjoying the play so strenuously, and they beheld
Charles Frohman and Bronson Howard. The critics
were puzzled. Here was a great playwright in the
flush of an enormous success and a rising young manager
evidently enjoying the performance. The mentors of
public taste were so impressed that they praised the
farce and started "The City Directory" on a career of
remarkable success. Frohman and Howard were re-
paying the good turn that Potter had done for "Shenandoah."

Charles Frohman now had a money-making success.
"Shenandoah" was the dramatic talk of the whole
country; it did big business everywhere, and its courageous young producer came in for praise and congratu-
lation on all sides.

The manager might well have netted what was in
those days a huge fortune out of this enterprise, but his
unswerving sense of honor led him to immediately discharge all his obligations. He wiped out the Wallack's
tour debts, and he eventually took up notes aggregating
forty-two thousand dollars that he had given to a well-
known Chicago printer who had befriended him in years
gone by. What was most important, he was now free
to unfurl his name to the breezes and to do business "on
his own."

Charles immediately launched himself on another sea
of productions. The most important was Gillette's
"All the Comforts of Home," which he put on at
Proctor's Twenty-third Street Theater. Frohman had
just acquired the lease of this theater. Already a big
idea was simmering in his mind, and the leasehold was

essential to its consummation. On May 8, 1890, he produced the new Gillette play, which scored a success.

This production marked another one of the many significant epochs in Frohman's life because it witnessed the first appearance of little Maude Adams under the Charles Frohman management.

Frohman had seen Miss Adams in "The Paymaster" down at Niblo's and had been much taken with her work. He had been unable, however, to find a part for her, so it was reserved for his brother Daniel to give her the first Frohman engagement at thirty-five dollars a week in "Lord Chumley." Subsequently Daniel released her so that she could appear in the same cast with her mother in Hoyt's "The Midnight Bell."

While trying "All the Comforts of Home" on the road there occurred an amusing episode. Frohman, who had been watching the rehearsals very carefully, said to Henry Miller, who was leading man:

"Henry, you are something of a matinée idol. I think it would help the play if you had a love scene with Miss Adams."

Accompanied by Rockwood, Frohman visited Gillette at his home at Hartford, got him to write the love scene, and then went on to Springfield, Massachusetts, for the "try-out."

That night the three assembled in the bleak drawing-room of the hotel. Frohman ordered a little supper of ham sandwiches and sarsaparilla, after which he rehearsed the love scene, which simply consisted of a tender little parting in a doorway. It served to bring out the wistful and appealing tenderness that is one of Maude Adams's great qualities.

"All the Comforts of Home" ran in Proctor's Theater

until October 18th. When the theater reopened it disclosed a venture that linked the name of Charles Frohman with high and artistic effort—his first stock company. With this organization he hoped to maintain the traditions established by Augustin Daly, A. M. Palmer, Lester Wallack, and the Madison Square Company.

He projected the Charles Frohman Stock Company in his usual lavish way. He engaged De Mille and Belasco to write the opening play. This was a very natural procedure: first, because of his intimate friendship with Belasco, and, second, because De Mille and Belasco had proved their skill as collaborators at Daniel Frohman's Lyceum Theater with such successes as "The Wife," "The Charity Ball," and "Lord Chumley." The result of their new endeavors was "Men and Women."

In this play the authors wrote in the part *Dora* especially for Maude Adams. They also created a rôle for Mrs. Annie Adams.

The cast of "Men and Women," like that of "Shenandoah," was a striking one, and it contained many names already established, or destined to figure prominently in theatrical history. Henry Miller had been engaged for leading man, but he retired during the rehearsals, and his place was taken by William Morris, who had appeared in the Charles Frohman production of "She" and in the road company of "Held by the Enemy." In the company that Frohman selected were Frederick de Belleville, who played *Israel Cohen*, one of the finest, if not the finest, Jewish characters ever put on the stage; Orrin Johnson; Frank Mordaunt; Emmet Corrigan; J. C. Buckstone; and C. Leslie Allen, brother of Viola Allen.

In addition to Maude Adams were Sydney Armstrong, who was the leading woman; Odette Tyler; and Etta Hawkins, who became the wife of William Morris during this engagement.

At the dress rehearsal of "Men and Women" occurred a characteristic Charles Frohman incident. When the curtain had gone down Frohman hurried back to William Morris's dressing-room and said, "Will, that dress-suit of yours doesn't look right."

"It's a brand-new suit, 'C. F.,'" he replied.

Frohman thought a moment and said: "Can you be at my office to-morrow morning at eight o'clock? I've got a good tailor."

Promptly at eight the next day they went over to Frohman's tailor, whom Frohman addressed as follows:

"I want you to make a dress-suit for William Morris by eight o'clock to-morrow night."

"Impossible!" said the man.

"Nothing is impossible," said Frohman. "If that dress-suit is not in Mr. Morris's dressing-room at eight o'clock you won't get paid for it."

The dress-suit showed up on time, and in it was a card, saying, "With Charles Frohman's compliments."

Charles inaugurated his first stock season at Proctor's on October 21, 1890. Although the notices were uniformly good, the start into public favor was a trifle slow. One reason was that a big bank failure had just shaken Wall Street, and there was considerable apprehension all over the city. By a curious coincidence there was a bank failure in the play. By clever publicity this fact was capitalized; the piece found its stride and ran for two hundred consecutive performances, when it was sent on the road with great success.

For this tour Charles also introduced another one of the many novelties that he put into theatrical conduct. He ordered a private car for the company, and they used it throughout the tour. It was considered an extravagance, but it was merely part of the Charles Frohman policy to make his people comfortable. With this private car he established a precedent that was observed in most of his traveling organizations.

With the stock company on tour in "Men and Women," the manager now organized the Charles Frohman Comedy Company to fill in the time at Proctor's. Once more he collected a brilliant aggregation of players, for they included Henrietta Crosman, Joseph Holland, Frederick Bond, and Thomas Wise. Each one became a star in the course of the next ten years.

The opening bill for the comedy company was Gillette's "Mr. Wilkinson's Widows," and was presented on March 30th, immediately following the run of "Men and Women." Henrietta Crosman subsequently withdrew from the cast, and Esther Lyons took her place.

Charles Frohman reopened the theater on August 27th with a revival of this play, in which Georgia Drew Barrymore, the mother of Ethel, appeared as *Mrs. Perrin*. Emily Bancker, afterward a star in "Our Flat," and Mattie Ferguson were in the cast.

On October 5th the company did Sardou's big drama of "Thermidor" for the first time on any stage, with another one of the casts for which Charles Frohman was beginning to become famous. It included a thin, gaunt Englishman whose name in the bill was simply J. F. Robertson, and who had just come from an engagement with John Hare in London. Subsequently the J. F. in his name came to be known as Johnston Forbes, because the man was Sir Johnston Forbes-Robertson.

In this company was Elsie De Wolfe, who later became a star and who years after left the theater to become an interior decorator. Among the male members of the company, besides Forbes-Robertson, was Jamison Lee Finney, who had graduated from the amateur ranks and who became one of the best-known comedians in the country.

In the mean time Charles had commissioned Henry C. De Mille to furnish a play for his stock company which was now on its way back from the coast. This play was "The Lost Paradise," which the American had adapted from Ludwig Fulda's drama. De Mille joined the company in Denver and rehearsals were begun there. By the time the company reached New York they were almost letter-perfect, and the opening at Proctor's on November 16th was a brilliant success. The play ran consecutively until March 1st.

The cast was practically the same as "Men and Women," with the addition of Cyril Scott, Odette Tyler, and Bijou Fernandez.

In "The Lost Paradise" Maude Adams scored the biggest success that she had made up to that time in New York. She played the part of *Nell*, the consumptive factory girl. This character, with its delicate and haunting interpretation, made an irresistible appeal to the audience.

"There's big talent in that girl," said Frohman in speaking of Miss Adams. He began to see the vision of what the years would hold for her.

By this time Charles Frohman had begun to make his

annual visit to London. Out of one of the earliest journeys came still another success of the many that now seemed to crowd upon him.

He had taken desk space with Abbey, Schoeffel & Grau in Henrietta Street in London. On the trip in question Belasco accompanied him. One night Frohman said:

"There is a little comedy around the corner called 'Jane.' Let's go and see it."

Frohman was convulsed with laughter, and the very next day sought out the author, William Lestocq, from whom he purchased the American rights. Out of this connection came another one of the lifelong friendships of Frohman. Lestocq, a few years later, became his principal English representative and remained so until the end.

Frohman was now in a whirlpool of projects. Although he was occupying himself with both the comedy and stock companies at Proctor's, he put on "Jane" as a midsummer attraction at the Madison Square Theater with a cast that included Katherine Grey, Johnstone Bennett, Jennie Weathersby, and Paul Arthur.

"Jane" became such an enormous success that Charles put out two road companies at once. In connection with "Jane" it may be said that his first real fortune—that is, the first money that he actually kept for a time—was made with this comedy.

Production after production now marked the Frohman career. Charles had always admired Henry E. Dixey, so he launched him as star in "The Solicitor" at Hermann's Theater, on September 8, 1891. It was the first time that the famous "Charles Frohman Presents" was used. In this company were Burr McIntosh, Sidney

Drew, and Joseph Humphreys. It was the failure of "The Solicitor" that led Frohman to put Dixey out again as star in a piece called "The Man with a Hundred Heads" at the Star Theater. This also failed, so he ventured with "The Junior Partner" at the same theater with a cast that included E. J. Ratcliffe, Mrs. McKee Rankin, Henrietta Crosman, and Louise Thorndyke-Boucicault.

Early the following year he tried his luck at Hermann's with "Gloriana," in which May Robson and E. J. Henley appeared. Hermann's Theater, however, seemed to be a sort of hoodoo, so Frohman returned to the Star, which had been his mascot, and made his first joint production with David Belasco in a musical piece called "Miss Helyett." Frohman had seen the play in Paris, and proceeded at once to buy the American rights from Charles Wyndham. This production not only marked the first joint presentation of Belasco and Charles, but it was the début of Mrs. Leslie Carter, who had become a protégée of Mr. Belasco. When the piece was moved to the Standard early in January, 1892, Mrs. Carter was starred for the first time.

By this time Charles Frohman was a personage to be reckoned with. "Shenandoah," the two stock companies, "Jane," and all the other enterprises both successful and otherwise, had made his name a big one in the theater. He now began to reach out for authors.

The first author to be approached was Augustus Thomas. He gave Charles a play called "Surrender." It was put on in Boston. The original idea in Thomas's mind was to write a satire on the war plays that had been so successful, like "Shenandoah" and "Held by the Enemy." "Surrender" began as a farce, but Charles Frohman and Eugene Presbrey, who produced it, wanted to make it serious.

The cast was a very notable one, including Clement Bainbridge, E. M. Holland, Burr McIntosh, Harry Woodruff, H. D. Blackmore, Louis Aldrich, Maude Bancks, Miriam O'Leary, Jessie Busley, and Rose Eytinge.

The rehearsals of "Surrender" were marked by many amusing episodes. Maude Bancks, for example, who was playing the part of a Northern girl in a Southern town, had to wear a red sash to indicate her Northern proclivities. This she refused to put on at the dress rehearsal because it did not match her costume. Bainbridge, an actor who played a Southern general, had a speech that he regarded as treason to his adopted country, and quit. But all these troubles were bridged over and the play was produced with some artistic success. It lasted sixteen weeks on the road.

After he had closed "Surrender" Frohman was telling a friend in New York that he had lost twenty-eight thousand dollars on this piece.

"But why did you permit yourself to lose so much money on a play that seemed bound to fail?"

"I believe in Gus Thomas. That is the reason," replied Frohman.

Although immersed in a multitude of enterprises, Frohman's activities now took a new and significant tack. Through all these crowded years his friendship for William Harris had been growing. Harris, who had graduated from minstrelsy to theatrical management and was the partner of Isaac B. Rich in the conduct of

the Howard Athenæum and the Hollis Street Theater
in Boston, now added the Columbia Theater in that
city to his string of houses. Charles at once secured
an interest in this lease, and it was his first out-of-town
theater. Quick to capitalize the opportunity, he put
one of the "Jane" road companies in it for a run and
called it the Charles Frohman Boston Stock Company.

VII

JOHN DREW AND THE EMPIRE THEATER

*T*HE year 1892 not only found Charles Frohman established as an important play-producing manager, but in addition he was reaching out for widespread theater management. It was to register a memorable epoch in the life of Charles and to record, through him, a significant era in the history of the American theater. From this time on his life-story was to be the narrative of the larger development of the drama and its people.

With the acquisition of his first big star, John Drew, he laid the corner-stone of what is the so-called modern starring system, which brought about a revolution in theatrical conduct. The story of Charles's conquest in securing the management of Drew, with all its attendant dramatic and sensational features, illustrates the resource and vision of the one-time minstrel manager who now began to come into his own as a real Napoleon of the stage.

Charles always attached importance and value to big names. He had paid dearly in the past for this proclivity with the Lester Wallack Company. Undaunted, he now turned to another investment in name that was to be more successful.

About this time John Drew had made his way to a unique eminence on the American stage. A member of a distinguished Philadelphia theatrical family, he had scored an instantaneous success on his first appearance at home and had become the leading man of Augustin Daly's famous stock company. He was one of "The Big Four" of that distinguished organization, which included Ada Rehan, Mrs. G. H. Gilbert, and James Lewis. They were known as such in America and England. Drew was regarded as the finest type of the so-called modern actor interpreting the gentleman in the modern play. He shone in the drawing-room drama; he had a distinct following, and was therefore an invaluable asset. The general impression was that he was wedded to the environment that had proved so successful and was so congenial.

Charles knew Drew quite casually. Their first meeting was characteristic. It happened during the great "Shenandoah" run. Henry Miller and Drew were old friends. It was Frohman's custom in those days to have after-theater suppers on Saturday nights at his rooms in the old Hoffman House, and sometimes a friendly game of cards.

One Saturday Miller called Frohman up and asked him if he could bring Drew down for supper.

"Certainly; with pleasure," said Frohman.

That night after the play Miller picked Drew up at Daly's and took him to the Hoffman House. Knowing the way to the Frohman rooms, he started for them unannounced, when he was stopped by a bell-boy, who said, "Mr. Frohman is expecting you in here," opening the door and ushering the guests into a magnificent private suite that Frohman had engaged for the occasion. It was the first step in the campaign for Drew.

Although Frohman was eager to secure Drew, he made

JOHN DREW

no effort to lure the actor away from what he believed was a very satisfactory connection.

As the friendship between the men grew, however, he discovered that Drew was becoming dissatisfied with his arrangement at Daly's. Up to that time "The Big Four" shared in the profits of the theater. Daly canceled this arrangement, and Drew suddenly realized that what seemed to be a most attractive alliance really held out no future for him.

Drew's dissatisfaction was heightened by his realization that Augustin Daly's greatest work and achievements were behind him. The famous old manager was undergoing that cycle of experience which comes to all of his kind when the flood-tide of their success begins to ebb.

Drew was speculating about his future when Frohman heard of his state of mind. He now felt that he would not be violating the ethics of the profession in making overtures looking to an alliance. He did not make a direct offer, but sent a mutual friend, Frank Bennett, once a member of the Daly company, who was then conducting the Arlington Hotel in Washington. Through him Frohman made a proposition to Drew to become a star. The actor accepted the offer, and a three-year contract was signed.

The capture of John Drew by Charles Frohman was more than a mere business stroke. Frohman never forgot that the great Daly had succeeded in ousting him from his first booking-offices in the Daly Theater Building. He found not a little humor in pre-empting the services of the Daly leading man as a sort of reciprocal stroke.

When Drew told Daly that he had signed a contract

with Frohman the then dictator of the American stage could scarcely find words to express his astonishment. He assured Drew that he was making the mistake of his life, because he regarded Frohman as an unlicensed interloper. Yet this "interloper," from the moment of the Drew contract, began a new career of brilliant and artistic development.

Frohman's starring arrangement with Drew created a sensation, both among the public and in the profession. It broke up "The Big Four," for Drew left a gap at Daly's that could not be filled.

There was also a widespread feeling that while Drew had succeeded in a congenial environment, and with an actress (Miss Rehan) who was admirably suited to him, he might not duplicate this success amid new scenes. Hence arose much speculation about his leading woman. A dozen names were bruited about.

Charles Frohman remained silent. He was keenly sensitive to the sensation he was creating, and was biding his time to launch another. It came when he announced Maude Adams as John Drew's leading woman. He had watched her development with eager and interested eye. She had made good wherever he had placed her. Now he gave her what was up to this time her biggest chance. The moment her name became bracketed with Drew's there was a feeling of satisfaction over the choice. How wise Charles Frohman was in the whole Drew venture was about to be abundantly proved.

Charles Frohman not only made John Drew a star, but the nucleus of a whole system. It was a time of rebirth for the whole American stage. Nearly all the old stars were gone or were passing from view. Forrest,

McCullough, Cushman, Janauschek were gone; Modjeska's power was waning; Clara Morris was soon to leave the stage world; Lawrence Barrett and W. J. Florence were dead; Edwin Booth had retired.

Frohman realized that with the passing of these stars there also passed the system that had created them. He knew that the public—the new generation—wanted younger people, popular names—somebody to talk about. He realized further that the public adored personality and that the strongest prop that a play could get was a fascinating and magnetic human being, whether male or female. The old stars had made themselves—risen from the ranks after years of service. Frohman saw the opportunity to accelerate this advance by providing swift and spectacular recognition. The new stars that were now to blossom into life under him owed their being to the initiative and the vision of some one else. Thus he became the first of the star-makers.

Charles was now all excitement. He had the making of his first big star, and he proceeded to launch him in truly magnificent fashion.

A play was needed that would bring out all those qualities that had made Drew shine in the drawing-room drama. The very play itself was destined to mark an epoch in the life of a man in the theater. Through Elizabeth Marbury, who had just launched herself as play-broker in a little office on Twenty-fourth Street, around the corner from Charles Frohman's, his attention was called to a French farcical comedy called "The Masked Ball," by Alexandre Bisson and Albert Carre. Frohman liked the story and wanted it adapted for American production. It was the beginning of his long patronage of French plays.

"I know a brilliant young man who could do this job for you very well," said Miss Marbury.

"What's his name?" asked Frohman.

"Clyde Fitch, and I believe he is going to have a great career," was the answer of his sponsor.

Fitch was given the commission. He did a most successful piece of adaptation, and in this way began the long and close relationship between the author of "Beau Brummel" (his first play) and the man who, more than any other, did so much to advance his career.

For Drew's début under his management Charles spared no expense. In addition to Maude Adams, the company included Harry Harwood (who was then coming into his own as a forceful and versatile character actor), C. Leslie Allen, Mrs. Annie Adams, and Frank E. Lamb.

With his usual desire to do everything in a splendid way, Frohman arranged for Drew's début at Palmer's Theater, the old Lester Wallack playhouse which was now under the management of A. M. Palmer, then one of the shining figures in the American drama, and located opposite Drew's former scenes of activity. Thus Drew's first stellar appearance was on a stage rich with tradition.

"The Masked Ball" opened October 3, 1892, in the presence of a representative audience. It was an instantaneous success. Drew played with brilliancy and distinction, and Frohman's confidence in him was amply justified.

The performance, however, had a human interest apart from the star. Maude Adams, for the first time in her career, had a real Broadway opportunity, and she made the most of it in such a fashion as to convince

CLYDE FITCH

HENRY ARTHUR JONES

Frohman and every one else that before many years were past she, too, would have her name up in electric lights. She played the part of *Zuzanne Blondet*, a more or less frivolous person, and it was in distinct contrast with the character that she had just abandoned, that of *Nell*, the consumptive factory-girl in "The Lost Paradise."

As *Zuzanne* in "The Masked Ball," Miss Adams

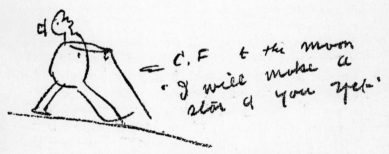

A CHARACTERISTIC FROHMAN BLUE PENCIL SKETCH

went to a ball and assumed tipsiness in order to influence her dissipated husband and achieve his ultimate reformation. The way she prepared for this part was characteristic of the woman. She wore a hat with a long feather, and she determined to make it a "tipsy feather." This feature became one of the comedy hits of the play, but in order to achieve it she worked for days and days to bring about the desired effect. The result of all this painstaking preparation was a brilliant performance. When the curtain went down on that memorable night at Palmer's Theater the general impression was:

"Maude Adams will be the next Frohman star."

The morning after the opening Frohman went to John Drew and said: "Well, John, you don't need me any more now. You're made."

"No, Charles; I shall need you always," was the reply.

Out of this engagement came the long and intimate friendship between Drew and Frohman. The first contract, signed and sealed on that precarious day when Frohman was seeing the vision of the modern star system, was the last formal bond between them. Though their negotiations involved hundreds of thousands of dollars in the years that passed, there was never another scrap of paper between them.

Seldom in the history of the American theater has another event been so productive of far-reaching consequence as "The Masked Ball." It brought Clyde Fitch into contact with the man who was to be his real sponsor; it made John Drew a star; it carried Maude Adams to the frontiers of the stellar realm; it gave Charles Frohman a whole new and distinguished place in the theater.

Frohman was quick to follow up this success. With
Drew he had made his first real bid for what was known
in those days as "the carriage trade"—that is, the patronage of the socially elect. He hastened to clinch this
with another stunning production at Palmer's. It was
Bronson Howard's play, "Aristocracy."

The play, produced on November 14, 1893, was done
in Frohman's usual lavish way. The company included
not less than half a dozen people who were then making
their way toward stardom—Wilton Lackaye, Viola Allen,
Blanche Walsh, William Faversham, Frederick Bond,
Bruce McRae, Paul Arthur, W. H. Thompson, J. W.
Piggott. "Aristocracy" was Bronson Howard's rever-
sion to the serenity of the society drama after the spectacle of war. The first night's audience was fashionable.
The distinction of the cast lent much to the success of
the occasion.

When John Drew called on Charles Frohman for the
first time at his offices at 1127 Broadway, his way was
impeded by a bright-eyed, alert young office-boy who
bore the unromantic name of Peter Daly. He incar-
nated every ill to which his occupation seems to be heir.
Without troubling himself to find out if Mr. Frohman
was in, he immediately said, after the grand fashion
of theatrical office-boys:

"Mr. Frohman is out and I don't know when he
will return."

"But I have an engagement with Mr. Frohman,"
said Drew.

"You will have to wait," said the boy.

Drew cooled his heels outside while Frohman waited
impatiently inside for him. When he emerged at lunch-

time he was surprised to find his man about to depart.

Daly was immediately discharged by Julius Cahn, who was office manager, but was promptly reinstated the next day by Frohman, who had been greatly impressed with the boy's quick wit and intelligence.

This office-boy, it is interesting to relate, became Arnold Daly, the actor. No experience of his life was perhaps more amusing or picturesque than the crowded year when he manned the outside door of Charles Frohman's office. Instead of attending to business, he spent most of his time writing burlesques on contemporary plays, which he solemnly submitted to Harry Rockwood, the bookkeeper.

During these days occurred a now famous episode. Young Daly was luxuriously reclining in the most comfortable chair in the reception-room one day when Louise Closser Hale, the actress, entered and asked to see Charles Frohman.

"He is out," said Daly.

"May I wait for him?" asked the visitor.

"Yes," answered Daly, and the woman sat down.

After three hours had passed she asked Daly, "Where is Mr. Frohman?"

"He's in London," was the reply.

Afterward Daly became "dresser" for John Drew, the virus of the theater got into his system, and before long he was an actor.

Thus even Charles Frohman's office-boys became stars.

Epochal as had been 1892, witnessing the first big Frohman star and a great artistic expansion, the new year that now dawned realized another and still greater dream of Charles Frohman, for it brought the dedication of his own New York theater at last, the famous Empire.

Ever since he had been launched in the metropolitan theatrical whirlpool, Frohman wanted a New York theater. As a boy he had witnessed the glories of the Union Square Theater under Palmer; as a road manager he had a part in the success of the Madison Square Theater activities; in his early managerial days he had been associated with the Lester Wallack organization; he had watched the later triumphs of the Lyceum Theater Company at home and on the road. Quite naturally he came to the conviction that he was ready to operate and control a big theater of his own.

The way toward its consummation was this:

One day toward the end of the 'eighties, William Harris came to New York to see Frohman about the booking of some attractions. He said:

"Charley, I want a theater in New York, and I know that you want one. Let's combine."

"All right," said Frohman. "You can get the Union Square. The lease is on the market."

"Very well," said Harris.

On the way down-stairs he met Al Hayman, who asked him where he was going.

"I am going over to lease the Union Square Theater," he replied.

"That's foolish," said Hayman. "Everything theatrical is going up-town."

"Well," answered Harris, "C. F. wants a theater, and I am determined that he shall have it, so I am going over to get the Union Square."

"If you and Frohman want a theater that badly, I will build one for you," he responded.

"Where?" asked Harris.

"I've got some lots at Fortieth and Broadway, and it's a good site, even if it is away up-town."

They went back to Frohman's office, and here was hatched the plan for the Empire Theater.

"I can't go ahead on this matter without Rich," said Harris.

"All right," said Frohman. "Wire Rich."

Rich came down next day, and the final details were concluded for the building of the Empire. Frank Sanger came in as a partner; thus the builders were Al Hayman, Frank Sanger, and William Harris. Without the formality of a contract they turned it over to Charles Frohman with the injunction that he could do with it as he pleased.

Frohman was in his element. He could now embark on another one of the favorite dream-enterprises.

He was like a child during the building of the theater. Every moment that he could spare from his desk he would walk up the street and watch the demolition of the old houses that were to make way for this structure. Often he would get Belasco and take him up the street to note the progress. One night as they stood before the skeleton of the theater that stood gaunt and gray in the gloom Charles said to his friend:

"David, just think; the great dream is coming true, and yet it's only a few years since we sat at 'Beefsteak John's' with only forty-two cents between us."

Naturally, Frohman turned to Belasco for the play to open the Empire. His old friend was then at work on "The Heart of Maryland" for Mrs. Leslie Carter. He explained the situation to Frohman. As soon as Mrs. Carter heard of it she went to Frohman and told him that she would waive her appearance and that Belasco must go ahead on the Empire play, which he did.

Just what kind of play to produce was the problem. Frohman still clung to the mascot of war. The blue coat and brass buttons had turned the tide for him with "Shenandoah," and he was superstitious in wanting another stirring and martial piece. Belasco had become interested in Indians, but he also wanted to introduce the evening-clothes feature. Hence came the inspiration of a ball at an army post in the far West during the Indian-fighting days. This episode proved to be the big dramatic situation of the new piece.

Then came the night when Belasco read the play to Frohman, who walked up and down the floor. When the author finished, Frohman rushed up to him with a brilliant smile on his face and said:

"David, you've done the whole business! You've got pepper and salt, soup, entrée, roast, salad, dessert, coffee; it's a real play, and I know it will be a success."

Having finished the work, which Belasco wrote in collaboration with Franklin Fyles, then dramatic editor of the New York *Sun*, they needed a striking name. So they sent the manuscript to Daniel, down at the Lyceum, for Charles always declared he had been happy in the selection of play titles. Back came the manuscript with his approval of the work, and with the title "The Girl I Left Behind Me." This they eagerly adopted.

Long before "The Girl I Left Behind Me" manuscript was ready to leave Belasco's hands, Frohman was assembling his company. Instead of having a star, he decided to have an all-round stock company. The success of this kind of institution had been amply proved at

Daly's, Wallack's, the Madison Square, and the Lyceum. Hence the Charles Frohman Stock Company, which had scored so heavily with "Men and Women" and "The Lost Paradise" at Proctor's Twenty-third Street Theater, now became the famous Empire Theater Stock Company and incidentally the greatest of all star factories. William Morris was retained as the first leading man, and the company included Orrin Johnson, Cyril Scott, W. H. Thompson, Theodore Roberts, Sydney Armstrong, Odette Tyler, and Edna Wallace. The child in the play was a precocious youngster called "Wally" Eddinger, who is the familiar Wallace Eddinger of the present-day stage.

The rehearsals for "The Girl I Left Behind Me" were held in the Standard Theater, which Frohman had already booked for productions, and were supervised by Belasco. Frohman, however, was always on hand, and his suggestions were invaluable.

"The Girl I Left Behind Me" was tried out for a week at Washington. The company arrived there on Sunday afternoon, but was unable to get the stage until midnight because Robert G. Ingersoll was delivering a lecture there. At the outset of this rehearsal Belasco became ill and had to retire to his bed, and Frohman took up the direction of this final rehearsal and worked with the company until long after dawn.

The week in Washington rounded out the play thoroughly, and the company returned to New York on the morning of January 25, 1893. Now came a characteristic example of Frohman's resource. At noon it was discovered that the new electric-light installation was not yet complete. Added to this was the disconcerting fact that the paint on the chairs was scarcely

dry. Sanger, Harris, and Rich urged Frohman to postpone the opening. "It will be useless to open under
these conditions," they said.

"The Empire must open to-night," said Frohman,
"if we have to open it by candle-light."

In saying this Charles Frohman emphasized what was
one of his iron-clad rules, for he never postponed an
announced opening.

That January night was a memorable one in the life
of Frohman. He sat on a low chair in the wings, and
alongside of him sat Belasco. His face beamed, yet he
was very nervous, as he always was on openings. At
the end of the third act, when the audience made insistent calls for speeches, Belasco tried to drag Frohman
out, but he would not go. "You go, David," he said.
And Belasco went out and made a speech.

"The Girl I Left Behind Me" was a complete success, and played two hundred and eighty-eight consecutive performances.

The opening of the Empire Theater strengthened
Charles Frohman's position immensely. More than this,
it established a whole new theatrical district in New
York. When it was opened there was only one up-town
theater, the Broadway. Within a few years other playhouses followed the example of the Empire, and camped
in its environs. Thus again Charles Frohman was a
pioneer.

The Empire Theater now became the nerve-center
of the Charles Frohman interests. He established his
offices on the third floor, and there they remained until
his death. He practically occupied the whole building,
for his booking interests, which had now grown to great
proportions, and which were in charge of Julius Cahn,

occupied a whole suite of offices. He now had his own New York theater, a star of the first magnitude, and a stock company with a national reputation.

When the Empire Stock Company began its second season in the August of 1893, in R. C. Carton's play, "Liberty Hall," Charles Frohman was able to keep the promise he had made to Henry Miller back in the 'eighties in San Francisco. That handsome and dashing young actor now succeeded William Morris as leading man of the stock company, Viola Allen became leading woman, and May Robson also joined the company. "Liberty Hall" ran until the end of October, when David Belasco's play, "The Younger Son," was put on. This added William Faversham to the ranks, and thus another star possibility came under the sway of the Star-Maker.

The Empire became the apple of Charles Frohman's eye, and remained so until his death. No star and no play was too good for it. On it he lavished wealth and genuine affection. To appear with the Empire Stock Company was to be decorated with the Order of Theatrical Merit. To it in turn came Robert Edison, Ethel Barrymore, Elita Proctor Otis, Jameson Lee Finney, Elsie De Wolfe, W. J. Ferguson, Ferdinand Gottschalk, J. E. Dodson, Margaret Anglin, J. Henry Benrimo, Ida Conquest, and Arthur Byron.

The Empire Stock Company became an accredited institution. A new play by it was a distinct event, its annual tour to the larger cities an occasion that was eagerly awaited. To have a play produced by it was the goal of the ambitious playwright, both here and abroad.

Through the playing of the Empire Company Frohman introduced Oscar Wilde to America, and with the stock-company opportunities he developed such playwrights as Henry Arthur Jones, Haddon Chambers, Sydney Grundy, Louis N. Parker, Madeline Lucette Ryley, Henry Guy Carleton, Clyde Fitch, Jerome K. Jerome, and Arthur Wing Pinero.

Having firmly established the Empire Theater, Charles now turned to a myriad of enterprises. He acquired the lease of the Standard Theater (afterward the Manhattan) and began there a series of productions that was to have significant effect on his fortunes.

In May, 1893, he produced a comedy called "Fanny," by George R. Sims, of London, in which W. J. Ferguson, Frank Burbeck, and Johnston Bennett appeared. It was a very dismal failure, but it produced one of the famous Frohman epigrams. Sims sent Frohman the following telegram a few days after the opening:

How is Fanny going?

Whereupon Frohman sent this laconic reply:

Gone.

Now came another historic episode in Frohman's career. He was making his annual visit to London. The lure and love of the great city was in him and it grew with each succeeding pilgrimage. He had learned to select successful English plays, as the case of "Jane" had proved. Now he was to go further and capture one of his rarest prizes.

Just about this time Brandon Thomas's farce, "Charley's Aunt," had been played at the Globe Theater as a Christmas attraction and was staggering along in great uncertainty. W. S. Penley, who owned the rights, played the leading part.

Suddenly it became a success, and the "managerial Yankee birds," as they called the American theatrical magnates, began to roost in London. All had their claws set for "Charley's Aunt."

Frohman had established an office in London at 4 Henrietta Street, in the vicinity of Covent Garden. His friendship with W. Lestocq, the author of "Jane," developed. Lestocq, who was the son of a publisher, and had graduated from a clever amateur actor into a professional, conceived a great liking for Frohman. While all the American managers were angling for "Charley's Aunt," he went to Penley, who was his friend, and said:

"Frohman has done so well with 'Jane' in America, he is the man to do 'Charley's Aunt.'"

Penley agreed to hold up all his negotiations for the play until Frohman arrived. A conference was held, and, through the instrumentality of Lestocq, Frohman secured the American rights to "Charley's Aunt."

At the end of this meeting Lestocq said in jest, "What do I get out of this?"

"I'll show you," said Frohman. "You shall represent me in London hereafter."

Out of this conference came one of the longest and most loyal associations in Charles's career, because from that hour until the day of his death Lestocq represented Charles Frohman in England with a fidelity of purpose and a devotion of interest that were characteristic of the men who knew and worked with Charles Frohman.

Frohman now returned to America to produce "Charley's Aunt." In spite of the success of the Empire, Frohman had "plunged" in various ways, and had

W. LESTOCQ

reached one of the numerous financial crises in his life. He looked upon "Charley's Aunt" as the agency that was to again redeem him. For the American production he imported Etienne Girardot, who had played the leading rôle in the English production. He surrounded Girardot with an admirable cast, including W. J. Ferguson, Frank Burbeck, Henry Woodruff, Nanette Comstock, and Jessie Busley.

Frohman personally rehearsed "Charley's Aunt." He tried it out first at Bethlehem, Pennsylvania, where the reception was not particularly cordial. He returned to New York in a great state of apprehension, although his good spirits were never dampened. On October 2, 1893, he produced the play at the Standard, and it was an immediate success. As the curtain went down on the first night's performance he assembled the company on the stage and made a short speech, thanking them for their co-operation. It was the first time in his career that he had done this, and it showed how keenly concerned he was. It was another "Shenandoah," because it recouped his purse, depleted from numerous outside ventures, inspired him with a fresh zeal, and enabled him to proceed with fresh enterprises. It ran for two hundred nights, and then duplicated its New York success on the road.

While gunning for "Charley's Aunt," Charles Frohman made his first London production with "The Lost Paradise." He put it on in partnership with the Gattis, at the Adelphi Theater in the Strand. It was a failure, however, and it discouraged him from producing in England for some little time.

These were the years when Frohman was making the few intimate friendships that would mean so much to him until the closing hours of his life. That of Charles Dillingham is an important one.

Dillingham had been a newspaper man in Chicago at a time when George Ade, Peter Dunne, and Frank Vanderlip (now president of the National City Bank) were his co-workers. He became secretary to Senator Squire, and at Washington wrote a play called "Twelve P.M." A manager named Frank Williams produced it in the old Bijou Theater, New York, just about the time that Charles Frohman was presenting John Drew across the street in "The Masked Ball." Dillingham had previously come on to New York, and his hopes, naturally, were in the play. "Twelve P.M." was a dismal failure, but it brought two unusual men together who became bosom friends. It came about in this extraordinary way:

During the second (and last) week of the engagement of "Twelve P.M." at the Bijou, Dillingham, who came every night to see his play, noticed a short, stout, but important-looking man pass into the playhouse.

"Who is that man?" he asked.

He was told it was Charles Frohman.

A few days later he received a letter from Frohman, which said:

> *Your play lacks all form and construction, but I like the lines very much. Would you like to adapt a French farce for me?*

Dillingham accepted this commission and thus met Frohman. Dillingham was then dramatic editor of the New York *Evening Sun*. One day he called on Frohman and asked him to send him out with a show.

"When do you want to go?"

"Right away."

"Very well," said Frohman, who would always have his little joke. "You can go to-morrow. I would like to get you off that paper, anyhow. You write too many bad notices of my plays."

Dillingham first went out ahead of the Empire Stock Company and afterward in advance of John Drew, in "That Imprudent Young Couple." He left the job, however, and soon returned to Frohman, seeking other work.

"What would you like to do?" asked Frohman.

"Take my yacht and go to England," said Dillingham, facetiously.

"All right," said Frohman. "We sail Saturday," and handed him fifty thousand dollars in stage money that happened to be lying on his desk. Dillingham thought at first he was joking, but he was not. They sailed on the *St. Paul*. Frohman had just established his first offices in Henrietta Street. There was not much business to transact, and the pair spent most of their time seeing plays. Dillingham acted as a sort of secretary to Frohman.

One day a haughty Englishman came up to the offices and asked Dillingham to take in his card.

"I have no time," said Dillingham, whose sense of humor is proverbial.

"What have you to do?" asked the man.

"I've got to wash the office windows first," was the reply.

The Englishman became enraged, strode in to Frohman, and told him what Dillingham had said. Frohman laughed so heartily that he almost rolled out of his chair. After the Englishman left he went out and congratulated

Dillingham on his jest. From that day dated a Damon and Pythias friendship between the two men. They were almost inseparable companions.

The time was at hand for another big star to twinkle in the Frohman heaven. During all these years William Gillette had developed in prestige and authority, both as actor and as playwright. The quiet, thoughtful, scholarly-looking young actor who had knocked at the doors of the Madison Square Theater with the manuscript of "The Professor," where it was produced after "Hazel Kirke," and whose road tours had been booked by Charles Frohman in his early days as route-maker, now came into his own. Curiously enough, his career was to be linked closely with that of the little man he first knew in his early New York days.

Frohman, who had booked and produced Gillette's play "Held By the Enemy," now regarded Gillette as star material of the first rank. Combined with admiration for Gillette as artist was a strong personal friendship. Gillette now wrote a play, a capital farce called "Too Much Johnson," which Frohman produced with the author as star. In connection with this opening was a typical Frohman incident.

The play was first put on at Waltham, Massachusetts. The house was small and the notices bad. Frohman joined the company next day at Springfield. Gillette was much depressed, and he met Frohman in this mood.

"This is terrible, isn't it? I'm afraid the play is a failure."

"Nonsense!" said Frohman. "I have booked it for New York and for a long tour afterward."

"Why?" asked Gillette in astonishment.

CHARLES DILLINGHAM

"I saw your performance," was the reply.

Frohman's confidence was vindicated, for when the play was put on at the Standard Theater in November, 1894, it went splendidly and put another rivet in Gillette's reputation.

Frohman now had two big stars, John Drew and William Gillette. A half-dozen others were in the making, chief among them the wistful-eyed little Maude Adams, who was now approaching the point in her career where she was to establish a new tradition for the American stage and give Charles Frohman a unique distinction.

VIII

*W*HEN Charles Frohman put Maude Adams opposite John Drew in "The Masked Ball" he laid the foundation of what is, in many respects, his most remarkable achievement. The demure little girl, who had made her way from child actress through the perils of vivid melodrama to a Broadway success, now set foot on the real highway to a stardom that is unique in the annals of the theater.

Brilliant as was his experience with the various men and women whom he raised from obscurity to fame and fortune, the case of Maude Adams stands out with peculiar distinctness. It is the one instance where Charles Frohman literally manufactured a star's future.

Yet no star ever served so rigorous or so distinguished an apprenticeship. Her five years as leading woman with John Drew tried all her resource. After her brilliant performance as *Zuzanne Blondet* in "The Masked Ball," she appeared in "The Butterflies," by Henry Guy Carleton. She had a much better part in "The Bauble Shop," which followed the next year.

John Drew's vehicle in 1895 was "That Imprudent Young Couple," by Henry Guy Carleton. This play not only advanced Miss Adams materially, but first served to bring forward John Drew's niece, Ethel Barrymore, a graceful slip of a girl, who developed a great friendship with Miss Adams. Following her appearance in the Carleton play came "Christopher Jr.," written by Madeline Lucette Ryley, in which Miss Adams scored the biggest hit of her career up to this time.

It remained for Louis N. Parker's charming play, "Rosemary," which was produced at the Empire Theater in 1896, to put Miss Adams into the path of the man who, after Charles Frohman, did more than any other person in the world to give her the prominence that she occupies to-day.

"Rosemary" was an exquisite comedy, and packed with sentiment. Maude Adams played the part of *Dorothy Cruikshank*, a character of quaint and appealing sweetness. It touched the hidden springs of whimsical humor and thrilling tenderness, qualities which soon proved to be among her chief assets.

Just about that time a little Scot, James M. Barrie by name, already a distinguished literary figure who had blossomed forth as a playwright with "Walker London" and "The Professor's Love Story," came to America for the first time. For three people destined from this time on to be inseparably entwined in career and fortune, it was a memorable trip. For Barrie it meant the meeting with Charles Frohman, who was to be his greatest American friend and producer; for Miss Adams it was to open the way to her real career, and for Frohman himself it was to witness the beginning of an intimacy that was perhaps the closest of his life.

Barrie's book, "The Little Minister," had been a tremendous success, and, not having acquired the formality of a copyright in America, the play pirates were busy with it. Frohman, after having seen the performance of "The Professor's Love Story," had cabled Barrie, asking him to make a play out of the charming Scotch romance. Barrie at first declined. Frohman, as usual, was insistent. Then followed the Scotchman's trip to America.

Under Frohman's influence he had begun to consider a dramatization of "The Little Minister," but the real stimulus was lacking because, as he expressed it to Frohman, he did not see any one who could play the part of *Babbie*.

Now came one of those many unexpected moments that shape lives. On a certain day Barrie dropped into the Empire Theater to see Frohman, who was out.

"Why don't you stop in down-stairs and see 'Rosemary'?" said Frohman's secretary.

"All right," said Barrie.

So he went down into the Empire and took a seat in the last row. An hour afterward he came rushing back to Frohman's office, found his friend in, and said to him, as excitedly as his Scotch nature would permit:

"Frohman, I have found the woman to play *Babbie* in 'The Little Minister'! I am going to try to dramatize it myself."

"Who is it?" asked Frohman, with a twinkle in his eye, for he knew without asking.

"It is that little Miss Adams who plays *Dorothy*."

"Fine!" said Frohman. "I hope you will go ahead now and do the play."

The moment toward which Frohman had looked for years was now at hand. He might have launched Miss Adams at any time during the preceding four or five seasons. But he desired her to have a better equipment, and he wanted the American theater-going public to know the woman in whose talents he felt such an ex-

MAUDE ADAMS

nounced that he would present her in a special all-star production of "Romeo and Juliet."

Charles Frohman himself was always frank enough to say that he had no great desire to produce Shakespeare. He lived in the dramatic activities of his day. It was shortly before this time that his brother Daniel, entering his office one day, found him reading.

"I am reading a new book," he said; "that is, new to me."

"What is that?" was the query?

"'Romeo and Juliet,'" he replied.

When Maude Adams dropped the rôle of *Babbie* to assume that of *Juliet* some people thought the transfer a daring one, to say the least. Even Miss Adams was a little nervous. Not so Frohman. To him Shakespeare was simply a playwright like Clyde Fitch or Augustus Thomas, with the additional advantage that he was dead, and therefore, as there were no royalties to pay, he could put the money into the production.

When Frohman went to rehearsal one day he noticed that the company seemed a trifle nervous.

"What's up?" he asked, abruptly.

Some one told him that the players were fearful lest all the details of the costume and play should not be carried out in strict accordance with history.

"Nonsense!" exclaimed Frohman. "Who's Shakespeare? He was just a man. He won't hurt you. I don't see any Shakespeare. Just imagine you're looking at a soldier, home from the Cuban war, making love to a giggling school-girl on a balcony. That's all I see, and that's the way I want it played. Dismiss all idea of costume. Be modern."

The production of "Romeo and Juliet" was super-

"Barbara Fritchie," with Julia Marlowe in the title rôle, came dangerously near closing because of discouraging business. Yet she came to New York, and with the exception of "When Knighthood was in Flower," registered the greatest popular triumph she has ever known. This was now the case with "The Little Minister."

Miss Adams was irresistible as *Lady Babbie*. As the quaint, slyly humorous, make-believe gipsy, she found full play for all her talents, and she captured her audience almost with her first speech.

Charles Frohman sat nervously in the wings during the performance. When the curtain went down his new star said to him:

"How did it go?"

"Splendidly," was his laconic comment.

"The Little Minister" ran at the Empire for three hundred consecutive performances, two hundred and eighty-nine of which were to "standing room only." The total gross receipts for the engagement were $370,000 —a record for that time.

On the last night of the run Miss Adams received the following cablegram from Barrie:

> *Thank you, thank you all for your brilliant achievement. "What a glory to our kirk."*
>
> BARRIE.

Maude Adams was now launched as a profitable and successful star. Like many other conscientious and idealistic interpreters of the drama, she had a great reverence for Shakespeare, and she burned with a desire to play in one of the great bard's plays. Charles Frohman knew this. Then, as always, one of his supreme ambitions in life was to gratify her every wish, so he an-

To the mastery of the part of *Lady Babbie* Maude Adams now consecrated herself with a fidelity of purpose which was very characteristic of her. Then, as always, she asked herself the question:

"What will this character mean to the people who see it?"

In other words, here, as throughout all her career, she put herself in the position of her audience. She devoted many weeks to a study of Scotch dialect. She fairly lived in a Scotch atmosphere. One of her friends of that time accused her of subsisting on a diet of Scotch broth.

As was his custom, Frohman gave the piece an out-of-town try-out. It opened on September 13, 1897, a date memorable in the Charles Frohman narrative, in the La Fayette Square Opera House in Washington. It was an intolerably hot night, and, added to the discomfort of the heat, there was considerable uncertainty about the success of the venture itself. This was not due to a lack of confidence in Miss Adams, but to the feeling that the play was excessively Scotch. A brilliant audience, including many people prominent in public life, witnessed the début and seemed most friendly.

Miss Adams regarded the first night as a failure. Financially the play limped along for a week, for the gross receipts were only $3,500. Yet when the play opened in New York two weeks later it was a spectacular success from the start.

Here is another curious example of the importance of the New York verdict. "Hazel Kirke," which became one of the historic successes of the American stage, tottered along haltingly for weeks in Philadelphia, Washington, and Baltimore. In the Quaker City, traordinary confidence. He announced with a suddenness that was startling, but which in reality conveyed no surprise to the few people who had watched Miss Adams's career up to this time, that he was going to launch her as star.

Some of his friends, however, objected

"Why split and separate a good acting combination?" was their comment, meaning the combination of John Drew and Miss Adams. To this objection Frohman made reply:

"I'll show you the wisdom of it. I'll put them both on Broadway at the same time."

He therefore launched Miss Adams in "The Little Minister" at the Empire and booked John Drew at Wallack's in "A Marriage of Convenience." His decision was amply vindicated, for both scored successes.

Charles Frohman now proceeded to present Miss Adams with his usual lavishness. First of all he surrounded her with a superb company. It was headed by Robert Edeson, who played the title rôle, and included Guy Standing, George Fawcett, William H. Thompson, R. Peyton Carter, and Wilfred Buckland.

With "The Little Minister" Charles Frohman gave interesting evidence of a masterful manipulation to make circumstances meet his own desires. He realized that the masculine title of the play might possibly detract from Miss Adams's prestige, so he immediately began to adapt several important scenes which might have been dominated by *Gavin Dishart*, the little minister, into strong scenes for his new luminary. These changes were made, of course, with Barrie's consent, and added much to the strength of the rôle of *Lady Babbie*.

vised by William Seymour. It was rehearsed in two sections. One half of the cast was in New York, with Faversham and Hackett; the other was on tour with Miss Adams in "The Little Minister." Seymour divided his time between the two wings, with the omnipresent spirit of Frohman over it all.

Miss Adams had made an exhaustive study of the part. After his first conference with her, Seymour wrote to Frohman as follows:

> *I thought I knew my Shakespeare, but Miss Adams has opened up a new and most wonderful field. An hour with her has given me more inspiration and ideas than twenty years of personal experience with it.*

As usual, Frohman surrounded Miss Adams with a magnificent cast. William Faversham played *Romeo;* James K. Hackett was *Mercutio;* W. H. Thompson was *Friar Lawrence;* Orrin Johnson played *Paris;* R. Peyton Carter was *Peter.* Others in the company were Campbell Gollan and Eugene Jepson.

"Romeo and Juliet" was produced at the Empire Theater May 8, 1899, and was a distinguished artistic success. Miss Adams's *Juliet* was appealing, romantic, lovely. It touched the chords of all her gentle womanliness and gave the character, so far as the American stage was concerned, a new tradition of youthful charm.

A unique feature of the first night's performance of "Romeo and Juliet" was the presence of Mary Anderson. This distinguished actress, who had just arrived from London for a brief visit, expressed a desire to see the new *Juliet*, and to feel once more the thrill of a Broadway first night. Miss Anderson herself had, of course, achieved great distinction as *Juliet*. She was regarded, in her day, as the physical and romantic ideal of the rôle.

When her desire to see the play was communicated to Charles, it was found that every box had been sold except the one reserved for his sisters. He therefore purchased this from them with a check for $200.

At the conclusion of the performance Miss Anderson was introduced to Miss Adams, and congratulated her on her success.

It was in 1900 that Miss Adams first played the part of a boy, a type of character that, before many years would pass, was to give her a great success. Her début as a lad, however, was under the most brilliantly artistic circumstances, because it was in Edmond Rostand's "L'Aiglon," adapted in English by Louis N. Parker. As the young Eaglet, son of the great Napoleon, she had fresh opportunity to display her versatility. It was a character in which romance, pathos, and tragedy were curiously entwined. Bernhardt had done it successfully in Paris, but Miss Adams brought to it the fidelity and brilliancy of youth. In "L'Aiglon" she was supported by Edwin Arden, Oswald Yorke, Eugene Jepson, J. H. Gilmour, and R. Peyton Carter.

When Charles Frohman put Miss Adams into "Romeo and Juliet" she received a whimsical letter from J. M. Barrie, saying, among other things:

> *Are you going to take Willie Shakespeare by the arm and l'ave me?*

The time was now at hand when she once more took the fascinating Scot by the arm. She now appeared in his "Quality Street," a new play with the real Barrie charm, in which she took the part of an exquisite English girl whose betrothed goes to the Napoleonic wars. She thinks he has forgotten her, and allows herself to externally fade into spinsterhood. When he comes back he does not recognize her. Then she suddenly blooms into exquisite youth—radiant and beguiling—and he discovers that it is his old love.

"Quality Street" was tried out in Toledo, Ohio, early in the season of 1901. On the opening night an incident occurred which showed Frohman's attitude toward new plays. The third act dragged somewhat toward the end, evidently on account of an anti-climax. On the following day Frohman asked his business manager to sit with him during the third act, saying:

"Last night Miss Adams played this act as Barrie wrote it. This afternoon she will play it as I want it."

The act went much more effectively, and it was never changed after that matinée performance.

"Quality Street" was another of what came to be known as a typical "Adams success."

For her next starring vehicle, Charles presented Maude Adams in "The Pretty Sister of José," a play which Mrs. Frances Hodgson Burnett made of her well-known story. She was supported by Harry Ainley, at that time England's great matinée idol. Here Miss Adams encountered for the first time something that resembled failure, because she was not adapted to the fiery, passionate character of the impetuous Spanish girl. The play, however, made its usual tour after the local season, and with much financial success.

The tour ended, Miss Adams suddenly disappeared from sight. There were even rumors that she had left the stage. As a matter of fact, she had retired to the seclusion of a convent at Tours, in France. There were two definite reasons for her retirement. One was that she wanted time for convalescence from an operation for appendicitis; the other, that she wished to perfect her French in order to fulfil a long-cherished desire to play *Juliet* to Sarah Bernhardt's *Romeo*. Unfortunately, this plan was never consummated, but it gave Miss Adams a very rare experience, for she lived with the simple French nuns for months. Later, when they were driven from France, she found them quarters near Birmingham, in England, saw to their comfort, and got them buyers for their lace.

Brilliant as had been Miss Adams's success up to this time, the moment was now at hand when she was to appear in the rôle that, more than all her other parts combined, would complete her conquest of the American heart. Once more she became a boy, this time the irresistible *Peter Pan*.

As *Peter Pan* she literally flew into a new fame. This play of Barrie's provided Frohman with one of the many sensations he loved, and perhaps no production of the many hundreds that he made in his long career as manager gave him quite so much pleasure as the presentation of the fascinating little Boy Who Never Would Grow Up.

The very beginning of "Peter Pan," so far as the stage presentation was concerned, was full of romantic interest. Barrie had agreed to write a play for Frohman, and met him at dinner one night at the Garrick Club in London. Barrie seemed nervous and ill at ease.

"What's the matter?" said Charles.

"Simply this," said Barrie. "You know I have an agreement to deliver you the manuscript of a play?"

"Yes," said Frohman.

"Well, I have it, all right," said Barrie, "but I am sure it will not be a commercial success. But it is a dream-child of mine, and I am so anxious to see it on the stage that I have written another play which I will be glad to give you and which will compensate you for any loss on the one I am so eager to see produced."

"Don't bother about that," said Frohman. "I will produce both plays."

Now the extraordinary thing about this episode is that the play about whose success Barrie was so doubtful was "Peter Pan," which made several fortunes. The manuscript he offered Frohman to indemnify him from loss was "Alice-Sit-By-The-Fire," which lasted only a season. Such is the estimate that the author often puts on his own work!

When Frohman first read "Peter Pan" he was so entranced that he could not resist telling all his friends about it. He would stop them in the street and act out the scenes. Yet it required the most stupendous courage and confidence to put on a play that, from the manuscript, sounded like a combination of circus and extravaganza; a play in which children flew in and out of rooms, crocodiles swallowed alarm-clocks, a man exchanged places with his dog in its kennel, and various other seemingly absurd and ridiculous things happened.

But Charles believed in Barrie. He had gone to an extraordinary expense to produce "Peter Pan" in England. He duplicated it in the United States. No other character in all her repertory made such a swift appeal to Miss Adams as *Peter Pan*. She saw in him the idealization of everything that was wonderful and wistful in childhood.

The way she prepared for the part was characteristic of her attitude toward her work. She took the manuscript with her up to the Catskills. She isolated herself for a month; she walked, rode, communed with nature, but all the while she was studying and absorbing the character which was to mean so much to her career. In the great friendly open spaces in which little *Peter* himself delighted, and where he was king, she found her inspiration for interpretation of the wondrous boy.

The try-out was made in Washington at the old National Theater. It went with considerable success, although the first-night audience was somewhat mystified and did not know exactly what to say or do.

It was when the play was launched on November 6, 1905, at the Empire Theater in New York, that little *Peter* really came into his own. The human birds, the droll humor, the daring allegory, above all the appealing, almost tragic, spectacle of *Peter* playing his pipe up in the tree-tops of the Never-Never Land, all contributed to an event that was memorable in more ways than one.

On this night developed the remarkable and thrilling feature in "Peter Pan" which made the adorable dream-child the best beloved of all American children. It came when *Peter* rushed forward to the footlights in the frantic attempt to save the life of his devoted little *Tinker Bell*, and asked:

"Do you believe in fairies?"

It registered a whole new and intimate relation between actress and audience, and had the play possessed no other distinctive feature, this alone would have at once lifted it to a success that was all its own.

MAUDE ADAMS

MAUDE ADAMS AS STAR

This episode became one of the many marvelous features of the memorable run of "Peter Pan" at the Empire. Nearly every child in New York—and subsequently, on the long and successful tours that Miss Adams made in "Peter Pan," their brothers everywhere —became acquainted with the episode and longed impatiently to have a part in it. On one occasion, fully fifteen minutes before Miss Adams made her appeal, a little child rose in a box at the Empire and said: "*I* believe in fairies."

"Peter Pan" recorded the longest single engagement in the history of the Empire. It ran from November 6, 1905, until June 9, 1906.

But "Peter Pan" did more than give Miss Adams her most popular part. It became a nation-wide vogue. Children were named after the fascinating little lad Who Never Would Grow Up; articles of wearing-apparel were labeled with his now familiar title; the whole country talked and loved the unforgetable little character who now became not merely a stage figure, but a real personal friend of the American theater-going people.

It was on a road tour of "Peter Pan" that occurred one of those rare anecdotes in which Miss Adams figures. Frohman always had a curious prejudice against the playing of matinées by his stars, especially Maude Adams. A matinée was booked at Altoona, Pennsylvania. Frohman immediately had it marked off his contract. The advance-agent of the company, however, ordered the matinée played at the urgent request of the local manager, but he did not notify the office in New York. When Charles got the telegram announcing the receipts, he was most indignant. "I'll discharge the person responsible for this matinée," he said.

In answer to his telegraphed inquiry he received the following wire:

> *The matinée was played at my request. I pre-*
> *ferred to work rather than spend the whole day*
> *in a bad hotel.*
>
> MAUDE ADAMS.

In connection with "Peter Pan" is a curious and tragic coincidence. Of all the Barrie plays that Charles produced he loved "Peter Pan" the best. Curiously enough, it was little *Peter* himself who gave him the cue for his now historic farewell as he stood on the sinking deck of the *Lusitania.*

At the end of one of the acts in "Peter Pan" the little boy says:

> *To die will be an awfully big adventure.*

These words had always made a deep impression on Frohman. They came to his mind as he stood on that fateful deck and said:

> *Why fear death? It is the most beautiful*
> *adventure in life.*

Having made such an enormous success with "Peter Pan," Miss Adams now turned to her third boy's part. It was that of "Chicot, the Jester," John Raphael's adaptation of Miguel Zamaceis's play "The Jesters." This was a very delightful sort of Prince Charming play, fragile and artistic. The opposite part was played by Consuelo Bailey. It was a great triumph for Miss Adams, but not a very great financial success.

Now came the first of her open-air performances.

During the season of "The Jesters" she appeared at Yale and Harvard as *Viola* in "Twelfth Night." She gave a charming and graceful performance of the rôle.

But Maude Adams could not linger long from the lure that was Barrie's. After what amounted to the practical failure of "The Jesters" she turned to her fourth Barrie play, which proved to be a triumph.

For over a year Barrie had been at work on a play for her. It came forth in his whimsical satire, "What Every Woman Knows." Afterward, in speaking of this play, he said that he had written it because "there was a Maude Adams in the world." Then he added, "I could see her dancing through every page of my manuscript."

Indeed, "What Every Woman Knows" was really written around Miss Adams. It was a dramatization of the roguish humor and exquisite womanliness that are her peculiar gifts.

As *Maggie Wylie* she created a character that was a worthy colleague of *Lady Babbie*. Here she had opportunity for her wide range of gifts. The rôle opposite her, that of *John Shand*, the poor Scotch boy who literally stole knowledge, was extraordinarily interesting. As most people may recall, the play involves the marriage between *Maggie* and *John*, according to an agreement entered into between the girl's brothers and the boy. The brothers agree to educate him, and in return he weds the sister. *Maggie* becomes *John's* inspiration, although he refuses to realize or admit it. He is absolutely without humor. He thinks he can do without her, only to find when it is almost too late that she has been the very prop of his success.

At the end of this play *Maggie* finally makes her husband laugh when she tells him:

> *I tell you what every woman knows: that Eve wasn't made from the rib of Adam, but from his funny-bone.*

This speech had a wide vogue and was quoted everywhere.

Curiously enough, in "What Every Woman Knows" Miss Adams has a speech in which she unconsciously defines the one peculiar and elusive gift which gives her such rare distinction. In the play she is supposed to be the girl "who has no charm." In reality she is all charm. But in discussing this quality with her brothers she makes this statement:

> *Charm is the bloom upon a woman. If you have it you don't have to have anything else. If you haven't it, all else won't do you any good.*

"What Every Woman Knows" was an enormous success, in which Richard Bennett, who played *John Shand*, shared honors with the star. Miss Adams's achievement in this play emphasized the rare affinity between her and Barrie's delightful art. They formed a unique and lovable combination, irresistible in its appeal to the public. Commenting on this, Barrie himself has said:

> *Miss Adams knows my characters and understands them. She really needs no directions. I love to write for her and see her in my work.*

Nor could there be any more delightful comment on Miss Adams's appreciation of all that Barrie has meant to her than to quote a remark she made not so very long ago when she said:

> *Wherever I act, I always feel that there is one unseen spectator, James M. Barrie.*

Maude Adams was now in what most people, both in and out of the theatrical profession, would think the very zenith of her career. She was the best beloved of American actresses, the idol of the American child. She was without doubt the best box-office attraction in the country. Yet she had made her way to this eminence by an industry and a concentration that were well-nigh incredible.

People began to say, "What marvelous things Charles Frohman has done for Miss Adams."

As a matter of fact, the career of Miss Adams emphasizes what a very great author once said, which, summed up, was that neither nature nor man did anything for any human being that he could not do for himself.

Miss Adams paid the penalty of her enormous success by an almost complete isolation. She concentrated on her work—all else was subsidiary.

Charles Frohman had an enormous ambition for Miss Adams, and that ambition now took form in what was perhaps his most remarkable effort in connection with her. It was the production of "Joan of Arc" at the Harvard Stadium. It started in this way:

John D. Williams, for many years business manager for Charles Frohman, is a Harvard alumnus. Realizing that the business with which he was associated had been labeled with the "commercial" brand, he had an ambition to associate it with something which would be considered genuinely esthetic. The pageant idea had suddenly come into vogue. "Why not give a magnificent pageant?" he said to himself.

One morning he went into Charles Frohman's office and put the idea to him, adding that he thought Miss Adams as *Joan of Arc* would provide the proper medium for such a spectacle. Frohman was about to go to Europe. With a quick wave of the hand and a swift "All right," he assented to what became one of the most distinguished events in the history of the American stage.

Schiller's great poem, "The Maid of Orléans," was selected. In suggesting the battle heroine of France, Williams touched upon one of Maude Adams's great admirations. For years she had studied the character of Joan. To her Joan was the very idealization of all womanhood. Bernhardt, Davenport, and others had tried to dramatize this most appealing of all tragedies in the history of France, and had practically failed. It remained for slight, almost fragile, Maude Adams to vivify and give the character an enduring interpretation.

"Joan of Arc," as the pageant was called, was projected on a stupendous scale. Fifteen hundred supernumeraries were employed. John W. Alexander, the famous artist, was employed to design the costumes. A special electric-lighting plant was installed in the stadium.

Miss Adams concentrated herself upon the preparations with a fidelity and energy that were little short of amazing. One detail will illustrate. As most people know, Miss Adams had to appear mounted several times during the play and ride at the head of her charging army.

This equestrianism gave Charles Frohman the greatest

solicitude. He feared that she would be injured in some way, and he kept cabling warnings to her, and to her associates who were responsible for her safety, to be careful.

Miss Adams, however, determined to be a good horsewoman, and for more than a month she practised every afternoon in a riding-academy in New York. Since the horse had to carry the trappings of clanging armor, amid all the tumult of battle, she rehearsed every day with all sorts of noisy apparatus hanging about him. Shots were fired, colored banners and flags were flaunted about her, and pieces of metal were fastened to her riding-skirt so that the steed would be accustomed to the constant contact of a sword.

Although the preparations for her own part were most exacting and onerous, Miss Adams exercised a supervising direction over the whole production, which was done in the most lavish fashion. She had every resource of the Charles Frohman organization at her command, and it was employed to the very last detail.

"Joan of Arc" was presented on the evening of June 22, 1909, in the presence of over fifteen thousand people. It was a magnificent success, and proved to be unquestionably the greatest theatrical pageant ever staged in this country. The elaborate settings were handled mechanically. Forests dissolved into regal courts; fields melted into castles. A hidden orchestra played the superb music of Beethoven's "Eroica," which accentuated the noble poetry of Schiller.

The first scene showed the maid of Domremy wandering in the twilight with her vision; the last revealed her dying of her wounds at the spring, soon to be buried under the shields of her captains.

The battle scene was an inspiring feature. It had been arranged that Miss Adams's riding-master should change places with her at the head of the charging troops and ride in their magnificent sweep down the field. It was feared that some mishap might befall her. When the charge was over and the stage-manager rushed up to congratulate the supposed riding-master on his admirable make-up, he was surprised to hear Miss Adams's voice issue forth from the armor, saying, "How did it go?" Strapped to her horse, she had led the charge herself and had seen the performance through.

"Joan of Arc" netted $15,000, which Charles Frohman turned over to Harvard University to do with as it pleased. There was unconscious irony in this, for the performance aroused great admiration in Germany, and the proceeds were devoted to the Germanic Museum in the university; in the end, the Germans were responsible for his death.

Accentuating this irony was the fact that Charles Frohman had made a magnificent vellum album containing the complete photographic record of the play, and sent it to the German Kaiser with the following inscription:

To His Majesty the German Emperor. This photographic record of the first English performance in America of Friedrich von Schiller's dramatic poem, "Jungfrau von Orleans," given for the Building Fund of the Germanic Museum of Harvard University under the auspices of the German Department in the Stadium, Tuesday, twenty-second of June, 1909, is respectfully presented by Charles Frohman.

178

MAUDE ADAMS AS STAR

There is no doubt that "Joan of Arc" was the supreme effort of Miss Adams's career. She was the living, breathing incarnation of the Maid. When she was told that Charles Frohman had refused an offer of $50,000 for the motion-picture rights, she said:

Of course it was refused. This performance is all poetry and solemnity.

The following June, in the Greek Theater of the University of California, at Berkeley, Miss Adams made her first and only appearance as *Rosalind* in "As You Like It." Ten thousand people saw the performance. Her achievement illustrates the extraordinary and indefatigable quality of her work. She rehearsed "As You Like It" during her transcontinental tour of "What Every Woman Knows," which extended from sea to sea and lasted thirty-nine weeks.

Most managers would have been content to rest with the laurel that such a performance as "Joan of Arc" had won. Not so with Charles Frohman. Every stupendous feat that he achieved merely whetted his desire for something greater. He delighted in sensation. Now he came to the point in his life where he projected what was in many respects the most unique and original of all his efforts, the presentation of Rostand's classic, "Chantecler."

It was on March 30, 1910, that Charles crossed over from London to Paris to see this play. It thrilled and stirred him, and he bought it immediately. He realized that it would either be a tremendous success or a colossal failure, and he was willing to stand or fall by it. In Paris the title rôle, originally written for the great Coquelin, had been played by Guitry. It was essentially

179

a man's part. But Frohman, with that sense of the spectacular which so often characterized him, immediately cast Miss Adams for it.

When he announced that the elf-like girl—the living *Peter Pan* to millions of theater-goers—was to assume the feathers and strut of the barnyard Romeo, there was a widespread feeling that he was making a great mistake, and that he was putting Miss Adams into a rôle, admirable artist that she was, to which she was absolutely unsuited. A storm of criticism arose. But Frohman was absolutely firm. Opposition only made him hold his ground all the stronger. When people asked him why he insisted upon casting Miss Adams for this almost impossible part he always said:

> *"Chantecler" is a play with a soul, and the soul of a play is its moral. This is the secret of "Peter Pan"; this is why Miss Adams is to play the leading part.*

Miss Adams was in Chicago when Frohman bought the play, and he cabled her that she was to do the title part. She afterward declared that this news changed the dull, dreary, soggy day into one that was brilliant and dazzling. "To play *Chantecler*," she said, "is an honor international in its glory."

The preparations for "Chantecler" were carried on with the usual Frohman magnificence. A fortune was spent on it. The costumes were made in Paris; John W. Alexander supervised the scenic effects.

The casting of the parts was in itself an enormous task. Frohman amused himself by having what he called "casting parties." For example, he would call up Miss Adams by long-distance telephone and say:

MAUDE ADAMS AS STAR

*I've got ten minutes before my train starts for
Atlantic City. Can you cast a peacock for me?*

Whereupon Miss Adams would say:

Ten minutes is too short.

Never, perhaps, in the history of the American stage
was the advent of a play so long heralded. The name
"Chantecler" was on every tongue. Long before the
piece was launched hats had been named after it, con-
troversies had arisen over its Anglicized spelling and pro-
nunciation. All the genius of publicity which was the
peculiar heritage of Charles Frohman was turned loose
to pave the way for this extraordinary production. It
was a nation-wide sensation.

For the first time in his life Charles had to postpone
an opening. It was originally set for the 13th of January,
1911, but the first night did not come until the 23d.
This added to the suspense and expectancy of the
public.

The demand for seats was unprecedented. A line began to form at four o'clock in the afternoon preceding
the day the sale opened. Within twenty-four hours
after the window was raised at the box-office as high
as $200 was offered in vain for a seat on the opening
night.

The Empire stage was too small, so the play was
produced at the Knickerbocker Theater. A brilliant
and highly wrought-up audience was present. Extraordinary interest centered about Miss Adams's performance as *Chantecler*. "Will she be able to do it?"
was the question on every tongue. On that memorable
opening-night Frohman, as usual, sat in the back seat

in the gallery and had the supreme satisfaction of seeing his star distinguish herself in a performance that in many respects revealed Miss Adams as she had never been revealed before. She was recalled twenty-two times.

Chantecler literally crowed and conquered!

Just how much "Chantecler" meant to Charles Frohman is attested by a remark he made soon after its inaugural. A friend was discussing epitaphs with him.

"What would you like to have written about you, C. F.?" asked the man.

The brilliant smile left Frohman's face for a moment, and then he said, solemnly:

"All that I would ask is this: 'He gave "Peter Pan" to the world and "Chantecler" to America.' It is enough for any man."

The last original production that Charles Frohman made with Maude Adams was "The Legend of Leonora," in which she returned once more to Barrie's exquisite and fanciful satire, devoted this time to the woman question. In England it had been produced under the title of "The Adored One."

It was in the part of *Leonora* that James M. Barrie saw Maude Adams act for the first time in one of his plays. He had come to America for a brief visit to Frohman, and during this period Miss Adams was having her annual engagement at the Empire Theater.

Of course, Barrie had Miss Adams in mind for the American production, and it is a very interesting commentary on his admiration for the American star that about the only instructions he attached to the manuscript of the play was this:

Leonora is an unspeakable darling, and this is all the guidance that can be given to the lady playing her.

On her last starring tour under the personal direction of Charles Frohman, Miss Adams combined with a revival of "Quality Street" a clever skit by Barrie called "The Ladies' Shakespeare," the subtitle being, "One Woman's Reading of 'The Taming of the Shrew.'" With an occasional appearance in Barrie's "Rosalind," it rounded out her stellar career under him.

Charles Frohman lived to see Maude Adams realize his highest desire for her success. She justified his confidence and it gave him infinite satisfaction.

Miss Adams's career as a star unfolds a panorama of artistic and practical achievement unequaled in the life of any American star. It likewise reveals a paradox all its own. While millions of people have seen and admired her, only a handful of people know her. The aloofness of the woman in her personal attitude toward the public represents Charles Frohman's own ideal of what stage artistry and conduct should be.

It is illustrated in what was perhaps the keenest epigram he ever made. He was talking about people of the stage who constantly air themselves and their views to secure personal publicity. It moved him to this remark:

"Some people prefer mediocrity in the limelight to greatness in the dark."

Herein he summed up the reason why Miss Adams has been an elusive and almost mysterious figure. By tremendous reading, solitary thinking, and extraordinary personal application she rose to her great eminence.

With her it has always been a creed of career first. Like Charles Frohman, she has hidden behind her activities, and they form a worthy rampart.

The history of the stage records no more interesting parallel than the one afforded by these two people— each a recluse, yet each known to the multitudes.

IX

THE BIRTH OF THE SYNDICATE

*C*HARLES FROHMAN'S talents and energies were very much like those of E. H. Harriman in that they found their largest and best expression when dedicated to a multitude of enterprises. Like Harriman, too, he did things in a wholesale way, for he had a contempt for small sums and small ventures.

Going back a little in point of time from the close of the preceding chapter, the final years of the last century found Frohman geared up to a myriad of activities. He had already assumed the rôle of Star-Maker, for Drew and Gillette were on his roster, and Maude Adams was about to be launched; the Empire Stock Company was an accredited institution with a national influence; he had started a chain of theaters; his booking interests in the West had assumed the proportions of an immense business; he had begun to make his presence felt in London. Yet no event of these middle 'nineties was more momentous in its relation to the future of the whole American theater than one which was about to transpire—one in which Charles Frohman had an important hand.

Despite the efforts made by the booking offices conducted by Charles Frohman and Klaw & Erlanger, the making of routes for theatrical attractions in the United

States was in a most disorganized and economically unsound condition. The local manager was still more or less at the mercy of the booking free-lance in New York. The booking agent himself only represented a comparatively few theaters and could not book a complete season for a traveling attraction.

In New York the manager was an autocrat who frequently dictated unbelievable terms to the traveling companies. Immense losses resulted from small traveling companies being pitted against one another in provincial towns that could only support one first-class attraction. Most theatrical contracts were not worth the paper they were written on.

Charles Frohman had first counted the cost of this theatrical demoralization when his great "Shenandoah" run at the old Star Theater had to be interrupted while playing to capacity because another attraction had been booked into that theater. He and all his representative colleagues in the business realized that some steps must be taken to rectify the situation. Piled on this was the general business depression that had followed the panic of 1893.

One day in 1896 a notable group of theatrical magnates met by chance at a luncheon at the Holland House in New York. They included Charles Frohman, whose offices booked attractions for a chain of Western theaters extending to the coast; A. L. Erlanger and Marc Klaw, who, as Klaw & Erlanger, controlled attractions for practically the entire South; Nixon & Zimmerman, of Philadelphia, who were conducting a group of the leading theaters of that city, and Al Hayman, one of the owners of the Empire Theater.

These men naturally discussed the chaos in the theatrical business. They decided that its only economic hope was in a centralization of booking interests, and they acted immediately on this decision. Within a few weeks they had organized all the theaters they controlled or represented into one national chain, and the open time was placed on file in the offices of Klaw & Erlanger. It now became possible for the manager of a traveling company to book a consecutive tour at the least possible expense. In a word, booking suddenly became standardized.

This was the beginning of the famous Theatrical Syndicate which, in a brief time, dominated the theatrical business of the whole country. It marked a real epoch in the history of the American theater because within a year a complete revolution had been effected in the business. The booking of attractions was emancipated from curb and café; a theatrical contract became an accredited and licensed instrument. The Syndicate became a clearing-house for the theatrical manager and the play-producer, and the medium through which they did business with each other. Charles Frohman contributed his growing chain of theaters to the organization and secured a one-sixth interest in it which he retained up to the time of his death.

Once launched, the Syndicate proceeded to ride the tempest, for the biggest storm in all American theatrical history soon began to develop. Out of the long turmoil came a whole new line-up in the business. It affected Charles Frohman less than any of his immediate associates in the big combination because, first of all, he was a passive member, and, second, he had a kingdom all his own. Yet the story of these turbulent years is so inseparably linked up with the development of the drama in this country that it is well worth rehearsing.

Although the Syndicate standardized the theatrical contract and made efficient and economical booking possible, it did not immediately secure the willing co-operation of some of the best-known traveling stars of the day. They included Mrs. Fiske, Richard Mansfield, Joseph Jefferson, Nat C. Goodwin, Francis Wilson (then in comic opera), and James A. Herne. They were great popular favorites and had been accustomed to appear at stated intervals in certain theaters in various parts of the country. They booked their own "time" and had a more or less personal relation with the lessees and managers of the theaters in which they appeared.

The Syndicate began to book these stars as it saw fit and as they could be best fitted into the country-wide scheme. A scale of terms was arranged that was regarded as equitable both to the attraction and the local manager.

These stars, however, refused to be booked in this way. They denied the right of the new organization to say when and where they should play. Out of this denial came the famous revolt against the Syndicate which blazed intermittently for more than two decades.

Chief among the insurgents was Mrs. Fiske, who had returned to the stage in "Tess of the D'Urbervilles," a dramatization of Thomas Hardy's great novel. Her husband and manager, Harrison Gray Fiske, was editor and publisher of *The Dramatic Mirror*, which became the voice of protest. Mrs. Fiske refused to appear in Syndicate theaters, and she hired independent houses all over the country. Such places were few and far be-

FRANCIS WILSON

WILLIAM COLLIER

tween in those days, and she was forced to play in public halls, even skating-rinks.

Mansfield became one of the leaders of the opposition to the Syndicate. He made speeches before the curtain, denouncing its methods. His lead was followed by Francis Wilson, and subsequently by James K. Hackett, David Belasco, and Henry W. Savage. The fight on the huge combination became a matter of nation-wide interest.

All the while the Syndicate was growing in power and authority. Gradually the revolutionists returned to the fold because desirable terms were made for them. Only Mrs. Fiske remained outside the ranks. In order to secure a New York City stage for her Mr. Fiske leased the Manhattan Theater for a long term.

It was during these strenuous years, and as one indirect result of the Syndicate fight, that a whole new theatrical dynasty sprang up. It took shape and centered in the growing importance of three then obscure brothers, Lee, Sam, and Jacob J. Shubert by name, who lived in Syracuse, New York. They were born in humble circumstances, and early in life had been forced to become breadwinners. The first to get into the theatrical business was Sam, the second son, who, as a youngster barely in his teens, became program boy and later on assistant in the box-office of the Grand Opera House in his native town. At seventeen he was treasurer of the Weiting Opera House there, and from that time until his death in a railroad accident in 1905 he was an increasingly powerful figure in the business.

Before Sam Shubert was twenty he controlled a chain of theaters with stock companies in up-state New York cities and had taken his two brothers into partnership with him. In 1900 he subleased the Herald Square Theater in New York City and thus laid the cornerstone of what came to be known as the "Independent Movement" throughout the country. He had initiative and enterprise. Gradually he and his brothers and their associates controlled a line of theaters from coast to coast. In these theaters they offered attractive bookings to the managers who were outside the Syndicate. The Shuberts also became producers and encouragers of productions on a large scale.

For the first time the Syndicate now had real opposition. A warfare developed that was almost as bitter and costly in its way as was the old disorganized method in vogue before the business was put on a commercial basis. It naturally led to over-production and to a surplus of theaters. Towns that in reality could only support one first-class playhouse were compelled to have a "regular" and an "independent" theater. Attractions of a similar nature, such as two musical comedies, were pitted against each other. In dividing the local patronage both sides suffered loss.

During the last year of Charles Frohman's life the Syndicate and the Shuberts, wisely realizing that such an uneconomic procedure could only spell disaster in a large way for the whole theatrical business, buried their differences. A harmonious working agreement was entered into that put an end to the destructive strife. Theatrical booking became an open field, and the producer can now play his attractions in both Syndicate and Shubert theaters.

Charles Frohman's activities were now nation-wide. Just as Harriman built up a transcontinental railroad system, so did the rotund little manager now set up an empire all his own. The building of the Empire Theater had given him a closer link with Rich and Harris. Through them he acquired an interest in the Columbia Theater, in Boston, and subsequently he became part owner of the Hollis Street Theater in that city. His third theater in Boston was the Park. By this time the firm name for Boston operation was Rich, Harris, and Charles Frohman. Their next venture was the construction of the magnificent Colonial Theater, on the site of the old Boston Public Library, which was opened with "Ben-Hur." With the acquisition of the Boston and Tremont playhouses, the firm controlled the situation at Boston.

Up to this time Frohman had controlled only one theater in New York—the Empire. In 1896 he saw an opportunity to acquire control of the Garrick in Thirty-fifth Street. He wrote to William Harris, saying, "I will take it if you will come on and run it." Harris assented, and the Garrick passed under the banner of Charles Frohman, who inaugurated his régime with John Drew in "The Squire of Dames." He put some of his biggest successes into this theater and some of his favorite stars, among them Maude Adams and William Gillette. To the chain of Charles Frohman controlled theaters in New York were added in quick order the Criterion, the Savoy, the Garden, and a part interest in the Knickerbocker.

During his early tenancy of the Garrick occurred an incident which showed Frohman's resource. He produced a play called "The Liars," by Henry Arthur Jones, in which he was very much interested. In the out-of-town try-out up-state Frohman heard that the critic of one of the most important New York newspapers had expressed great disapproval of the piece on account of some personal prejudice. He did not want this prejudice to interfere with the New York verdict, so he went to Charles Dillingham one day shortly before the opening and said:

"Can you get me some loud laughers?"

Dillingham said he could.

"All right," said Frohman; "I want you to plant one on either side of Mr. Blank," referring to the critic who had a prejudice against the play.

This was done, and on the opening night the "prop" laughers made such a noisy demonstration that the critic said it was the funniest farce in years.

Charles Frohman's first foreign star, who paved the way for so many, was Olga Nethersole. His management of her came about in a curious way. A difference had arisen between Augustin Daly and Ada Rehan, his leading woman. Miss Rehan had decided to withdraw from the company, and in casting about quickly for a successor had decided upon Olga Nethersole, then one of the most prominent of the younger English actresses. While the deal was being consummated Daly and Miss Rehan adjusted their differences, and the arrangements for Miss Nethersole's appearance in America were abrogated.

Miss Nethersole was left without an American manager. Daniel Frohman, then manager of the Lyceum Theater, stepped in and became her American sponsor, forming a partnership with his brother Charles to handle her interests. Jointly they now conducted an elaborate tour for her covering two years, in which she appeared in "Denise," "Frou-Frou," "Camille," and "Carmen."

MARGARET ANGLIN

ANNIE RUSSELL

The sensational episode of her tour was the production of "Carmen." The fiery, impetuous, emotional, and sensuous character of the Spanish heroine appealed to Miss Nethersole's vivid imagination, and she gave a realistic portrayal of the rôle that became popular and spectacular. In all parts of the country the "Carmen Kiss" became a byword. The play, in addition to its own merits as a striking drama, and its vogue at the opera through Madame Calvé's performance of the leading rôle, became a very successful vehicle for Miss Nethersole's two tours. Miss Nethersole was the first star outside of Charles Frohman's own force who appeared at the Empire Theater, where she played a brief engagement with "Camille" and "Carmen."

From his earliest theatrical day Charles believed implicitly in melodrama. His first production on any stage was a thriller. The play that turned the tide in his fortunes was a spine-stirrer. He now turned to his favorite form of play by producing "The Fatal Card," by Haddon Chambers and B. C. Stephenson, at Palmer's Theater. He did it with an admirable cast that included May Robson, Agnes Miller, Amy Busby, E. J. Ratcliffe, William H. Thompson, J. H. Stoddart, and W. J. Ferguson.

A big melodrama now became part of his regular season. He leased the old Academy of Music at Fourteenth Street and Irving Place in New York, where, as a boy, he had seen his brother Gustave sell opera librettos, and where he became fired with the ambition to make money. Here he produced a notable series of melodramas in lavish fashion. The first was "The Sporting Duchess." This piece, which was produced in

England as "The Derby Winner," was a sure-enough thriller. The cast included E. J. Ratcliffe, Francis Carlyle, J. H. Stoddart, Alice Fischer, Cora Tanner, Agnes Booth, and Jessie Busley.

Charles Frohman's next melodrama at the Academy was the famous "Two Little Vagrants," adapted from the French by Charles Klein. In this cast he brought forward a notable group destined to shine in the drama, for among them were Dore Davidson, Minnie Dupree, Annie Irish, George Fawcett, and William Farnum, the last named then just beginning to strike his theatrical stride.

Still another famous melodrama that Charles introduced to the United States at the famous old playhouse was "The White Heather," in which he featured Rose Coghlan, and in which Amelia Bingham made one of her first successes. With this piece Charles emphasized one of the customs he helped to bring to the American stage. He always paid for the actresses' clothes. He told Miss Coghlan to spare no expense on her gowns, and she spent several thousand dollars on them. When she saw Frohman after the opening, which was a huge success, she said:

"I am almost ashamed to see you."

"Why?" he asked.

"Because I spent so much money on my gowns."

"Nonsense!" said Frohman. "You did very wisely. You and the gowns are the hit of the piece."

Frohman here established a new tradition for the production of melodrama in the United States. Up to his era the producer depended upon thrill rather than upon accessory. Frohman lavished a fortune on each production. Any competition with him had to be on the same elaborate scale.

Fully a year before Maude Adams made her stellar début Frohman put forth his first woman star in Annie Russell. This gifted young Englishwoman, who had appeared on the stage at the age of seven in "Pinafore," had made a great success in "Esmeralda," at the Madison Square Theater. Frohman, who was then beginning his managerial career, was immediately taken with her talent. She appeared in some of his earlier companies. He now starred her in a play by Bret Harte called "Sue." He presented her both in New York and in London.

Under Frohman, Miss Russell had a long series of starring successes. When she appeared in "Catherine," at the Garrick Theater, in her support was Ethel Barrymore, who was just beginning to emerge from the obscurity of playing "bits." In succession Miss Russell did "Miss Hobbs," "The Royal Family," "The Girl and the Judge," "Jinny the Carrier," and "Mice and Men."

In connection with "Mice and Men" is a characteristic Frohman story. Charles ordered this play written from Madeleine Lucette Ryley for Maude Adams. When he read the manuscript he sent it back to Miss Ryley with the laconic comment, "Worse yet." She showed it to Gertrude Elliott, who bought it for England. When Charles heard of this he immediately accepted the play, and it proved to be a success. The moment a play was in demand it became valuable to him.

Spectacular success seemed to have taken up its abode with Charles. It now found expression in the production of "Secret Service," the most picturesque and profitable of all the Gillette enterprises. The way it came to be written is a most interesting story,

Frohman was about to sail for Europe when Gillette sent him the first act of this stirring military play. Frohman read it at once, sent for the author and said:

"This is great, Gillette. Let me see the second act."

Gillette produced this act forthwith, and Frohman's enthusiasm increased to such an extent that he postponed his sailing until he received the complete play. Frohman's interest in "Secret Service" was heightened by the fact that he had scored two tremendous triumphs with military plays, "Held by the Enemy" and "Shenandoah." He felt that the talisman of the brass button was still his, and he plunged heavily on "Secret Service."

It was first put on in Philadelphia. Even at that time there obtained the superstition widely felt in the theatrical business that what fails out of town must succeed in New York. Frohman, who shared this superstition, was really eager not to register successfully in the Quaker capital.

But "Secret Service" smashed this superstition, because it scored heavily in Philadelphia and then had an enormous run at the Garrick Theater in New York. In "Secret Service" Maurice Barrymore had the leading part, and he played it with a distinction of bearing and a dash of manner that were almost irresistible.

William Gillette always proved to be one of Charles Frohman's mascots. Practically whatever he touched turned to gold. He and Frohman had now become close friends, and the actor-author frequently accompanied the manager on his trips to London.

During their visit in 1899, "Sherlock Holmes" had become the literary rage. Everybody was talking about the masterful detective of Baker Street.

"We must get those Doyle stories," said Frohman to Gillette.

"All right," said the author.

Frohman personally went to see Conan Doyle and made a bid for the rights.

"Certainly, Mr. Frohman," replied Doyle, "but I shall make one stipulation. There must be no love business in 'Sherlock Holmes.'"

"All right," said Frohman; "your wishes shall be respected."

Frohman now engaged Gillette to make the adaptation, but he said absolutely nothing about the condition that Doyle had made. Gillette, as most American theater-goers know, wove a love interest into the strenuous life of the famous detective.

A year later, Gillette and Frohman again were in England, Gillette to read the manuscript of the play to Doyle. The famous author liked the play immensely and made no objection whatever to the sentimental interest. In fact, his only comment when Gillette finished reading the manuscript was:

"It's good to see the old chap again."

He referred, of course, to *Sherlock Holmes*, who, up to this time, had already met his death on four or five occasions.

"Sherlock Holmes" proved to be another "Secret Service" in every way. Gillette made an enormous success in the title rôle, and after a long run at the Garrick went on the road. Frohman revived it again and again until it had almost as many "farewells" as Adelina Patti. The last business detail that Charles discussed with Gillette before sailing on the fatal trip in 1915 was for a revival of this play at the Empire.

The Frohman Star Factory was now working full time. Next in output came William Faversham. This brilliant young Englishman had started with Daniel Frohman's company at the Lyceum in a small part. At a rehearsal of "The Highest Bidder" Charles singled him out.

"Where did you get your cockney dialect?" he asked.

"Riding on the top of London 'buses," was the reply.

"Well," answered Charles, "I want to do that myself some day."

This was the first contact between two men who became intimate friends and who were closely bound up in each other's fortunes.

During his Lyceum engagement Faversham wanted to widen his activities. He read in the papers one day that Charles was producing a number of plays, so he made up his mind he would try to get into one of them. He went to Frohman's office every morning at half-past nine and asked to see him or Al Hayman. Sometimes he would arrive before Frohman, and the manager had to pass him as he went into his office. He invariably looked up, smiled at the waiting actor, and passed on. Faversham kept this up for weeks. One day Alf Hayman asked him what he wanted there.

"I am tired of hanging round the Lyceum with nothing to do. I want a better engagement," was the answer.

Hayman evidently communicated this to Frohman and Al Hayman, but they made no change in their attitude. Every day they passed the waiting Faversham as they arrived in the morning and went out to lunch, and always Frohman smiled at him.

Finally one morning Charles came to the door, looked intently at Faversham, puffed out his cheeks as was

WILLIAM FAVERSHAM

his fashion, and smiled all over his face. Turning to Al Hayman, who was with him, he said:

"Al, we've got to give this fellow something to do or we won't be able to go in and out of here much longer."

In a few moments Frohman emerged again, asked Faversham how tall he was. When he was told, he invited Faversham into his office and inquired of him if he could study a long part and play it in two days. Faversham said he could. The result was his engagement for Rider Haggard's "She." Such was the unusual beginning of the long and close association between Faversham and Charles Frohman.

Faversham became leading man of the Empire Stock Company, and his distinguished career was a matter of the greatest pride to Charles. He now was caught up in the Frohman star machine and made his first appearance under the banner of "Charles Frohman Presents," in "A Royal Rival," at the Criterion in August, 1901.

Charles not only made Faversham a star, but provided him with a wife, and a very charming one, too. In the spring of 1901 an exquisite young girl, Julie Opp by name, was playing at the St. James Theater in London. Frohman sent for her and asked her if she could go to the United States to act as leading woman for William Faversham.

"I have been to America once," she said, "and I want to go back as a star."

When Frohman let loose the powers of his persuasiveness, Miss Opp began to waver.

"I don't want to leave my nice London flat and my English maid," she protested.

"Take the maid with you," said Frohman. "We can't

box the flat and take that to New York, but we have flats in New York that you can hire."

"I hate to leave all my friends," continued Miss Opp.

"Well, I can't take over all your friends," replied Frohman, "but you will have plenty of new admirers in New York."

Miss Opp asked what she thought were unreasonable terms. Frohman said nothing, but sent Charles Dillingham to see her next day. He said Frohman wanted to know if she was joking about her price. "Of course," he said, "if you are not joking he will pay it anyhow, because when he makes up his mind to have anybody he is going to have him."

This shamed Miss Opp. She asked a reasonable fee, went to the United States, and not only became Faversham's leading woman, but his wife. Frohman always took infinite delight in teasing the Favershams about having been their matchmaker.

Charles, who loved to create a sensation in a big way, was now able to gratify one of his favorite emotions with the production of "The Conquerors." Like many of the Frohman achievements, it began in a picturesque way.

During the summer of 1897, Frohman and Paul Potter, being in Paris, dropped in at that chamber of horrors, the Grand Guignol, in the Rue Chaptal. There they saw "Mademoiselle Fifi," a playlet lasting less than half an hour, adapted by the late Oscar Metenier from Guy de Maupassant's short story. It was the tale of a young Prussian officer who gets into a French country house during the war of 1870, abuses the aristocrats who live there, shoots out the eyes of the family portraits, entertains at supper a number of loose French girls from Rouen, and is shot by one of the girls for vilifying Frenchwomen. Frohman was deeply impressed.

"Why can't you make it into a long play?" said Frohman.

"I can," said Potter.

"How?" queried Frohman.

"By showing what happened to the French aristocrats while the Prussian officer was shooting up the place," answered the author.

"Do it," said Frohman, "and I'll open the season of the Empire Stock Company in this drama, and get George Alexander interested for London."

As "The Conquerors" the play went into rehearsal about Christmas. Mrs. Dazian, wife of Henry Dazian, the costumier, was watching a scene in which William Faversham plans the ruin of Viola Allen, the leading woman.

"Well," said Mrs. Dazian, "if New York will stand for that it will stand for anything."

Frohman jumped up in excitement. "What is wrong with it?" he cried. "The manuscript was shown to a dozen people of the cleanest minds. They found nothing wrong. I've done the scene a dozen times. I have it up-stairs on my shelves at this moment in 'The Sporting Duchess.'"

Mrs. Dazian was obdurate. "It is awful," she said.

The first night approached. Potter was to sail for Europe next day. Frohman had provided him with sumptuous cabin quarters on the *New York*. After the dress rehearsal, Potter appeared on the Empire stage, where he found Frohman. The latter was worried.

"Paul," said he, "the first three acts are fine; the

last is rotten. You must stay and rewrite the last act."

Potter had to postpone his trip. At ten next morning the new act was handed in; the company learned and rehearsed it by three in the afternoon, and that night Frohman and the author stood in the box-office watching the audience file in.

"How's the house, Tommy?" demanded Frohman of Thomas Shea, his house manager.

"Over seventeen hundred dollars already," said Shea.

"You can go to Europe, Paul," said Frohman. "Your last act is all right. We don't want you any more."

The American public agreed with Mrs. Dazian. They thought the play excruciatingly wicked, but they were just as eager to see it on the Fourth of July as they had been six months earlier.

A dozen details combined to make "The Conquerors" a storm-center. First of all it was attacked because of its alleged immorality. In the second place the author was charged with having appropriated some of Sardou's "La Haine." In the third place, this play marked the first stage appearance of Mrs. Clara Bloodgood, wife of "Jack" Bloodgood, one of the best-known men about town in New York. Mr. Bloodgood became desperately ill during rehearsals, and his wife divided her time between watching at his bedside and going to the theater. Of course, the newspapers were filled with the account of the event which was agitating all society, and it added greatly to popular interest in the play.

"The Conquerors" not only brought Paul Potter and Frohman a great success, but it sped William Faversham on to the time when he was to become a star. The cast was one of the most distinguished that Froh-

HENRY MILLER

man had ever assembled, and it included among its women five future stars—Viola Allen, Blanche Walsh, Ida Conquest, Clara Bloodgood, and May Robson.

By this time Henry Miller had left the Empire Stock Company and had gone on the road with a play called "Heartsease," by Charles Klein and J. I. C. Clark. It failed in Cincinnati, and Miller wrote Frohman about it. A week later the men met on Broadway. Miller still believed in "Heartsease" and asked Frohman if he could read it to him.

"All right," replied Frohman; "come to-morrow and let me hear it."

Miller showed up the next morning and left Klein and Clark, who had accompanied him, in a lower office. Frohman locked the door, as was his custom, curled himself up on a settee, lighted a cigar, and asked for the manuscript.

"I didn't bring it. I will act it out for you."

Miller knew the whole production of the play depended upon his performance. He improvised whole scenes and speeches as he went along, and he made a deep impression. When he finished, Frohman sat still for a few moments. Then he rang a bell and Alf Hayman appeared. To him he said, quietly:

"We are going to do 'Heartsease.'"

Miller rushed down-stairs to where Klein and Clark were waiting, and told them to get to work revising the manuscript.

When the play went into rehearsal, Frohman, who sat in front, spoke to Miller from time to time, asking, "Where is that line you spoke in my office?"

This incident is cited to show Charles's amazing

memory. Miller, of course, had improvised constantly during his personal performance of the play, and Frohman recognized that these improvisations were missing when the piece came into rehearsal.

Charles now added a third star to his constellation in Henry Miller. He first produced "Heartsease" in New Haven. Charles Dillingham sat with him during the performance. When the curtain went down on a big scene, and the audience was in a tumult, demanding star and author, Frohman leaned over to speak to his friend. Dillingham thought he was about to make a historic remark, inspired by the enormous success of the play before him. Instead, Frohman whispered:

"Charley, I wonder if they have any more of that famous apple-pie over at Hueblein's?"

He was referring to a famous article of food that had added almost as much glory to New Haven as had its historic university, and for which Frohman had an inordinate love.

Henry Miller now became an established Frohman star. After "Heartsease" had had several successful road seasons, Frohman presented Miller in "The Only Way," an impressive dramatization of Charles Dickens's great story, "A Tale of Two Cities."

Charles Dillingham's friendship with Frohman had now become one of the closest of his life. He always accompanied Frohman to England, and was regarded as his right-hand man. Frohman had always urged his friend to branch out for himself. The result was that Dillingham assumed the managership of Julia Marlowe.

Dillingham presented Miss Marlowe at the Knickerbocker Theater in New York in "The Countess Valeska."

Frohman liked the play so much that he became interested in the management of Miss Marlowe, and together
they produced "Colinette," adapted from the French
by Henry Guy Carleton, at this theater. "Colinette"
inspired one of the many examples of Frohman's quick
retort.

The "try-out" was at Bridgeport, and Dillingham
had engaged a private chair car for the company. When
Frohman tried to get on this car at Grand Central Station the porter turned him down, saying:

"This is the Marlowe car."

Whereupon Frohman spoke up quickly and said:
"I am Mr. Marlowe," and stepped aboard.

The production of "Colinette" marked the beginning
of another one of Frohman's intimate associations.
He engaged William Seymour to rehearse and produce
the play. Seymour later directed some of the greatest
Frohman undertakings and eventually became general
stage-manager for his chief. Frohman was now actively
interested in Miss Marlowe's career. Under the joint
Frohman-Dillingham management she played in "As
You Like It" and "Ingomar."

By this time Clyde Fitch had steadily made his way
to the point where Frohman had ceased to regard him
as a "pink tea" author, but as a really big playwright.
They became great friends. He gave Fitch every possible encouragement. The time was at hand when Fitch
was to reward that encouragement, and in splendid
fashion.

Once more the Civil War proved a Charles Frohman
mascot, for Fitch now wrote "Barbara Fritchie," founded
on John G. Whittier's famous war poem. He surrounded
the star with a cast that included W. J. Lemoyne,

Arnold Daly, Dodson Mitchel, and J. H. Gilmour. The play opened at the Broad Street Theater in Philadelphia. At the dress rehearsal began an incident which showed Charles's ready resource.

In the second act the business of the play required that Miss Marlowe take a gun and shoot a man. No gun was at hand. It was decided to send the late Byron Ongley, assistant stage-manager of the company, to the Stratford Hotel, where the star lived, with a gun and show her how to use it there.

When Frohman, who came to see the rehearsal, heard of this he had an inspiration for a fine piece of publicity.

"Why can't Ongley pretend to be a crank and appear to be making an attempt on Miss Marlowe's life?"

He liked Ongley, and he really conceived the idea more to play one of his numerous practical jokes than to capitalize the event.

Without saying a word to Ongley, Dillingham notified the Stratford management that Miss Marlowe had received a threatening letter from a crank who might possibly appear and make an attempt on her life. When Ongley entered the hotel lobby innocently carrying the gun he was beset by four huge porters and borne to the ground. The police were summoned and he was haled off to jail, where he spent twenty-four hours. The newspapers made great capital of the event, and it stimulated interest in the performance.

When "Barbara Fritchie" opened at the Criterion Theater in New York, which had passed under the Frohman control, it scored an immediate success. It ran for four months. Not only was Miss Marlowe put into the front rank of paying stars, but the success of the play

WILLIAM H. CRANE

gave Clyde Fitch an enormous prestige, for it was his first big triumph as an original playwright. From this time on his interest was closely linked with that of Charles Frohman, who became his sponsor.

In connection with Julia Marlowe is a characteristic Frohman story. The manager always refused to accept the new relation when one of his women stars married. This incident grew out of Julia Marlowe's marriage to Robert Taber.

One day his office-boy brought in word that Mrs. Taber would like to see him.

"I don't know her."

After an interval of a few moments a dulcet voice came through the door, saying, "Won't you see me?"

"Who are you?"

"Mrs. Taber."

"I don't know Mrs. Taber, but Julia Marlowe can come in."

Charles was now in a whirlwind of activities. He was not only making stars, but also, as the case of Clyde Fitch proved, developing playwrights. In the latter connection he had a peculiar distinction.

One day some years before, Madeline Lucette Ryley came to see him. She was a charming English *ingénue* who had been a singing soubrette in musical comedies at the famous old Casino, the home of musical comedies, where Francis Wilson, De Wolf Hopper, Jefferson De Angelis, and Pauline Hall had achieved fame as comic-opera stars. She had also appeared in a number of serious plays.

Mrs. Ryley made application for a position. Frohman said to her:

"I don't need actresses, but I need plays. Go home and write me one."

Mrs. Ryley up to that time had written plays only as an amateur. She went home and wrote "Christopher Jr." and it started her on a notably successful career as a playwright. In fact, she was perhaps the first of the really successful women playwrights.

Charles Frohman celebrated the opening theatrical season of the new twentieth century by annexing a new star and a fortune at the same time. It was William H. Crane in "David Harum" who accomplished this.

Again history repeated itself in a picturesque approach to a Frohman success. One morning, at the time when both had apartments at Sherry's, Frohman and Charles Dillingham emerged from the building after breakfast. On the sidewalk they met Denman Thompson, the old actor. Frohman engaged him in conversation. Suddenly Thompson began to chuckle.

"What are you laughing at?" asked Frohman.

"I was thinking of a book I read last night, called 'David Harum,'" replied Thompson.

"Was it interesting?"

"The best American story I ever read," said the actor.

Frohman's eyes suddenly sparkled. He winked at Dillingham, who hailed a cab and made off. Frohman engaged Thompson in conversation until he returned. In his pocket he carried a copy of "David Harum."

Frohman read the book that day, made a contract for its dramatization, and from the venture he cleared nearly half a million dollars.

Frohman considered four men for the part of *David Harum*. They were Denman Thompson, James A.

Hearne, Sol Smith Russell, and Crane. Thompson was too old, Hearne had been associated too long with the "Shore Acres" type to adapt himself to the Westcott hero, and Sol Smith Russell did not meet the requirements. Frohman regarded Crane as ideal.

His negotiations with Crane for this part were typical of his business arrangements. It took exactly five minutes to discuss them. When the terms had been agreed upon, Frohman said to Crane:

"Are you sure this is perfectly satisfactory to you?"

"Perfectly," replied Crane.

Frohman reached over from his desk and shook his new star by the hand. It was his way of ratifying a contract that was never put on paper, and over which no word of disagreement ever arose. Crane's connection with Charles Frohman lasted for nine years.

Frohman personally rehearsed "David Harum." Much of its extraordinary success was due to his marvelous energy. It was Frohman, and not the dramatist, who introduced the rain-storm scene at the close of the second act which made one of the biggest hits of the performance. Throughout the play there were many evidences of Frohman's skill and craftsmanship.

It was just about this time that the real kinship with Augustus Thomas began. Frohman, after his first meeting with Thomas years before in the box-office of a St. Louis theater, had produced his play "Surrender," and had engaged him to remodel "Sue." Now he committed the first of the amazing quartet of errors of judgment with regard to the Thomas plays that forms one of the curious chapters in his friendship with this distinguished American playwright.

Thomas had conceived the idea of a cycle of American plays, based on the attitude toward women in certain sections of the country. The first of these plays had been "Alabama," the second "In Mizzoura." Thomas now wrote "Arizona" in this series. When he offered the play to Frohman, the manager said:

"I like this play, Gus, but I have one serious objection to it. I don't see any big situation to use the American flag. Perhaps I am superstitious about it. I have had such immense luck with the flag in "Shenandoah" and "Held by the Enemy" that I have an instinct that I ought not to do this play, much as I would like to."

As everybody knows, the play went elsewhere and was one of the great successes of the American stage.

Frohman now realized his mistake. He sent for Thomas and said: "I want you to write me another one of those rough plays."

The result was "Colorado," which Frohman put on at the Grand Opera House in New York with Wilton Lackaye in the leading rôle, but it was not a success.

A few years later Frohman made another of the now famous mistakes with Thomas. Thomas had seen Lawrence D'Orsay doing his usual "silly ass" part in a play. He also observed that the play lagged unless D'Orsay was on the stage. He therefore wrote a play called "The Earl of Pawtucket," with D'Orsay in mind, and Frohman accepted it. When the time came to select the cast, Thomas suggested D'Orsay for the leading part.

"Impossible!" said Frohman. "He can't do it."

Thomas was so convinced that D'Orsay was the ideal man that Frohman made this characteristic concession: "I think well of your play, and it will probably be a

AUGUSTUS THOMAS

SIR ARTHUR WING PINERO

success," he said, "but I do not believe that D'Orsay is the man for it. If you can get another manager to do it I will turn back the play to you, and if you insist upon having D'Orsay I will release him from his contract with me."

Kirk La Shelle took the play and it was another "Arizona."

Frohman produced a whole series of Thomas successes, notably "The Other Girl," "Mrs. Leffingwell's Boots," and " De Lancey." To the end of his days the warmest and most intimate friendship existed between the men. It was marked by the usual humor that characterized Frohman's relations. Here is an example:

Thomas conducted the rehearsals of "The Other Girl" alone. Frohman, who was up-stairs in his offices at the Empire, sent him a note on a yellow pad, written with the blue pencil that he always used:

"How are you getting along at rehearsals without me?"

"Great!" scribbled Thomas.

The next day when he went up-stairs to Frohman's office, he found the note pinned on the wall.

Such was the mood of the man who had risen from obscurity to one of commanding authority in the whole English-speaking theater.

X

THE RISE OF ETHEL BARRYMORE

*W*HILE the star of Maude Adams rose high in the theatrical heaven, another lovely luminary was about to appear over the horizon. The moment was at hand when Charles Frohman was to reveal another one of his protégés, this time the young and beautiful Ethel Barrymore. It is an instance of progressive and sympathetic Frohman sponsorship that gave the American stage one of its most fascinating favorites.

Some stars are destined for the stage; others are born in the theater. Ethel Barrymore is one of the latter. Two generations of eminent theatrical achievement heralded her advent, for she is the granddaughter of Mrs. John Drew, mistress of the famous Arch Street Theater Company of Philadelphia, and herself, in later years, the greatest *Mrs. Malaprop* of her day. Miss Barrymore's father was the brilliant and gifted Maurice Barrymore; her mother the no less witty and talented Georgia Drew, while, among other family distinctions, she came into the world as the niece of John Drew.

Despite the royalty of her theatrical birth, no star in America had to labor harder or win her way by more persistent and conscientious effort. At fourteen she was playing child's parts with her grandmother. A few years later she came to New York to get a start. Though she bore one of the most distinguished and honored names in the profession, she sat around in agents' offices for six months, beating vainly at the door of opportunity. Finally she got a chance to understudy Elsie De Wolfe, who was playing with John Drew, in "The Bauble Shop," at the Empire. One day when that actress became ill this seventeen-year-old child played the part of a thirty-two-year-old woman with great success. Understudies then became her fate for several years. While playing a part on the road with her uncle in "The Squire of Dames," Charles Frohman saw her for the first time. He looked at her sharply, but said nothing. Later, during this engagement, she met the man who was to shape her career.

About this time Miss Barrymore went to London. Charles had accepted Haddon Chambers's play "The Tyranny of Tears," in which John Drew was to star in America. She got the impression that she would be cast for one of the two female parts in this play, and she studied the costuming and other details. With eager expectancy she called on Frohman in London. Much to her surprise Frohman said:

"Well, Ethel, what can I do for you?"

"Won't I play with Uncle John?" she said.

"No, I am sorry to say you will not," replied Frohman.

This was a tragic blow. It was in London that Miss Barrymore received this first great disappointment, and it was in London that she made her first success. Charles Frohman, who from this time on became much impressed with her appealing charm and beauty, gave her a small rôle with the company he sent over with Gillette to play "Secret Service" in the British capital. Odette Tyler played the leading comedy part. One night when Miss Barrymore was standing in the wings the stage-manager rushed up to her and said, excitedly:

"You will have to play Miss Tyler's part."

"But I don't know her lines," said Miss Barrymore.

"That makes no difference; you will have to play. She's gone home sick."

"How about her costume?" said Miss Barrymore.

"Miss Tyler was so ill that we could not ask her to change her costume. She wore it away with her," was the reply.

Dressed as she was, Miss Barrymore, who had watched the play carefully, and who has an extremely good memory, walked on, played the part, and made a hit.

When the "Secret Service" company returned to America, Miss Barrymore remained in London. She lived in a small room alone. Her funds were low and she had only one evening gown. But she had the Barrymore wit and charm, her own beauty, and was in much social demand. By the time she prepared to quit England the one gown had seen its best days. She had arranged to sail for home on a certain Saturday. The night before sailing she was invited to a supper at the home of Anthony Hope. Just as she was about to dress she received a telegram from Ellen Terry, who was playing at the Lyceum Theater, saying:

Do come and say good-by before you go.

When she arrived at the Lyceum, the first thing that Miss Terry said was, "Sir Henry wants to say good-by to you."

On going into the adjoining dressing-room the great actor said to her:

"Wouldn't you like to stay in England?"

"Of course," said Miss Barrymore.

"Would you like to play with me?" he asked.

Coming at her hour of discouragement and despair, it was like manna from heaven. Her knees quaked, but she managed to say, "Y-e-s."

"All right," said Sir Henry. "Go down-stairs. Loveday has a contract that is ready for you to sign."

With this precious contract stuffed into her bosom, Miss Barrymore now rode in triumph to the Hope supper-party.

"What a pity that you have got to leave England," said Sir Herbert Beerbohm Tree.

"But I am going to stay," said Miss Barrymore.

A gasp ran around the table.

"And with whom?" asked Tree.

"With Sir Henry and Miss Terry," was the proud response.

Miss Barrymore played that whole season most acceptably with Irving and Terry in "The Bells" and "Waterloo," and afterward with Henry B. Irving in "Peter the Great."

When she returned to America in 1898 she had a new interest for Charles Frohman. Yet the Nemesis of the Understudy, which had pursued her in America, still held her in its grip, for she was immediately cast as understudy for Ida Conquest in a play called "Catherine" that Frohman was about to produce at the Garrick Theater. She had several opportunities, however, to play the leading part, and at her every appearance she was greeted most enthusiastically. Her youth and appealing beauty never failed to get over the footlights.

Frohman was always impressed by this sort of thing. It was about this time that he said to a friend of his:

"There is going to be a big development in one of my companies before long. There's a daughter of 'Barry' [meaning Maurice Barrymore] who gets a big reception wherever she goes. She has got the real stuff in her."

Miss Barrymore's first genuine opportunity came when Charles cast her for the part of *Stella De Gex* in Marshall's delightful comedy "His Excellency the Governor," which was first put on at the Empire in May, 1899. The grace and sprightliness that were later to bloom so delightfully in Miss Barrymore now found their first real expression. Both in New York and on the road she made a big success.

While rehearsing "His Excellency the Governor," Charles sat in the darkened auditorium of the Empire one day. When the performance was over he walked back on the stage and, patting Miss Barrymore on the shoulder, said:

"You're so much like your mother, Ethel. You're all right."

Frohman was not the type of man to lag in interest. He realized what the girl's possibilities were, so early in 1901 he sent for Miss Barrymore and said to her:

"Ethel, I have a nice part for you at last."

It was the rôle of *Madame Trentoni* in Clyde Fitch's charming play of old New York, "Captain Jinks." Now came one of those curious freaks of theatrical fortune. "Captain Jinks" opened at the Walnut Street Theater in Philadelphia, and seemed to be a complete failure from the start. Although the Quakers did not like the play, they evinced an enormous interest in the lovely leading woman. From the gallery they cried down:

"We loved your grandmother, Ethel, and we love you."

RISE OF ETHEL BARRYMORE

It was a tribute to the place that Mrs. John Drew had in the affections of those staid theater-goers.

Despite the bad start in Philadelphia, Charles believed in Miss Barrymore, and he had confidence in "Captain Jinks." He brought the play into New York at the Garrick. The expectation was that it might possibly run two weeks. Instead, it remained there for seven months and then played a complete season on the road.

Now came the turn in the tide of Ethel Barrymore's fortunes. She was living very modestly on the top floor of a theatrical boarding-house in Thirty-second Street. With the success of "Captain Jinks" she moved down to a larger room on the second floor. But a still greater event in her life was now to be consummated.

During the third week of the engagement she walked over from Thirty-second Street to the theater. As she passed along Sixth Avenue she happened to look up, and there, in huge, blazing electric lights, she saw the name "Ethel Barrymore." She stood still, and the tears came to her eyes. She knew that at last she had become a star.

Charles had said absolutely nothing about it to her. It was his unexpected way of giving her the surprise of arriving at the goal of her ambition.

The next day she went to Frohman and said, "It was a wonderful thing for you to do."

Whereupon Frohman replied, very simply, "It was the only thing to do."

Ethel Barrymore was now a star, and from this time on her stage career became one cycle of ripening art and expanding success. A new luminary had entered the Frohman heaven, and it was to twinkle with increasing brilliancy.

15

Her next appearance was in a double bill, "A Country Mouse" and "Carrots," at the Savoy Theater, in October, 1902. Here came one of the first evidences of her versatility. "A Country Mouse" was a comedy; "Carrots," on the other hand, was impregnated with the deepest tragedy. Miss Barrymore played the part of a sad little boy, and she did it with such depth of feeling that discriminating people began to realize that she had great emotional possibilities.

Her appearance in "Cousin Kate" the next year was a return to comedy. In this play Bruce McRae made his first appearance with her as leading man, and he filled this position for a number of years. He was as perfect an opposite to her as was John Drew to Ada Rehan. Together they made a combination that was altogether delightful.

It was while playing in a piece called "Sunday" that Miss Barrymore first read Ibsen's "A Doll's House." She was immensely thrilled by the character. She said to Frohman at once: "I must do this part. May I?"

"Of course," he said.

Here was another revelation of the Barrymore versatility, for she invested this strange, weird expression of Ibsen's genius with a range of feeling and touch of character that made a deep impression.

Charles now secured the manuscript of "Alice-Sit-By-the-Fire." He was immensely taken with this play, not only because it was by his friend Barrie, but because he saw in it large possibilities. Miss Barrymore was with him in London at this time. Frohman told her the story of the play in his rooms at the Savoy, acting it out as he always did with his plays. There were two important women characters: the mother, played in

London by Ellen Terry, who philosophically accepts the verdict of the years, and the daughter, played by the popular leading woman Irene Vanbrugh, who steps into her place.

"Would you like to play in 'Alice'?" asked Frohman.

"Yes," said Miss Barrymore.

"Which part?"

"I would rather have you say," said Miss Barrymore.

Just then the telephone-bell rang. Barrie had called up Frohman to find out if he had cast the play.

"I was just talking it over with Miss Barrymore," he replied.

Then there was a pause. Suddenly Frohman turned from the telephone and said:

"Barrie wants you to play the mother."

"Fine!" said Miss Barrymore. "That is just the part I wanted to do."

In "Alice-Sit-By-the-Fire" Miss Barrymore did a very daring thing. Here was an exquisite young woman who was perfectly willing to play the part of the mother of a boy of eighteen rather than the younger rôle, and she did it with such artistic distinction that Barrie afterward said of her:

"I knew I was right when I wanted her to play the mother. I felt that she would understand the part."

"Alice-Sit-By-the-Fire" was done as a double bill with "Pantaloon," in which Miss Barrymore's brother, John Barrymore, who was now coming to be recognized as a very gifted young actor, scored a big success. Later another brother, Lionel, himself a brilliant son of his father, appeared with her.

The theater-going world was now beginning to look upon Ethel Barrymore as one of the really charming fixtures of the stage. What impressed every one, most of all Charles Frohman, was the extraordinary ease with which she fairly leaped from lightsome comedy to deep and haunting pathos. Her work in "The Silver Box," by John Galsworthy, was a conspicuous example of this talent. Frohman gave the manuscript of the play to Miss Barrymore to read and she was deeply moved by it.

"Can't we do it?" she said.

"It is very tragic," said Frohman.

"I don't mind," said Miss Barrymore. "I want to do it so much!"

In "The Silver Box" she took the part of a charwoman whose life moves in piteous tragedy. It registered what, up to that time, was the most poignant note that this gifted young woman had uttered. Yet the very next season she turned to a typical Clyde Fitch play, "Her Sister," and disported herself in charming frocks and smart drawing-room conversation.

Miss Barrymore's career justified every confidence that Charles had felt for her. It remained, however, for Pinero's superb if darksome play "Midchannel" to give her her largest opportunity.

When Frohman told her about this play he said: "Ethel, I have a big play, but it is dark and sad. I don't think you want to do it."

After she had heard the story she said, impulsively: "You are wrong. I want to play this part very much."

"All right," said Frohman. "Go ahead."

As *Zoe Blundell* she had a triumph. In this character she was artistically reborn. The sweetness and girlishness now stood aside in the presence of a somber and

ETHEL BARRYMORE

haunting tragedy that was real. Miss Barrymore literally made the critics sit up. It recorded a distinct epoch in her career, and, as in other instances with a Pinero play, the American success far exceeded its English popularity.

When Miss Barrymore did "The Twelve-Pound Look," by Barrie, the following year, she only added to the conviction that she was in many respects the most versatile and gifted of the younger American actresses. Frohman loved "The Twelve-Pound Look" as he loved few plays. Its only rival in his regard was "Peter Pan." He went to every rehearsal, he saw it at every possible opportunity. Like most others, he realized that into this one act of intense life was crowded all the human drama, all the human tragedy.

Miss Barrymore now sped from grave to gay. When the time came for her to rehearse Barrie's fascinating skit, "A Slice of Life," Frohman was ill at the Knickerbocker Hotel. He was very much interested in this little play, so the rehearsals were held in his rooms at the hotel. There were only three people in the cast— Miss Barrymore, her brother John, and Hattie Williams. It was so excruciatingly funny that Frohman would often call up the Empire and say:

"Send Ethel over to rehearse. I want to forget my pains."

Charles Frohman lived to see his great expectations of Ethel Barrymore realized. He found her the winsome slip of a fascinating girl; he last beheld her in the full flower of her maturing art. He was very much interested in her transition from the seriousness of "The Shadow" into the wholesome humor and womanliness of "Our Mrs. McChesney," a part he had planned for her before his final departure. It was one of the many swift changes that Miss Barrymore has made, and had he lived he would have found still another cause for infinite satisfaction with her.

Another star now swam into the Frohman ken. This was the way of it:

Paul Potter was making a periodical visit to New York in 1901. David Belasco came to see him at the Holland House.

"Paul," said he, "C. F. and I want you to make us a version of Ouida's 'Under Two Flags' for Blanche Bates."

"I never read the novel," said Potter.

"You can dramatize it without reading it," remarked Belasco, and in a month he was sitting in Frohman's rooms at Sherry's and Potter was reading to them his dramatization of "Under Two Flags," throwing in, for good measure, a ride from "Mazeppa" and a snow-storm from "The Queen of Sheba."

"I like all but the last scene," said Frohman. "When *Cigarette* rides up those mountains with her lover's pardon, the pardon is, to all intents and purposes, delivered. The actual delivery is an anti-climax. What the audience want to see is a return to the garret where the lovers lived and were happy."

As they walked home that night Belasco said to Potter:

"That was a great point which C. F. made. What remarkable intuition he has!"

Frohman and Potter used to watch Belasco at work, teaching the actors to act, the singers to sing, the dancers to dance.

Then came a hitch.

"Gros, our scene-painter," said Frohman, "maintains

that *Cigarette* couldn't ride up any mountains near the Algerian coast, for the nearest mountains are the Atlas Mountains, eight hundred miles away."

He undertook to convert Mr. Gros. Fortunately for him the author of the play stood in the Garden Theater while Belasco was rehearsing a dance.

"Oh," said he, "if it's a comic opera you can have all the mountains you please. I thought it was a serious drama."

Then Frohman ventured to criticize the mountain torrent.

"What's the matter with the torrent?" called Belasco, while *Cigarette* and her horse stood on the slope.

"It doesn't look like water at all," said Frohman.

Just then the horse plunged his nose into the torrent and licked it furiously. Criticism was silenced. The play was a big, popular success, and with it Blanche Bates arrived as star.

One day, a year later, Frohman remarked to Potter in Paris, "What do you say to paying Ouida a visit in Florence?"

He and Belasco had paid her considerable royalties. He thought she would be gratified by a friendly call. Frohman and Potter obtained letters of introduction from bankers, consuls, and Florentine notables, and sent them in advance to Ouida. The landlord of the inn gave them a resplendent two-horse carriage, with a liveried coachman and a footman. Frohman objected to the footman as undemocratic. The landlord insisted that it was Florentine etiquette, and shrugged his shoulders when they departed, seeming to think that they were bound on a perilous journey.

Through the perfumed, flower-laden hills they climbed,

the Arno gleaming below. The footman took in their cards to the villa of Mlle. de la Ramée. He promptly returned.

"The signora is indisposed," he remarked.

The visitors sent him back to ask if they might come some other day. Again he returned.

"The signora is indisposed," was the only answer he could get.

Potter and Frohman drove away. Frohman was hurt. He did not try to conceal it.

"That's the first author," he said, "who ever turned me down. Anyway, the pancakes at lunch were delicious." He met rebuff—as he met loss—with infinite humor.

Stars now crowded quick and fast into the Frohman firmament. Next came Virginia Harned. Daniel Frohman had seen her in a traveling company at the Fourteenth Street Theater and engaged her to support E. H. Sothern. She later came under Charles's control, and he presented her as star in "Alice of Old Vincennes," "Iris," and "The Light that Lies in Woman's Eyes."

Effie Shannon and Herbert Kelcey followed. Their first venture with him, "Manon Lescant," was a direful failure, but it was followed up with "My Lady Dainty," which was a success.

Charles Frohman had various formulas for making stars. Some he discovered outright, others he developed. Here is an example of his Christopher Columbus proclivities:

One day he heard that there was a very brilliant young Hungarian actor playing a small part down at the Irving Place German Theater in New York City. He went to see him, was very much impressed with his ability, sent for him, and said:

JULIA MARLOWE

"If you will study English I will agree to take care of you on the English-speaking stage."

The man assented, and Frohman paid him a salary all the while he was studying English. Before many years he was a well-known star. His name was Leo Ditrichstein.

Frohman now got Ditrichstein to adapt "Are You a Mason?" from the German, put it on at Wallack's Theater, and it was a huge success. Besides Ditrichstein, this cast, which was a very notable one, included John C. Rice, Thomas W. Wise, May Robson, Arnold Daly, Cecil De Mille, and Sallie Cohen, who had played Topsy in the stranded "Uncle Tom's Cabin" Company, whose advance fortunes Frohman had piloted in his precarious days on the road.

Just as Frohman led the American invasion in England, so did he now bring about the English invasion of America. He had inaugurated it with Olga Nethersole. He now introduced to American theater-goers such artists as Charles Hawtrey, Mrs. Patrick Campbell, Charles Warner, Sir Charles Wyndham, Mary Moore, Marie Tempest, and Fay Davis, in whose career he was enormously interested. He starred Miss Davis in a group of plays ranging from "Lady Rose's Daughter" to "The House of Mirth."

In connection with Mrs. Campbell's first tour occurred another one of the famous Frohman examples of quick retort. He was rehearsing this highly temperamental lady, and made a constructive criticism which nettled her very much. She became indignant, called him to the footlights, and said:

"I want you to know that I am an artist?"

Frohman, with solemn face, instantly replied:

"Madam, I will keep your secret."

One of the early English importations revealed Frohman's utterly uncommercialized attitude toward the theater. He was greatly taken with the miracle play "Everyman," and brought over Edith Wynne Mathison and Charles Rann Kennedy to do it. He was unable to get a theater, so he put them in Mendelssohn Hall.

"You'll make no money with them there," said a friend to him.

"I don't expect to make any," replied Frohman, "but I want the American people to see this fine and worthy thing."

The play drew small audiences for some time. Then, becoming the talk of the town, it went on tour and repaid him with a profit on his early loss.

One of the happiest of Charles Frohman's theatrical associations now developed. In 1903, when the famous Weber and Fields organization seemed to be headed toward dissolution, Charles Dillingham suggested to Willie Collier that he go under the Frohman management. Collier went to the Empire Theater and was ushered into Frohman's office.

"It took you a long time to get up here," said the magnate. "How would you like to go under my management?"

"Well," replied Collier, with his usual humor, "I didn't come up here to buy a new hat."

The result was that Collier became a Frohman star and remained one for eleven years. He and Frohman were constantly exchanging witty telegrams and letters. Frohman sent Collier to Australia. At San Francisco the star encountered the famous earthquake. He wired Frohman:

"San Francisco has just had the biggest opening in its history."

Whereupon Frohman, who had not yet learned the full extent of the calamity, wired back:

"Don't like openings with so many 'dead-heads.'"

All the while, William Gillette had been thriving as a Frohman star. Like many other serious actors, he had an ambition to play *Hamlet*. With Frohman the wishes of his favorite stars were commands, so he proceeded to make ready a production. Suddenly Barrie's remarkable play "The Admirable Crichton" fell into his hands. He sent for Gillette and said:

"Gillette, I am perfectly willing that you should play *Hamlet*, but I have just got from Barrie the ideal play for you."

When Gillette read "The Admirable Crichton," he agreed with Frohman, and out of it developed one of his biggest successes. "Hamlet," with its elaborate production, still awaits Gillette.

In presenting Clara Bloodgood as star in Clyde Fitch's play "The Girl with the Green Eyes," Frohman achieved another one of his many sensations. The smart, charming girl who had made her début under sensational circumstances in "The Conquerors," now saw her name up in electric lights for the first time. Frohman's confidence in her, as in many of his protégés, was more than fulfilled.

Charles Frohman, who loved to dazzle the world with his Napoleonic coups, launched what was up to this time, and which will long remain, the most spectacular of theatrical deals. He greatly admired E. H. Sothern, who had been associated with him in some of his early ventures. The years that Julia Marlowe had played under his joint management had endeared her to him. One day he had an inspiration. There had been no big Shakespearian revival for some time, so he said:

"Why not unite Sothern and Marlowe and tour the country in a series of magnificent Shakespearian productions?"

At that time Julia Marlowe had reverted to the control of Charles Dillingham, while Sothern was still under the management of Daniel Frohman. Charles now brought the stars together, offered them a guarantee of $5,000 a week for a forty weeks' engagement and for three seasons. In other words, he pledged these two stars the immense sum of $200,000 for each season, which was beyond doubt the largest guarantee of the kind ever made in the history of the American theater.

It was just about this time that Joseph Humphreys, Frohman's seasoned general stage-manager, succumbed to the terrific strain under which he had worked all these years, as both actor and producer. William Seymour stepped into his shoes, and has retained that position ever since.

Charles was constantly bringing about revolutions. Through him Francis Wilson, for example, departed from musical comedy, in which he had made a great success, and took up straight plays. He began with Clyde Fitch's French adaptation of "Cousin Billy," and thus commenced a connection under Charles Frohman that lasted many years. With him, as with all his other stars, there was never a scrap of paper.

Frohman and Wilson met at the Savoy Hotel in Lon-

E. H. SOTHERN

don one day. Frohman had often urged him to quit musical comedy, and he now said he was ready to make the plunge.

"All right," said Frohman. "I will give you so much a week and a percentage of the profits."

"It's done," said Wilson.

"Do you want a contract?" asked Frohman.

"No."

This was about all that ever happened in the way of arrangements between Frohman and his stars, to some of whom he paid fortunes.

During these years Charles had watched with growing interest the development of a young girl from Blooming-ton, Illinois, Margaret Illington by name. She had appeared successfully in the old Lyceum Stock Company when it was transferred by Daniel Frohman to Daly's, and had played with James K. Hackett and E. H. Sothern. Charles now cast her in Pinero's play "A Wife Without a Smile." Afterward she appeared in Augustus Thomas's piece "Mrs. Leffingwell's Boots," and made such a strong impression that Frohman made her leading woman with John Drew in Pinero's "His House in Order."

Just about this time Charles, whose interest in French plays had constantly increased through the years, singled out Henri Bernstein as the foremost of the younger French playwrights. He secured his remarkable play "The Thief" for America. He now produced this play at the Lyceum with Miss Illington and Kyrle Bellew as co-stars, and it proved to be an enormous success, continuing there for a whole season, and then duplicating its triumph on the road, where Frohman at one time had four companies playing it in various parts of the country.

XI

THE CONQUEST OF THE LONDON STAGE

GREAT as were Charles Frohman's achievements in America, they were more than matched in many respects by his activities in England. He was the one American manager who made an impress on the British drama; he led the so-called "American invasion." As a matter of fact, he *was* the invasion. No phase of his fascinatingly crowded and adventurous career reflects so much of the genius of the man, or reveals so many of his finer qualities, as his costly attempt to corner the British stage. Here, as in no other work, he showed himself in really Napoleonic proportions.

Behind Charles's tremendous operations in London were three definite motives. First of all, he really loved England. He felt that the theater there had a dignity and a distinction far removed from theatrical production in America. There was no sneer of "commercialism" about it. To be identified with the stage in England was something to be proud of. He often said that he would rather make fifteen pounds in London than fifteen thousand dollars in America. It summed up his whole attitude toward the theater in Great Britain.

In the second place, he knew that a strong footing in England was absolutely necessary to a mastery of the situation in America. Just as important as any of his other reasons was the conviction in his own mind that to produce the best English-speaking plays in the United States he must know English playwrights and English authors on their own ground, and to produce, if possible, their own works on their home stages.

This latter desire led him to the long and brilliant series of productions that he made in London, and which amounted to what later became an almost complete monopoly on British dramatic output for the United States.

The net result was that he became a sort of Colossus of the English-speaking theater. Figuratively, he stood astride the mighty sea in which he was to meet his death, with one foot planted securely in England and the other in New York.

Charles's first visits to England were made in the most unostentatious way, largely to look over the ground and see what he could pick up for America. His first offices in Henrietta Street were very modest rooms. Unpretentious as they were, they represented a somewhat historic step, because Frohman was absolutely the first American manager to set up a business in England. Augustin Daly had taken over a company, but he allied himself in no general way with British theatrical interests.

When Frohman first engaged W. Lestocq as his English manager, as has already been recorded, he made a significant remark:

"You know I am coming into London to produce plays. But I am coming in by the back door. I shall get to the front door, however, and you shall come with me."

No sooner had he set foot in London than his productive activities were turned loose. With A. and S. Gatti he put on one of his New York successes, "The Lost Paradise," at the Adelphi Theater. In this instance he merely furnished the play. It failed, however. Far from discouraging Frohman, it only filled him with a desire to do something big.

This play marked the beginning of one of his most important English connections. The Gattis, as they were known in England, were prominent figures in the British theater. They were Swiss-Italians who had begun life in England as waiters, had established a small eating-house, and had risen to become the most important restaurateurs of the British capital. They became large realty-owners, spread out to the theater, and acquired the Adelphi and the Vaudeville.

Charles Frohman's arrangement with them was typical of all his business transactions. Some years afterward a well-known English playwright asked Stephen Gatti:

What is your contract with Frohman?"

"We have none. When we want an agreement from Charles Frohman about a business transaction it is time to stop," was his reply.

With the production of a French farce called "A Night Out," which was done at the Vaudeville Theater in 1896, Frohman began his long and intimate association with George Edwardes. This man's name was synonymous with musical comedy throughout the amusement world. As managing director of the London Gaiety Theater, the most famous musical theater anywhere, he occupied a unique position. Charles was the principal American importer of the Gaiety shows, and through this and various other connections he had much to do with Edwardes.

Frohman and Edwardes were the joint producers of "A Night Out," and it brought to Charles his first taste of London success. This was the only play in London in which he ever sold his interest. Out of this sale grew a curious example of Frohman's disregard of money. For his share he received a check of four figures. He carried it around in his pocket for weeks. After it had become all crumpled up, Lestocq persuaded him to deposit it in the bank. Only when the check was almost reduced to shreds did he consent to open an account with it.

It remained for an American play, presenting an American star, to give Charles his first real triumph in London. With the production of "Secret Service," in 1897, at the Adelphi Theater, he became the real envoy from the New World of plays to the Old. It was an ambassadorship that gave him an infinite pride, for it brought fame and fortune to the American playwright and the American actor abroad. Frohman's envoyship was as advantageous to England as it was to the United States, because he was the instrument through which the best of the modern English plays and the most brilliant of the modern English actors found their hearing on this side of the water.

Frohman was immensely interested in the English production of "Secret Service." Gillette himself headed the company. Both he and Frohman were in a great state of expectancy. The play hung fire until the third act. When the big scene came British reserve melted and there was a great ovation. It was an immediate success and had a long run.

One feature of the play that amused the critics and

theater-goers generally in London was the fact that the spy in "Secret Service," who was supposed to be the bad man of the play, received all the sympathy and the applause, while the hero was arrested and always had the worst of it, even when he was denouncing the spy. Gillette's quiet but forceful style of acting was a revelation to the Londoners.

It was during this engagement that an intimate friend said to Terriss, the great English actor who was distinguished for his impulsiveness:

"Chain yourself to a seat at the Adelphi some night and learn artistic repose from Gillette."

Concerning the first night of "Secret Service" is another one of the many Frohman stories. When a London newspaper man asked the American manager about the magnificent celebration that he was sure had been held to commemorate Gillette's triumph, Frohman said:

"There was nothing of the sort. Mr. Dillingham, my manager, and I joined Mr. Gillette in his rooms at the Savoy. We had some sandwiches and wine and then played 'hearts' for several hours."

This episode inspired Frohman to give utterance to what was the very key-note of his philosophy about an actor and his work. Talking with a friend in England shortly after the opening of "Secret Service," about the modest way in which Gillette regarded his success, he said:

"Nothing so kills the healthy growth of an actor and brings his usefulness to an end so soon, as the idea that social enjoyment is a means to public success, and that industrious labor to improve himself is no longer necessary."

ELSIE FERGUSON

Frohman always regarded the success of "Secret Service" as the corner-stone of his great achievements in England. Once, in speaking of this star's hit, he said:

"You know, what tickles me is the fact that it was left for England to discover that Gillette is a great actor. It's one on America."

A few years later, Frohman made his first Paris production with "Secret Service." The masterful little man always regarded the world as his field; hence the annexation of Paris. He had a version made by Paul de Decourcelle, and the play was put on at the Renaissance Theater. Guitry, the great French actor, played Gillette's part. A very brilliant audience saw the opening performance, but the French did not get the atmosphere of the play. They could not determine whether it was serious or comic. The character of *General Nelson* was almost entirely omitted in the play because the actors themselves could not tell whether it was humor or tragedy. Besides, the French actors wanted to do it their own way.

Dillingham, who had charge of the production in Paris, realizing on the opening night that it would be a failure, and knowing that he had to send Frohman some sort of telegram, cabled, with his customary humor, the following:

> *The tomb of Napoleon looks beautiful in the moonlight.*

As was the case in England, Charles was the only American manager who made any impression upon the French drama. From his earliest producing days he had a weakness for producing adapted French plays.

From France came some of his hugest successes, especially those of Bernstein. He "bulled" the French market on prices. The French playwright hailed him with joy, for he always left a small fortune behind him.

Having established a precedent with Gillette, he now presented his first American woman star in England. It was Annie Russell in Bret Harte's story "Sue." He was very fond of this play, having already produced it in the United States, and he was very proud of the impression that Miss Russell made in London.

Up to this time Frohman had made his English productions in conjunction with the Gattis or George Edwardes at the Adelphi, the Vaudeville, or the Garrick theaters. This would have satisfied most people. But Frohman, who wanted to do things in a big way, naturally desired his own English theater, where he could unfurl his own banner and do as he pleased.

Early in 1897, therefore, he took what was up to that time his biggest English step, for he leased the Duke of York's Theater for nineteen years. His name went over the doorway and from that time on this theater was the very nerve-center, if not the soul, of Charles Frohman's English operations. It was one of the best known and the most substantial of British playhouses, located in St. Martin's Lane, in the very heart of the theatrical district. He took a vast pride in his control of it. He even emblazoned the announcement of his London management on the walls of the Empire on Broadway in New York. In his affections it was in England what the Empire was to him in America. It was destined to be the background of his distinguished artistic endeavors, perhaps the most distinguished.

Charles now embarked on a sea of lavish productions. Typical of his attitude was his employment of the best-known and highest-salaried producer in London. This man was Dion Boucicault, son of the famous playwright of the same name, who was himself a very finished and versatile actor. He gave the Frohman productions a touch of genuine distinction, and his wife, the accomplished Irene Vanbrugh, added much to the attractiveness of the Frohman ventures.

The Frohman sponsorship of the Duke of York's was celebrated with a magnificent production of Anthony Hope's "The Adventure of Lady Ursula," which had been a success in New York with E. H. Sothern. It ran the entire season. The play was put on in the usual Frohman way, so much so that the British critics said that "the production, from first to last, was correct down to a coat-button."

Until the end of his life the Duke of York's Theater had a large place in his heart. At the back of private box F, which was his own box, and which was also used for royalty when it visited the play, was a comfortable retiring-room, charmingly decorated in red. Here Frohman loved to sit and entertain his friends, especially such close intimates as Sir James M. Barrie, Haddon Chambers, Sir Arthur Pinero, Henry Arthur Jones, Michael Morton, and other English playwrights.

These busy days at the Duke of York's furnished Frohman with many amusing episodes. On one occasion he was caught in the self-operating elevator of the theater and was kept a prisoner in it for over an hour. His employees were in consternation. When he was finally extricated they began to apologize most profusely.

"Nonsense!" said Frohman. "I am glad I got stuck. It's the first vacation I have had in two years."

The lobby of the Duke of York's illustrates one of Charles's distinctive ideas. Instead of ornamenting it with pictures of dead dramatic heroes like Shakespeare and Garrick, he filled it with photographs of his live American stars. The English theater-goers who went there saw huge portraits of Maude Adams, Ethel Barrymore, Marie Doro, John Drew, Otis Skinner, and William Gillette.

On one occasion he was held up at the entrance of the Duke of York's by a new doorkeeper who asked for his ticket.

"I am Frohman," said the manager.

"Can't help it, sir; you've got to have a ticket."

"You're quite right," said Frohman, who went to the box-office and bought himself a stall seat. When the house-manager, James W. Matthews, threatened to discharge the doorkeeper, Frohman said:

"Certainly not. The man was obeying orders. If he had done otherwise you should have discharged him."

Frohman so loved the Duke of York's that he would go back to it and witness the same play twenty times. During his last visit to England, when his right knee was troubling him, he telephoned down one night to have his box reserved. Matthews, to spare him any trouble, had a little platform built so that he would not have to walk up the steps. Two weeks later, Frohman again telephoned that he wanted the box held, and added:

"I am better now. Don't bother to build a theater for me."

Curiously enough, the first failure that Charles had

at the Duke of York's was "The Christian," which had scored such an enormous success in America. But failure only spurred him on to further efforts. When an English friend condoled with him about his loss on this occasion he said:

"Forget it. Don't let's revive the past. Let's get busy and pulverize the future."

To the average mind the extent of Frohman's London productions is amazing. When the simple fact is stated that he made one hundred and twenty-five of these, one obtains at a glance the immense scope of the man's operations there. Many of them stand out brilliantly. Early among them was the Frohman-Belasco presentation of Mrs. Leslie Carter in two of her greatest successes at the Garrick Theater.

The first was "The Heart of Maryland." It was during this engagement that Charles bought the English rights to "Zaza," then a sensational success in Paris. It was his original intention to star Julia Marlowe in this play. When Belasco heard of the play he immediately saw it was an ideal vehicle for Mrs. Carter, and Frohman generously turned it over to him. After its great triumph in the United States, Frohman and Belasco produced "Zaza" in London.

It was a huge success and made the kind of sensation in which Frohman delighted. There was much question as to its propriety, so much so that the Lord Chamberlain himself, who supervised the censorship, came and witnessed the performance. He made no objection, however.

An amusing incident, which shows the extraordinary devotion of Charles Frohman's friends, occurred on the first night. While attending the rehearsals at the Garrick, Frohman caught cold and went to bed with a slight attack of pneumonia. On the inaugural night he lay bedridden. He was so eager for news of the play that he said to Dillingham:

"Send me all the news you can."

Dillingham organized a bicycle service, and every fifteen minutes sent encouraging and cheering bulletins to Frohman, who was so elated that he was able to emerge from bed the next morning a well man.

Now the interesting thing about this episode is that Dillingham fabricated most of the messages, because, until the end of the play and for several days thereafter, its success was very much in doubt. Indeed, it took more than a week for it to "catch on."

Charles followed up "Zaza" with a superb production of "Madame Butterfly," in which he used Belasco's beautiful equipment. This production put the artistic seal on Frohman's achievement as a London manager. Up to this time there were some who believed that, despite the lavishness of his policy, there was the germ of the commercial in him. "Madame Butterfly" removed this, but if there had been any doubt remaining, it would have been wiped out by his exquisite presentation of "The First Born." Associated with this play is a story that shows Frohman's dogged determination and resource.

Belasco had made the production of "The First Born" in America in lavish fashion. He brought to it all his love and knowledge of Chinese art.

A rival manager, W. A. Brady, wishing to emulate the success of "The First Born," got together a production of "The Cat and the Cherub," another Chinese

EDNA MAY

play, and secured time in London, hoping to beat Frohman out. It now became a race between Frohman and Brady for the first presentation in London. Both managers were in America. Brady got his production off first. When Frohman heard of it he said:

"We must be in London first."

"But there are no sailings for a week," said one of his staff.

"Then we will hire a boat," was his retort.

However, there proved to be no need for this enterprise, because a regular sailing developed.

"The Cat and the Cherub" won the race across the Atlantic and was produced first. It took the edge off the novelty of "The First Born," which was a failure, but its fine quality gave Charles the premier place as an artistic producer in England, and he never regretted having made the attempt despite the loss.

Frohman became immersed in a multitude of things. In September, 1901, for example, he was interested in five English playhouses—the Aldwych, the Shaftesbury, the Vaudeville, and the Criterion, as well as the Duke of York's. He had five different plays going at the same time—"Sherlock Holmes," "Are You a Mason?" "Bluebell in Fairyland," "The Twin Sister," and "The Girl from Maxim's." This situation was typical of his English activities from that time until his death.

The picturesqueness of detail which seemed to mark the beginning of so many of Charles Frohman's personal and professional friendships attended him in England, as the case of his first experience with Edna May shows.

One hot night late in the summer season of 1900 Frohman was having supper alone on his little private balcony at the Savoy Hotel overlooking the Thames. It was before the Strand wing of the hostelry had been built. As he sat there, clad only in pajamas and smoking a large black cigar, he heard a terrific din on the street below. There was cheering, shouting, and clapping of hands. Summoning a waiter, he asked:

"What's all that noise about?"

"Oh, it's only Miss Edna May coming to supper, sir."

"Why all this fuss?" continued Frohman.

"Well, you see, sir," answered the servant, "they are bringing her back in triumph."

When Frohman made investigation he found that the doctors and nurses at the Middlesex Hospital in London, where Edna May frequently sang for the patients, had engaged the whole gallery of the Shaftesbury Theater where she was singing in "The American Beauty," and attended in a body. After the play they had surrounded her at the stage entrance, unhitched the horse from her little brougham, and hauled her through the streets to the Savoy.

This episode made a tremendous impression on Frohman. He was always drawn to the people who could create a stir. He had heard that Edna May was nearing the end of her contract with George Lederer, so he entered into negotiations with her, and that autumn she passed under his management and remained so until she retired in 1907.

In the case of Edna May there could be no starmaking. The spectacular rise of this charming girl from the chorus to the most-talked-of musical comedy rôle in the English-speaking world—that of the Salvation Army girl in "The Belle of New York"—had given her a great reputation. Frohman now capitalized that reputation in his usual elaborate fashion. He first presented Miss May in "The Girl from Up There."

She appeared under his management in various pieces, both in New York and in London. Her company in New York included Montgomery and Stone, Dan Daly, and Virginia Earle. When he presented Miss May at the Duke of York's in "The Girl from Up There" the result was the biggest business that the theater had known up to that time. In succession followed "Kitty Gray," which ran a year in London, "Three Little Maids," and "La Poupée."

All the while there was being written for Miss May a musical piece in which she was to achieve one of her greatest successes, and which was to bring Charles into contact with another one of his future stars. It was "The School Girl," which Frohman first did in May, 1903, in London, and afterward put on with great success at Daly's in New York.

In the English production of this play was a petite, red-haired little girl named Billie Burke, who sang a song called "Put Me in My Little Canoe," which became one of the hits of the play. Frohman was immensely attracted by this girl, and afterward took her under his patronage and she became one of his best-known stars.

Edna May, under Frohman's direction, was now perhaps the best known of the musical comedy stars in England and America. He took keen delight in her success. In "The Catch of the Season," which he did at Daly's in New York in August, 1905, she practically bade farewell to the American stage. Henceforth Frohman kept her in England. In "The Belle of Mayfair" she was succeeded by Miss Burke in the leading part.

Frohman's production of "Nelly Neil" at the Aldwych Theater in 1907 was one of the most superb musical comedy presentations ever made. For this Frohman imported Joseph Coyne from America to do the leading juvenile rôle. He became such a great favorite that he has remained in England ever since.

Just as Edna May had bidden farewell to America in "The Catch of the Season," so she now bade farewell to the English stage in "Nelly Neil." She had become engaged to Oscar Lewisohn, who insisted on an early marriage. About this time Frohman and George Edwardes secured the English rights to "The Merry Widow." They both urged Miss May to postpone her marriage and appear in it. Miss May was now compelled to decide between matrimony and what would have been perhaps her greatest success, and she chose matrimony.

Her good-by appearance on the stage, May 1, 1907, was one of the most extraordinary events in the history of the English theater. This lovely, unassuming American girl had so completely endeared herself to the hearts of the London theater-goers that she was made the center of a tumultuous farewell. The day the seat-sale opened there was a queue several blocks long. During the opening performance Charles sat in his box alone. When some friends entered he was in tears. He had a genuine personal affection for Miss May, and her retirement touched him very deeply.

In connection with "Nelly Neil" there is a little story which illustrates Charles's attitude toward his productions. He had spent a fortune on "Nelly Neil," and it was not a financial success. After giving it every chance he instructed Lestocq to put up the two weeks' notice. Lestocq remarked that it was a shame to end such a

BILLIE BURKE

magnificent presentation. Whereupon Frohman turned around quickly and said:

"Shut up, or I'll run it another month. You know, Lestocq, if I don't keep a hand on myself sometimes my sentiment will be the ruin of me."

By this time Frohman and James M. Barrie had become close friends. The manager had produced "Quality Street" at the Vaudeville Theater with great success. He now approached a Barrie production which gave him perhaps more pleasure than anything he did in his whole stage life. The advent of "Peter Pan" was at hand. The remarkable story of how Charles got the manuscript of "Peter Pan" has already been told in this biography.

The original title that Barrie gave the play was "The Great White Father," which Frohman liked. Just as soon as Barrie suggested that it be named after its principal character, Frohman fairly overflowed with enthusiasm. In preparing for "Peter Pan" in England, Charles was like a child with a toy. Money was spent lavishly; whole scenes were made and never used. He regarded it as a great and rollicking adventure.

The first production of the Barrie masterpiece on any stage took place at the Duke of York's Theater, London, on December 27, 1904. Frohman was then in America. At his country place up at White Plains, only his close friend, Paul Potter, with him, he eagerly awaited the verdict. It was a bitterly cold night, and a snow-storm was raging. Frohman's secretary in the office in New York had arranged to telephone the news of the play's reception which Lestocq was expected to cable from London. On account of the storm the message was delayed.

Frohman was nervous. He kept on saying, "Will it never come?" His heart was bound up in the fortunes of this beloved fairy play. While he waited with Potter, Frohman acted out the whole play, getting down on all-fours to illustrate the dog and crocodile. He told it as *Wendy* would have told it, for *Wendy* was one of his favorites. Finally at midnight the telephone-bell rang. Potter took down the receiver. Frohman jumped up from his chair, saying, eagerly, "What's the verdict?" Potter listened a moment, then turned, and with beaming face repeated Lestocq's cablegram:

> *Peter Pan all right. Looks like a big success.*

This was one of the happiest nights in Frohman's life.

The first *Peter* in England was Nina Boucicault, who played the part with great wistfulness and charm. She was the first of a quartet which included Cissy Loftus, Pauline Chase, and Madge Titheradge.

Charles so adored "Peter Pan" that he produced it in Paris, June 1, 1909, at the Vaudeville Theater, with an all-English cast headed by Pauline Chase. Robb Harwood was *Captain Hook*, and Sibyl Carlisle played *Mrs. Darling*. It was produced under the direction of Dion Boucicault. The first presentation was a great hit, and the play ran for five weeks. On the opening night Barrie and Frohman each had a box. Frohman was overjoyed at its success, and Barrie, naturally, could not repress his delight. What pleased them most was the spectacle of row after row of little French kiddies, who, while not understanding a word of the narrative, seemed to be having the time of their lives.

From the date of its first production until his death, "Peter Pan" became a fixed annual event in the English life of Charles Frohman. He revived it every year at holiday-time. No occasion in his calendar was more important than the annual appearance of the fascinating boy who had twined himself about the American manager's heart.

Charles was now a conspicuous and prominent figure in English theatrical life. The great were his friends and his opinion was much quoted. In addition to his sole control of the Duke of York's, he had interests in a dozen other playhouses. He liked the English way of doing business. Yet, despite what many people believed to be a strong pro-British tendency, he was always deeply and patriotically American, and he lost several fortunes in pioneering the American play and the American actor in England.

To name the American plays that he produced in London would be to give almost a complete catalogue of American drama revealed to English eyes. Curiously enough, at least two plays, "The Lion and the Mouse" and "Paid in Full," that had made enormous successes in America, failed utterly in England under his direction. He gave England such typically American dramas as "The Great Divide," "Brewster's Millions," "Alias Jimmy Valentine," "Years of Discretion," "A Woman's Way," "On the Quiet," and "The Dictator."

In addition to Gillette he presented Billie Burke in "Love Watches," William Collier in "The Dictator" and "On the Quiet," and Ethel Barrymore in "Cynthia."

With his presentation of Collier he did one of his characteristic strokes of enterprise. Marie Tempest was playing at the Comedy in London. He had always been anxious to try Collier's unctuous American humor on the British, so the American comedian swapped engagements with Miss Tempest. She came over to the Criterion in New York to do "The Freedom of Suzanne," while Collier took her time at the Comedy in "The Dictator." He scored a great success and remained nearly a year.

The time was now ripe for the most brilliant of all the Charles Frohman achievements in England. Had he done nothing else than the Repertory Theater he would have left for himself an imperishable monument of artistic endeavor. The extraordinary feature of this undertaking was that it was left for an American to finance and promote in the very cradle of the British drama the highest and finest attempt yet made to encourage that drama. The Repertory Theater would have proclaimed any manager the open-handed patron of drama for drama's sake.

The National or Repertory Theater idea, which was the antidote for the long run, the agency for the production of plays that had no sustained box-office virtue, which took the speculative feature out of production, had been preached in England for some time. Granville Barker had tried it at the Court Theater, where the Shaw plays had been produced originally. The movement lagged; it needed energy and money.

Barrie had been a disciple of the Repertory Theater from the start. He knew that there was only one man in the world who could make the attempt in the right way. One day in 1909 he said to Frohman:

"Why don't you establish a Repertory Theater?"

Then he explained in a few words what he had in mind.

Without a moment's hesitation Frohman said, briskly: "All right, I'll do it."

With these few words he committed himself to an enterprise that cost him a fortune. But it was an enterprise that revealed, perhaps as nothing in his career had revealed, the depths of his artistic nature.

With his marvelous grasp of things, Frohman swiftly got at the heart of the Repertory proposition. When he launched the enterprise at the Duke of York's he said:

> *Repertory companies are usually associated in the public mind with the revival of old masterpieces, but if you want to know the character of my repertory project at the Duke of York's, I should describe it as the production of new plays by living authors. Whatever it accomplishes, it will represent the combined resources of actor and playwright working with each other, a combination that seems to me to represent the most necessary foundation of any theatrical success.*

Frohman stopped at nothing in carrying out the Repertory Theater idea. He engaged Granville Barker to produce most of the plays. Barker in turn surrounded himself with a superb group of players. The most brilliant of the stage scenic artists in England, headed by Norman Wilkinson, were engaged to design the scenes. Every possible detail that money could buy was lavished on this project.

The result was a series of plays that set a new mark for English production, that put stimulus behind the so-called "unappreciated" play, and gave the English-speaking drama something to talk about—and to remember. The mere unadorned list of the plays pro-

17   249

duced is impressive. They were "Justice," by John Galsworthy; "Misalliance," by Bernard Shaw; "Old Friends" and the "The Twelve-Pound Look," by James M. Barrie; "The Sentimentalists," by George Meredith; "Madras House," by Granville Barker; "Chains," by Elizabeth Baker; "Prunella," by Lawrence Housman and Granville Barker; "Helena's Path," by Anthony Hope and Cosmo Gordon Lenox, and a revival of "Trelawney of the Wells," by Sir Arthur Pinero.

The way "The Twelve-Pound Look" came to be produced is interesting. When the repertory for the theater was being discussed one day by Barrie and Barker at the former's flat in Adelphi Terrace House, Barker said:

"Haven't you got a one-act play that we could do?"

Barrie thought a moment, scratched his head, and said:

"I think I wrote one about six months ago when I was recovering from malaria. You might find it somewhere in that desk." He pointed toward the flat-top table affair on which he had written "The Little Minister" and "Peter Pan."

Barker rummaged around through the drawers and finally found a manuscript written in Barrie's hieroglyphic hand. It was "The Twelve-Pound Look."

The production of "Justice" was generally regarded in England as the finest example of stage production that has been made within the last twenty-five years. Despite the expense, and the fact that Frohman insisted upon making each play a splendid production, the Repertory Theater prospered. It ran from February 21, 1910, until the middle of May. Its run was temporarily terminated by the death of King Edward VII.,

PAULINE CHASE

and it was impossible to revive the project successfully after the formal period of mourning closed.

Frohman's constantly widening activities in London made it necessary for him to have more spacious quarters. The story of his offices really tells the story of his work, for they increased in scope as his operations widened. When he leased the Aldwych Theater he set up his headquarters there. With the acquisition of the Globe he needed more room, and this theater became the seat of his managerial operations. In 1913, and with characteristic lavishness, he engaged what is perhaps the finest suite of theatrical offices in London. They were in a marble structure known as Trafalgar House, in Waterloo Place, one of the choicest and most expensive locations in the city.

Here he had a suite of six rooms. Like the man himself, his own personal quarters were very simple. There was a long, high-ceiled room, with a roll-top desk, which was never used, at one end, and a low morris-chair at the other. From this morris-chair and from his rooms at the Savoy Hotel he ruled his English realm.

Charles's love for his stars never lagged, and wherever it was possible for him to surround himself with their pictures he did so. As a result, the visitor to his London rooms found him surrounded by the familiar faces of Maude Adams, Ethel Barrymore, Ann Murdock, Marie Doro, Julia Sanderson, William Gillette, and John Drew. On the roll-top desk, side by side, were the pictures of his two *Peter Pans*, Miss Adams and Pauline Chase.

Charles's last London production, strangely enough, consisted of two plays by his closest friend, Barrie.

This double bill was "The New Word," a fireside scene, which was followed by "Rosy Rapture."

By a strange coincidence his first English venture was a failure, and so was his last. Yet the long and brilliant journey between these two dates was a highway that any man might have trod with pride. The English-speaking drama received an impetus and a standard that it never would have had without his unflagging zeal and his generous purse. He left an influence upon the English stage that will last.

What endeared him perhaps more than anything else to England was the smiling serenity with which he met criticism and loss. There may have been times when the English resented his desire for monopoly, but they forgot it in tremendous admiration for his courage and his resource. He revolutionized the economics of the British stage; he invested it with life, energy, action; he established a whole new relation between author and producer. Here, as in America, he was the pioneer and the builder.

XII

BARRIE AND THE ENGLISH FRIENDSHIPS

*T*HE fortunes of Charles Frohman's English productions ebbed and flowed; actors and actresses
came and went; to him it was all part of a big and
fascinating game. What really counted and became
permanent were the man's friendships, often made in the
theatrical world of make-believe, but always cemented
in the domain of very sincere reality. In England were
some of his dearest personal bonds.

They grew out of the fact that Charles had the rare
genius of inspiring loyal friendship. He gave much and
he got much. Yet, like Stevenson, it was a case of "a
few friends, but these without capitulation."

In England he seemed to be a different human being.
The inaccessibility that hedged him about in America
vanished. He emerged from his unsocial shell; he
gave out interviews; he relaxed and renewed his youth
in jaunt and jest. His annual trip abroad, therefore, was
like a joyous adventure. It mattered little if he made
or lost a fortune each time.

Frohman was happy in London. He liked the soft,
gray tones of the somber city. "It's so restful," he
always said. Even the "bobbie" delighted him. He
would watch the stolid policeman from the curb and say,
admiringly: "He is wonderful; he raises his hand and

253

all London stops." He was greatly interested in the traffic regulations.

Although he had elaborate offices, his real London headquarters were in the Savoy Hotel. Here, in the same suite that he had year after year, and where he was known to all employees from manager to page, he literally sat enthroned, for his favorite fashion was to curl up on a settee with his feet doubled under him. More than one visitor who saw him thus ensconced called him a "beaming Buddha."

From his informal eminence he ruled his world. Around him assembled the Knights of the Dramatic Round Table. Wherever Frohman sat became the unofficial capitol of a large part of the English-speaking stage. In those Savoy rooms there was made much significant theatrical history. To the little American came Barrie, Pinero, Chambers, Jones, Sutro, Maugham, Morton, with their plays; Alexander, Tree, Maude, Hicks, Barker, Bouchier, with their projects.

Like Charles Lamb, Frohman loved to ramble about London. Often he would stop in the midst of his work, hail a taxi, and go for a drive in the green parks. The Zoological Gardens always delighted him. He frequently stopped to watch the animals. The English countryside always lured him, especially the long green hedges, which held a peculiar fascination. He walked considerably in the country and in town, and he took great delight in peering in shop windows.

In London, as in New York, the theater was his life and inspiration. Almost without exception he went to a performance of some kind every evening. At most of the London theaters he was always given the royal box whenever possible. He liked the atmosphere of

JAMES M. BARRIE

the British playhouse. He always said it was more like a drawing-room than a place of amusement.

To Charles, London meant J. M. Barrie, and to be with the man who wrote "Peter Pan" was one of his supreme delights. The devotion between these two men of such widely differing temperaments constitutes one of the really great friendships of modern times. Character of an unusual kind, on both sides, was essential to such a communion of interest and affection. Both possessed it to a remarkable degree.

No two people could have been more opposite. Frohman was quick, nervous, impulsive, bubbling with optimism; Barrie was the quiet, canny Scot, reserved, repressed, and elusive. Yet they had two great traits in common—shyness and humor. As Barrie says:

"Because we were the two shyest men in the world, we got on so well and understood each other so perfectly."

There was another bond between these two men in the fact that each adored his mother. In Charles's case he was the pride and the joy of the maternal heart; with Barrie the root and inspiration of all his life and work was the revered "Margaret Ogilvy." He is the only man in all the world who ever wrote a life of his mother.

There was still another and more tangible community of interest between these two remarkable men. Each detested the silk hat. Frohman had never worn one since the Haverly Minstrel days, when he had to don the tile for the daily street parade. Barrie, in all his life, has had only one silk hat. It is of the vintage of the early 'seventies. The only occasion when he wears the much-detested headgear is at the first rehearsal of the companies that do his plays. Then he attires himself in morning clothes, goes to the theater, nervously holds the hat in his hand while he is introduced to the actors and actresses. Just as Charles used to hide his silk hat as soon as the minstrel parade was over and put on a cap, so does Barrie send the objectionable headgear home as soon as these formalities are over and welcome his more comfortable bowler as an old friend.

Curiously enough, Frohman and Barrie did not drift together at once. When the little Scotchman made his first visit to America in 1896 and "discovered" Maude Adams as the inspired person to act *Lady Babbie*, he met the man who was to be his great friend in a casual business way only. The negotiations for "The Little Minister" from England were conducted through an agent.

But when Frohman went abroad the following year the kinship between the men started, and continued with increasing intimacy. The men became great pals. They would wander about London, Barrie smoking a short, black pipe, Frohman swinging his stick. On many of these strolls they walked for hours without saying a word to each other. Each had the great gift of silence—the rare sense of understanding.

Barrie and his pipe are inseparable, as the world knows. There is a legend in London theatrical lore that Frohman wanted to drive to Barrie's flat one night. He was in his usual merry mood, so the instruction he gave was this:

"Drive to the Strand, go down to Adelphi Terrace, and stop at the first smell of pipe smoke."

Frohman never tired of asking Barrie about "Peter

Pan." It was a curious commentary on the man's tenacity of interest and purpose that, although he made nearly seven hundred productions in his life, the play of the " Boy Who Would Never Grow Up " tugged most at his heart. Nor did Barrie ever weary of telling him how the play began as a nursery tale for children; how their insistent demand to "tell us more" made it the "longest story in the world"; how, when one pirate had been killed, little Peter (the original of the character, now a soldier in the great war) excitedly said: "One man isn't enough; let's kill a lot of them."

No one will be surprised to know that in connection with "Peter Pan" is one of the most sweetly gracious acts in Frohman's life. The original of *Peter* was sick in bed at his home when the play was produced in London. The little lad was heartsick because he could not see it. When Frohman came to London Barrie told him about it.

"If the boy can't come to the play, we will take the play to the boy," he said.

Frohman sent his company out to the boy's home with as many "props" as could be jammed into the sick-room. While the delighted and excited child sat propped up in bed the wonders of the fairy play were unfolded before him. It is probably the only instance where a play was done before a child in his home.

As most people know, Barrie, at his own expense, erected a statue of *Peter Pan* in Kensington Gardens as his gift to the children of London who so adored his play. It was done as a surprise, for the statue stood revealed one May Day morning, having been set up during the night.

When he planned this statue Barrie mentioned it casually to Frohman, and said nothing more about it.

Frohman never visited the park to see it, but when the model was put on exhibition at the Academy he said to Lestocq one day:

"Where is that *Peter Pan* model?" When he was told he said: "I want to see it, but do I have to look at anything else in the gallery?" On being assured that he did not, he said, "All right."

Frohman went to the Academy, bolted straight for the sculpture-room, and stood for a quarter of an hour gazing intently at the graceful figure of *Peter* playing his pipe. Then he walked out again, without stopping to look at any of the lovely things about him. It was characteristic of Frohman to do just the thing he had in mind to do and nothing else.

Frohman and Barrie seldom wrote to each other. When they did it was a mere scrawl that no other human being in the world could read. The only cablegram that Barrie ever sent Frohman was about "What Every Woman Knows." Hilda Trevelyan played *Maggie Wylie*. Barrie liked her work so much that he cabled Frohman about it on the opening night. When the actress went down to breakfast the next morning to read what the newspapers said about her she found on her plate a cable from Frohman doubling her salary. It was Frohman's answer to Barrie.

Frohman's faith in Barrie was marvelous. It was often said in jest in London that if Barrie had asked Frohman to produce a dramatization of the Telephone Directory he would smile and say with enthusiasm:

"Fine! Who shall we have in the cast?"

One of the great Frohman-Barrie adventures was in Paris. It illustrates so completely the relation between these men that it is worth giving in detail.

Frohman was in Paris, and after much telegraphic insistence persuaded his friend to come over on his first visit to the French capital. Frohman was aglow with anticipation. He wanted to give Barrie the time of his life.

"What would a literary man like to do in Paris?" was the question he asked himself.

In his usual generous way he planned the first night, for Barrie was to arrive in the afternoon. He was then living at the Hôtel Meurice, in the Rue Royale, so he engaged a magnificent suite for his guest. He ordered a sumptuous dinner at the Café de Paris, bought a box at the Théâtre Français, and engaged a smart victoria for the evening.

Barrie was dazed at the splendor of the Meurice suite, but he survived it. When Frohman spoke of the Café de.Paris dinner he said he would rather dine quietly at the hotel, so the elaborate meal was given up.

"Now what would you like to do this evening?" asked his host.

"Are there any of those country fairs around here, where they have side shows and you can throw balls at things?" asked Barrie.

Frohman, who had box seats for the most classic of all Continental theaters in his pocket, said:

"Yes, there is one in Neuilly."

"All right," said Barrie, "let's go there."

"We'll drive out in a victoria," meekly suggested Frohman.

"No," said Barrie, "I think it would be more fun to go on a 'bus."

With the unused tickets for the Théâtre Français in his waistcoat, and the smart little victoria still waiting in front of the Meurice (for Frohman forgot to order the man home), the two friends started for the country fair, where they spent the whole evening throwing balls at what the French call "Aunt Sally." It is much like the old-fashioned side-show at an American county fair. A negro pokes his head through a hole in the canvas, and every time the thrower hits the head he gets a knife. When Frohman and Barrie returned to the Meurice that night they had fifty knives between them. The next night they repeated this performance until they had knives enough to start a hardware-store. This was the simple and childlike way that these two men, each a genius in his own way, disported themselves on a holiday.

One more incident will show the amazing accord between Frohman and Barrie. They were constantly playing jokes on each other, like two youngsters. One day they were talking in Frohman's rooms at the Savoy when a certain actress was announced.

"I would like to know what this woman really thinks of me," said Barrie. "I have never met her."

"All right," said Frohman, "you pretend to be my secretary."

The woman came up and had a long talk with Frohman, during which she gave her impressions, not very flattering, of British playwrights in general and Barrie in particular. All the while the little Scot sat solemnly at a near-by desk, sorting papers and occasionally handing one to Frohman to sign. When the woman left they nearly exploded with laughter.

One of Frohman's delights when in England was to go to Barrie's flat in London, overlooking the Victoria Embankment. He liked this place, first of all, because it was Barrie's. Then, too, he could sit curled up in the corner on a settee, smoking a fat, black cigar, and look out on the historic Thames. Here he knew he would not have to talk. It was the place of Silence and Understanding. He was in an atmosphere he loved. In the flat above lives John Galsworthy; down-stairs dwells Granville Barker; while just across the street is the domicile of Bernard Shaw, whose windows face Barrie's.

When Barrie wanted to notify Shaw that Frohman was with him, he would throw bread-crusts against Shaw's window-panes. In a few moments the sash would fly up and the familiar, grinning, bearded face would pop out. On one of the occasions Shaw yelled across:

"Are you inviting me to a feast, Barrie—are you casting bread upon the troubled waters or is it just Frohman?"

In view of Frohman's perfect adoration of Barrie—and it amounted to nothing else—it is interesting, as a final glimpse of the relation between these men, to see what the American thought of his friend's work. In analyzing Barrie's work once, Frohman said:

"Barrie's distinctive note is humanity. There is rich human blood in everything he writes. He is a satirist whose arrows are never barbed with vitriol, but with the milk of human kindness; a humanist who never surfeits our senses, but leaves much for our willing imagination; an optimist whose message is as compelling for its reasonableness as it is welcome for its gentleness."

Through Barrie and "Peter Pan" came another close and devoted friendship in Charles Frohman's life—the one with Pauline Chase. This American girl had been engaged by one of Frohman's stage-managers for a small part with Edna May in "The Girl from Up There." Frohman did not even know her in those days. After she made her great success as the Pink Pajama girl in "Liberty Belles," at the Madison Square Theater, Frohman engaged her and sent her to England, where, with the exception of one visit to the United States in "Our Mrs. Gibbs," she has remained ever since.

It was not until she played "Peter Pan" that the Frohman-Chase friendship really began. The way in which Miss Chase came to play the part is interesting. Cissie Loftus, who had been playing *Peter*, became ill, and Miss Chase, who had been playing one of the twins, and was her understudy, went on to do the more important part at a matinée in Liverpool. Frohman said to her:

"Barrie and I are coming down to see you act. If we like you well enough to play *Peter*, I will send you back a sheet of paper with a cross mark on it after the play."

At the end of the first act an usher rapped on Miss Chase's dressing-room door and handed her the much-desired slip with the cross. Frohman sent word that he could not wait until the end of the play, because he and Barrie were taking a train back to London. In this unusual way Pauline Chase secured the part which helped to endear her to the man who was her friend and sponsor.

Frohman, Barrie, and Miss Chase formed a trio who went about together a great deal and had much in common, aside from the kinship of the theater. It was for Miss Chase that Barrie wrote "Pantaloon," in which she appeared in conjunction with "Peter Pan," and which gave her a considerable reputation in England.

When Pauline Chase was confirmed in the little church in Marlow-on-the-Thames, Barrie was her godfather and Miss Ellen Terry was her godmother. Frohman attended this ceremony, and it made a tremendous impression on him. He saw the spectacular side of the ceremony, and the spiritual meaning was not lost on him.

The personal comradeship with Pauline Chase was one of the really beautiful episodes in Frohman's life. He was genuinely interested in this girl's career, and in tribute to her confidence in him she made him, in conjunction with Barrie, her father confessor. Here is an episode that is tenderly appealing, and which shows another of the many sides of his character:

Frohman and Barrie were both afraid that Miss Chase would marry without telling them about it, so a compact was made by the three that the two men should be her mentors. There were many applicants for the hand of this lovely American girl. The successful suitor eventually was Alec Drummond, member of a distinguished English family, who went to the front when the war began.

One reason for Miss Chase's devotion to Charles lay in the fact that the American manager had the body of her mother removed from its resting-place in Washington to the dreamy little churchyard at Marlow-on-the-Thames. It is near Marlow that Miss Chase lived through all the years of the Frohman-Barrie comradeship. Her little cottage at Tree Tops, Farnham Common, five miles from Marlow, was one of the places he loved to visit. On the vine-embowered porch he liked to sit and smoke. On the lawn he indulged in his only exercise, croquet, frequently with Barrie or Captain Scott, who died in the Antarctic, and Haddon Chambers, who lived near by. Often he went with his hostess to feed the chickens.

But wherever he went he carried plays. No matter how late he retired to his room, he read a manuscript before he went to bed. He probably read more plays than any other manager in the world.

Frohman went to Marlow nearly every Saturday in summer. His custom was to alight from the train at Slough, where Miss Chase would meet him in her car and drive him over to Marlow, where they lunched at The Compleat Angler, a charming inn on the river.

Miss Chase sometimes playfully performed the office of manicure for Frohman. Once when she was in Paris he sent her this telegram:

Nails.

Whereupon she wired back:

I am afraid you will have to bite them.

Frohman then sent her the telegram by mail, and under it wrote:

I have.

Of all spots in England, and for that matter in all the world, Charles loved Marlow best. It is typical of the many contrasts in his crowded life that he would seek peace and sanctuary in this drowsy English town that nestled between green hills on the banks of the Thames. He always said that it framed the loveliest memories of his life.

PAUL POTTER

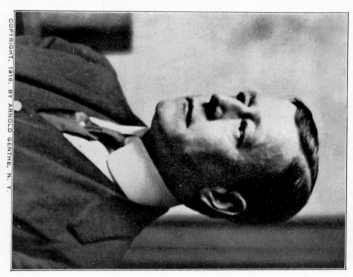

HADDON CHAMBERS

ENGLISH FRIENDSHIPS

When Miss Chase wrote Frohman that she was to be confirmed in the little church in Marlow, she got the following reply from him, which showed how dear the drowsy place was in his affection:

Dear Pauline:—I am glad about Marlow. That little church is the only one in the world I care for—that one across the river at Marlow. Whenever I see it I want to die and stay there.
And Marlow with its long street and nobody on it is fine.

It was Haddon Chambers who first took Frohman to Marlow. It came about in a natural way, because Maidenhead, which is a very popular resort in England (much frequented by theatrical people) is only a short distance away. One day Chambers, who was with Frohman at Maidenhead, said, "There is a lovely, quiet village called Marlow not far away. Let's go over there." So they went.

On this trip occurred one of the many humorous adventures that were always happening when Frohman and Chambers were together. Chambers had the tickets and went on ahead. When he reached the train he found that Frohman was not there. On returning he found his friend held up by the gateman, who demanded a ticket. Quick as a flash Chambers said to him:

"Why do you keep His Grace waiting?"

The gateman immediately became flurried and excited and made apologies. In the mean time Frohman, who took in the situation with his usual quickness, looked solemn and dignified and then passed in like a peer of the realm.

Chambers rented a cottage at Marlow each summer, and one of the things to which Frohman looked forward most eagerly was a visit with him there. Frequent visits to Marlow made the manager known to the whole town. The simplicity of his manner and his keen interest, humor, and sympathy won him many friends. His arrival was always more or less of an event in the little township.

It is a one-street place, with many fascinating old shops. Frohman loved to prowl around, look in the shop windows, and talk to the tradesmen, who came to know and love him and look forward to his advent with the keenest interest. To them he was not the great American theatrical magnate, but a simple, kindly, interested human being who inquired about their babies and who had a big and generous nature.

Frohman once made this remark about the Marlow antique shops: "They're great. When I buy things the proprietor always tells me whether they are real or only fake stuff. That's because I'm one of his friends." It was typical of the man that he was as proud of this friendship as with that of a prince.

On the tramps through Marlow he was often accompanied by Miss Chase and Haddon Chambers. He had three particular friends in the town. One was Muriel Kilby, daughter of the keeper of The Compleat Angler. When Frohman first went to Marlow she was a slip of a child. He watched her grow up with an increasing pride. This great and busy man found time in New York to write her notes full of friendly affection. A few days before the *Lusitania* went down she received a note from him saying that he was soon to sail, and looked forward with eagerness to his usual stay at Marlow.

Through Miss Kilby Frohman became more intimately a part of the local life of Marlow. She was head of the Marlow Amateur Dramatic Society, which gave an amateur play every year. Frohman became a member, paid the five shillings annual dues, and whenever it was possible he went to their performances. As a matter of fact, the Marlow Dramatic Society has probably the most distinguished non-resident membership in the world, for besides Frohman (and through him) it includes Barrie, Haddon Chambers, Pauline Chase, Marie Lohr, William Gillette, and Marc Klaw. Frohman always took his close American friends to Marlow. One of the prices they paid was membership in the amateur dramatic society.

Like every really great man, Charles Frohman was tremendously simple, as his friendship with W. R. Clark, the Marlow butcher, shows. Clark is a big, ruddy, John Bull sort of man, whose shop is one of the main sights of High Street in the village. Frohman regarded his day at Marlow incomplete without a visit to Clark. One day he met Clark dressed up in his best clothes. He asked Clark where he was going.

"I am going to visit my pigs," replied the butcher. Frohman thought this a great joke, and never tired of telling it.

Once when Frohman gave out an interview about his friends in Marlow, he sent the clipping to his friend Clark, who wrote him a letter, which contained, among other things:

> *I can assure you I quite appreciate your kind-*
> *ness in sending the cutting to me. When the*
> *township of Marlow has obtained from His*

Majesty King George the necessary charter to become a county borough, and you offer yourself for the position of Mayor, I will give you my whole-hearted support and influence to secure your election.

Then, too, there was Jones, the Marlow barber, who shaved Frohman for a penny because he was a regular customer.

"Jones is a great man," Frohman used to say. "He never charges me more than a penny for a shave because I am one of his regular customers. Otherwise it would be twopence. I always give his boy a sixpence, however, but Jones doesn't know that."

Indeed, the people of Marlow looked upon Frohman as their very own. He always said that he wanted to be buried in the churchyard by the river. This churchyard had a curious interest for him. He used to wander around in it and struck up quite an acquaintance with the wife of the sexton. She was always depressed because times were so bad and no one was dying. Then an artist died and was buried there, and the old woman cheered up considerably. Frohman used to tell her that the only funeral that he expected to attend was his own.

"And mark you," he said, for he could never resist a jest, "you must take precious good care of my grave."

His wish to lie in Marlow was not attained, but in tribute to the love he had for it the memorial that his friends in England have raised to him—a fountain—stands to-day at the head of High Street in the little town where he loved to roam, the place in which he felt, perhaps, more at home than any other spot on earth. Had he made the choice himself he would have preferred this simple, sincere tribute, in the midst of simple, unaffected people who knew him and loved him, to stained glass in the stateliest of cathedrals.

Charles cared absolutely nothing for honors. He was content to hide behind the mask of his activities. He would never even appear before an audience. Almost unwillingly he was the recipient of the greatest compliment ever paid an American theatrical man in England. It happened in this way:

One season when Frohman had lost an unusual amount of money, Sir John Hare gathered together some of his colleagues.

"Frohman has done big things," Hare said to them. "He loses his money like a gentleman. Let us make him feel that he is not just an American, but one of us."

A dinner was planned in his honor at the Garrick Club. He is the only American theatrical manager to be elected to membership in this exclusive club. When Frohman was apprised of the dinner project he shrank from it.

"I don't like that sort of thing," he said. "Besides, I can't make a speech."

"But you won't have to make a speech," said Sir Arthur Pinero, who headed the committee.

Frohman tried in every possible way to evade this dinner. Finally he accepted on the condition that when the time came for him to respond he was merely to get up, bow his acknowledgment, and say, "Thank you." This he managed to do.

At this dinner, over which Sir John Hare presided, Frohman was presented with a massive silver cigarette-box, on which was engraved the facsimile signatures of every one present. These signatures comprise the "Who's Who" of the British theater. These princes of the drama were proud and glad to call themselves "A few of his friends," as the inscription on the box read.

The signers were, among others, Sir Arthur Pinero, Sir Charles Wyndham, Sir John Hare, Sir Herbert Beerbohm Tree, Sir James M. Barrie, Alfred Sutro, Cyril Maude, H. B. Irving, Lawrence Irving, Louis N. Parker, Anthony Hope, A. E. W. Mason, Seymour Hicks, Robert Marshall, W. Comyns Carr, Weedon Grossmith, Gerald Du Maurier, Eric Lewis, Dion Boucicault, A. E. Matthews, Arthur Bouchier, Cosmo Hamilton, Allan Aynesworth, R. C. Carton, Sam Sothern, and C. Aubrey Smith.

Nothing gave Charles more satisfaction in England perhaps than his encouragement of the British playwright. He inherited Pinero from his brother Daniel, and remained his steadfast friend and producer until his death. Pinero would not think of submitting a play to any other American manager without giving Frohman the first call. In all the years of their relations, during which Charles paid Pinero a large fortune, there was not a sign of contract between them.

Frohman practically made Somerset Maugham in America. His first association with this gifted young Englishman was typical of the man's method of doing business. Maugham had written a play called "Mrs. Dot," in which Marie Tempest was to appear. Frederick Harrison, of the Haymarket Theater, had an option on it, which had just expired. Another manager wanted

the play. Frohman heard of it, and asked to be allowed
to read it. Maugham then said:

"It must be decided to-night."

It was then dinner-time.

"Give me three hours," said Frohman.

At one o'clock in the morning he called up Maugham
at his house and accepted the play, which was probably
the quickest reading and acceptance on record in England.

Another experience with Maugham shows how Frohman really inspired plays.

He was riding on the train with the playwright when
he suddenly said to him:

"I want a new play from you."

"All right," said Maugham.

Frohman thought a moment, and suddenly flashed
out:

"Why not rewrite 'The Taming of the Shrew' with
a new background?"

"All right," said Maugham.

The result was Maugham's play "The Land of
Promise," which was really built around Frohman's idea.

Frohman produced all of Maugham's plays in America,
and most of them were great successes. He also did
the great majority of them in England. Maugham
waxed so prosperous that he was able to buy a charming
old residence in Chesterfield Street which he remodeled
in elaborate fashion. On its completion his first dinner
guest was Charles Frohman. When Maugham sent
him the invitation it read:

> *Will you come and see the house that Froh-*
> *man built?*

In the same way he developed men like Michael Morton. He would see a French farce in the Paris theaters, and, although he could not understand a word of French, he got the spirit and the meaning through its action. He would buy the play, go to London with the manuscript, and get Morton or Paul Potter to adapt it for American consumption.

Life in London to Charles Frohman was one series of adventures. Like Harun-al-Rashid in the *Arabian Nights*, he delighted to wander about, often with Barrie, sometimes with Lestocq, seeking out strange and picturesque places in which to eat.

These adventures began in his earliest days in England. Here is a characteristic experience:

One day Madeline Lucette Ryley, the playwright, came to see him in his office in Henrietta Street. A battered old man was hanging around the door.

"Did you see that man outside?" asked Frohman.

"Yes," said Mrs. Ryley. "Is he the bailiff?"

"Oh no," said Frohman, "he is a Maidenhead cabby." This is the story of how he came there.

The day before Frohman had been down to Maidenhead alone for luncheon. At the station he hailed a cabby who was driving a battered old fly.

"Where to, Governor?" asked the man.

"Number 5 Henrietta Street," said Frohman.

"No such place in Maidenhead," said the driver.

"Oh, I mean the place opposite Covent Garden in London."

The old cabby wasn't a bit flustered, but he said, "I will have to get a new horse."

He changed horses and they made the long way to

London, arriving there considerably after nightfall. When Frohman asked for his bill the old man said, with some hesitation:

"I'm afraid it will cost you five pounds."

"That's all right," said Frohman, and paid the bill.

To his great surprise, the cabby showed up next morning, saying: "I like London. I think I'll stay here." It was with the greatest difficulty that Frohman got rid of him. When the cabby finally started to go he said:

"Well, Governor, if you want to go back to Maidenhead I'll do it for half-price."

A short time after this incident Frohman, whose purse was none too full then, asked some people to dine with him at the Hotel Cecil. By some mistake he and his party were shown into a room that had been arranged for a very elaborate dinner. Before he realized it the waiter began to serve the meal. He soon knew that it was not the menu he had ordered, and was costing twenty times more. But he was game and stuck to it. It was midwinter, and when the fresh peaches came on he said to the woman on his right:

"This will break me, I know, but we might as well have a good time."

Frohman almost invariably took one of his American friends to England with him. It was usually Charles Dillingham, Paul Potter, or William Gillette.

On one of Gillette's many trips with him Frohman got up an elaborate supper for Mark Twain at the Savoy and invited a brilliant group of celebrities, including all three of the Irvings, Beerbohm Tree, Chauncey M. Depew, Sir Charles Wyndham, Haddon Chambers, Nat Goodwin, and Arthur Bouchier. In his inconspicuous way, however, he made it appear that Gillette was giving the supper.

Midnight arrived, and Twain had not shown up. It was before the days of taxis, so Dillingham was sent after him in a hansom. After going to the wrong address, he finally located the humorist in Chelsea. He found Mark Twain sitting in his dressing-gown, smoking a Pittsburg stogie and reading a book.

"Did you forget all about the supper?" asked Dillingham.

"No," was the drawling reply, "but I didn't know where the blamed thing was. I had a notion that some one of you would come for me."

Mark Twain and Frohman were great friends. They were often together in London. Their favorite diversion was to play "hearts."

The great humorist once drew a picture of Charles, and under it wrote:

> *N. B. I cannot make a good mouth. There-*
> *fore leave it out. There is enough without it,*
> *anyway. Done with the best ink.*
>
> *M. T.*

Underneath this inscription he wrote:

To Charles Frohman, Master of Hearts.

Few things in England pleased Frohman more than to play a joke on Gillette, for the author of "Secret Service," like his great friend, relaxed when he was on the other side. When Frohman produced "Sue" in England an amusing incident happened.

Frohman had brought over Annie Russell and Ida Conquest for his piece. The actresses were very much

OTIS SKINNER

excited before the first night, and went without dinner. After the play they were very hungry. On going to the Savoy they encountered the English prohibition against serving women at night when unaccompanied by men. After trying at several places they went to their lodging in Langham Place almost famished.

In desperation they telephoned to Dillingham, who was playing "hearts" at the Savoy with Frohman and Gillette. He hurriedly got some food together in a basket, and with his two friends drove to where the young women were staying. The house was dark; fruitless pulls at the door-bell showed that it was broken. It was impossible to raise any one.

Dillingham knew that the actresses were occupying rooms on the second floor front. He had five large English copper pennies in his pocket, and so he started to throw them up to the window to attract their attention. He threw four, and each fell short.

"This is the last copper," he said to Frohman. "If we can't reach the girls with this they will have to go hungry."

Whereupon Frohman said: "Let Gillette throw it. He can make a penny go further than any man in the world."

Such was Charles Frohman's English life. It was joyous, almost rollicking, and pervaded with the spirit of adventure. Yet behind all the humor was something deep, searching, and significant, because in England, as in America, this man was a vital and constructive force, and where he went, whether in laughter or in seriousness, he left his impress.

XIII

A GALAXY OF STARS

*T*HE last decade of Charles Frohman's life was one of continuous star-making linked with far-flung enterprise. He now had a chain of theaters that reached from Boston by way of Chicago to Seattle; his productions at home kept on apace; his prestige abroad widened.

Frohman had watched the development of Otis Skinner with great interest. That fine and representative American actor had thrived under his own management. Early in the season of 1905 he revived his first starring vehicle, a costume play by Clyde Fitch, called "His Grace de Grammont." It failed, however, and Skinner looked about for another piece. He heard that Frohman, who had a corner on French plays for America, owned the rights to Lavedan's play "The Duel," which had scored a big success in Paris. He knew that the leading rôle ideally fitted his talent and temperament.

Skinner went to Frohman and asked him if he could produce "The Duel" in America.

"Why don't you do it under my management?" asked the manager.

"All right," replied the actor, "I will."

With these few remarks began the connection between Charles Frohman and Otis Skinner.

It was during the closing years of Frohman's life that his genius for singling out gifted young women for eminence found its largest expression. Typical of them was Marie Doro, a Dresden-doll type of girl who made her first stage appearance, as did Billie Burke and Elsie Ferguson, in musical comedy.

Charles Frohman saw her in a play called "The Billionaire" at Daly's Theater in New York, in which she sang and danced. He had an unerring eye for beauty and talent. With her, as with others that he transported from musical pieces to straight drama, he had an uncanny perception. He engaged her and featured her in a slender little play called "Friquette."

Miss Doro made such an impression on her first appearance that Frohman now put her in "Clarice," written by William Gillette, in which he also appeared. Her success swept her nearer to stardom, for she next appeared in a Frohman production which, curiously enough, reflected one of Frohman's sentimental moods.

For many years Mrs. G. H. Gilbert was a famous figure on the American stage. She had been one of the "Big Four" of Augustin Daly's company for many years, and remained with Daly until his death. She was the beloved first old woman of the dramatic profession. When the Daly company disbanded Mrs. Gilbert did not prepare to retire. She was hearty and active.

Frohman realized what a warm place this grand old woman had in the affection of theater-goers after all the years of faithful labor, so he said to himself:

"Here is a wonderful old woman who has never been a star. She must have this great experience before she dies."

He engaged Clyde Fitch to write a play called

"Granny," in which Mrs. Gilbert was starred. It made her very happy, and she literally died in the part.

In the cast of "Granny" Miss Doro's youthful and exquisite beauty shone anew. Her success with the press and the public was little short of phenomenal. Charles now saw Miss Doro as star. He held youth, beauty, and talent to be the great assets, and he seldom made a mistake. It was no vanity that made him feel that if an artist pleased him she would likewise please the public.

Frohman now starred Miss Doro in the stage adaptation of William J. Locke's charming story, "The Morals of Marcus." She became one of his pet protégées. With her, as with the other young women, he delighted to nurse talent. He conducted their rehearsals with a view of developing all their resources, and to show every facet of their temperaments. Failure never daunted him so long as he had confidence in his ward. This was especially the case with Miss Doro, who was unfortunate in a long string of unsuccessful plays. Frohman's faith in her, however, was at last justified, when she played *Dora* in Sardou's great play, "Diplomacy," with brilliant success a year in London and later in New York.

With the exception of Maude Adams and Ann Murdock, no Frohman star had so swift or spectacular a rise as Billie Burke. Her story is one of the real romances of the Frohman star-making.

Billie Burke was the daughter of a humble circus clown in America. From him she probably inherited her mimetic gifts. At the beginning of her career she had obscure parts in American musical pieces.

MARIE DORO

It was in London, however, that she first came under the observation of Charles. She had graduated from the chorus to a part in Edna May's great success, "The School Girl." She had a song called "Put Me in My Little Canoe," which made a great hit. Frohman became so much interested that he thought of sending Miss Burke to America in the piece. He transferred the song to Miss May, which left Miss Burke with scarcely any opportunity. Subsequently she was put in "The Belle of Mayfair," and afterward replaced Miss May when she retired.

Louis N. Parker saw her in this piece and agreed with Frohman that the girl had possibilities as a serious actress. She was cast for her first dramatic part in "The Honorable George," the play he was then producing in London.

When Michael Morton adapted a very beguiling French play called "My Wife," Frohman saw that here was Miss Burke's opportunity for America. He secured her release from the Gattis, who controlled her English appearances, and made her John Drew's leading woman. She met his confidence by adapting herself to the rôle with great brilliancy and effect. Indeed, with Miss Burke, Frohman introduced a distinct and piquant reddish-blond type of beauty to the American stage. It became known as the "Billie Burke type." Realizing this, Frohman was very careful to adapt her personal appearance, humor, and temperament to her plays. He literally had plays written about her peculiar gifts.

Miss Burke's great success in "My Wife" projected her into the Frohman stellar heaven. She was launched as a star in "Love Watches," an adaptation from the French, securely established herself in the favor of theater-goers, and from that time on her appearance in a *chic*, smart play became one of the distinct features of the annual Frohman season. Her most distinguished success was with Pinero's play "Mind the Paint Girl," in which Frohman was greatly interested.

Few of Frohman's "discoveries" justified his confidence with lovelier success than Julia Sanderson. Her first public appearance on the stage had been in vaudeville. When Frohman sought a comedienne with a certain dainty, lady-like quality for the English musical play called "The Dairymaids," which he produced at the Criterion in 1907, his attention was called to this charming girl, then doing musical numbers in a New York vaudeville theater. Frohman went to see her, and was fascinated by her beauty and charm. He noted, most of all, a certain gentle quality in her personality, and with his peculiar genius in adapting plays to people and people to plays, she fairly bloomed under his persuasive and sympathetic sponsorship.

Frohman now obtained "The Arcadians," in which Miss Sanderson was featured. Of all the musical plays that he produced, this was perhaps his favorite. He liked it so much that he told Miss Sanderson one day during rehearsal:

"If the public does not like 'The Arcadians,' then I am finished with light opera."

"The Arcadians," however, proved to be a gratifying success, and Frohman's confidence was vindicated. Frohman was undergoing his long and almost fatal illness at the Knickerbocker Hotel when "The Arcadians" was being rehearsed. He was so fond of the music that whenever possible the rehearsals in which Miss Sanderson sang were conducted in his rooms at the hotel.

JULIA SANDERSON

He always said that he could see the whole performance in her singing. In rehearsing her he always seemed to well-nigh break her heart, but it was his way, as he afterward admitted, of provoking her emotional temperament.

He next gave her a strong part in "The Siren," and subsequently made her a co-star with Donald Brian in "The Sunshine Girl," which brought out to the fullest advantage, so far, her exquisite and alluring qualities.

The last star to twinkle into life under the Frohman wand was Ann Murdock. Here is presented an extraordinary example of the way that Charles literally "made" stars, for seldom, if ever, before has a young actress been so quickly raised from obscurity to eminence. Almost overnight he lifted her into fame.

Miss Murdock, who was born in New York, and had spent her childhood in Port Washington, Long Island, was not a stage-struck girl. She went on the stage because she made up her mind that she wanted more nice frocks than she was having. She rode over to New York one day and went to Henry B. Harris's office to get a position. As she sat waiting among a score of applicants, Harris came out. He was so much taken with her striking Titian beauty and unaffected girlish charm that he immediately asked her to come in ahead of the rest, and gave her a small part in one of "The Lion and the Mouse" road companies. When Harris saw her act he took her out of the cast and put her in a new production that he was making in New York.

At the end of the season she wanted to get under Charles Frohman's management, so she went to the Empire Theater to try her luck. There she met William

Gillette, who was making one of his numerous revivals of "Secret Service." The moment he saw this fresh, appealing young girl he immediately cast her in his mind for the part of the young Southern girl. After he had talked with her, however, he said:

"I think it would be best if I wrote a part for you. I am now working on a play, and I think you had better go in that."

Miss Murdock now appeared in Gillette's new play, "Electricity," in which Marie Doro was starred. Charles Frohman saw her at the opening rehearsal for the first time.

"Electricity" was a failure. Instead of following up her connection with the Frohman office, she went to the cast of "A Pair of Sixes," in which she played for a whole season on Broadway, displaying qualities which brought her conspicuously before the public and to the notice of the man who was to do so much for her.

One night Charles stopped in to see this farce. He had never forgotten the lovely young girl who had played in "Electricity." The next day he sent for Miss Murdock, offered her an engagement, and made another of those simple arrangements, for he said to her:

"You are with me for life."

This was Frohman's way of telling an actor or actress that, without the formality of a contract, they were to look to him each season for employment and that they need not worry about engagements.

From this time on Frohman took an earnest interest in Miss Murdock's career. He saw in her, as he had seen in only a few of his women stars, an immense opportunity to create a new and distinct type.

Just about this time he became very much interested

ANN MURDOCK

in the English adaptation of a French play which he called "The Beautiful Adventure," which was, curiously enough, one of the plays uppermost in his mind on the day he went to his death.

He now did a daring but characteristic Frohman thing. He believed implicitly in Miss Murdock's talents; he felt that the part of the ingenuous young girl in this play was ideally suited to her pleading personality, so, in conjunction with Mrs. Thomas Whiffen and Charles Cherry, he featured her in the cast. Miss Murdock's characterization amply justified Frohman's confidence, but the play failed in New York and on the road. He wrote to Miss Murdock:

> *I am afraid our little play is too gentle for the West. Come back. I have something else for you.*

He now put Miss Murdock into Porter Emerson Browne's play "A Girl of To-day," which had its first presentation in Washington. Frohman, Miss Murdock, and her mother were riding from the station in Washington to the Shoreham Hotel. As they passed the New National Theater, where the young actress was to appear, Miss Murdock suddenly looked out of the cab and saw the following inscription in big type on the bill:

> *Charles Frohman presents Ann Murdock in "A Girl of To-day."*

It was the first intimation that she had been made a star, and she burst into tears. In this episode Frohman had repeated what he had done in the case of Ethel Barrymore ten years before.

Frohman had predicted great things for Miss Murdock, for at the time of his death there was no doubt of the fact that she was destined, in his mind, for a very remarkable career.

But those last years of Frohman's life were not confined exclusively to the pleasant and grateful task of making lovely women stars. The men also had a chance, as the case of Donald Brian shows. Frohman had been much impressed with his success in "The Merry Widow," so he put him under his management and starred him in "The Dollar Princess," which was the first of a series of Brian successes.

Frohman saw that Brian had youth, charm, and pleasing appearance. He was an unusually good singer and an expert dancer. He was equipped to give distinction to the musical play Frohman wanted to present. He had watched the interest of his audiences, and saw that young Brian was a distinct favorite with women as well as men, and his success as star justified all these plans.

While Frohman was making new stars, older ones came under his control in swift succession, among them Madame Nazimova, William Courtnay, James K. Hackett, Kyrle Bellew, Mrs. Fiske, Charles Cherry, John Mason, Martha Hedman, Alexandra Carlisle, William Courtleigh, Nat Goodwin, Blanche Bates, Hattie Williams, Gertrude Elliott, Constance Collier, Richard Carle, and Cyril Maude.

Frohman now reached the very apex of his career. At one time he had twenty-eight stars under his management; and in addition fully as many more companies bore his name throughout the country. To be a Frohman star was the acme of stage ambition, for it not only meant professional distinction, but equitable and honorable treatment.

The year 1915 dawned with fateful significance for Charles Frohman. With its advent began a chain of happenings that, in the light of later events, seemed almost prophetic of the fatal hour which was now closing in.

Perhaps the most picturesque and significant of these events was the reconciliation with his old friend David Belasco. Twelve years before, through an apparently trivial thing, a breach had developed between these two men whose fortunes had been so intimately entwined. They had launched their careers in New York together; the old Madison Square Theater had housed their first theatrical ambition; they had kept pace on the road to fame; their joint productions had been features of the New York stage. Yet for twelve years they had not spoken.

Frohman became ill, and lay stricken at the Knicker-bocker Hotel. That he had thought much of his old comrade, so long estranged, was evident. A remarkable coincidence resulted. It was like an act in any one of the many plays they had produced.

One afternoon Belasco, who had heard of the serious plight of Frohman, sat in his studio on the top floor of the Belasco Theater. There, amid his Old World curios, he pondered over the past.

"'C. F.' is lying ill at the Knickerbocker," he said to himself. "He may die. I must see him. This quarrel of ours is a great mistake."

He started to write a note to his old friend, when the telephone-bell rang. It was his business manager, Benjamin Roeder, who said:

"I have just had a telephone message from Charles Frohman. He wants to see you."

When Belasco told Roeder that he was just in the act of writing to Frohman to tell him that he wanted to see him, both men were amazed at the coincidence.

That night, when the few friends who gathered each evening at Frohman's bedside had gone, Belasco entered the sick-room at the Knickerbocker. Frohman was so weak that he could hardly raise his hand. Belasco went to him, took his right hand in both of his, and the old comrades put together again the thread of their friendship just where it had been broken twelve years before.

They talked over the old days. Frohman, whose mind was always on the theater, suddenly said:

"Let's do a play together, David."

"All right," said Belasco.

"You name the play. I will get the cast, and we will rehearse it together," added Frohman.

Out of this reconciliation came the magnificent revival of "A Celebrated Case," by D'Ennery and Cormon. The cast included Nat Goodwin, Otis Skinner, Ann Murdock, Helen Ware, Florence Reed, and Robert Warwick. On Frohman's recovery he undertook the rehearsals. Belasco came in at the end, but he had little to do.

Frohman and Belasco not only resumed their joint production of plays, but they resumed part of their old life together. Now began again their favorite diet of pumpkin and meringue pie and tea after the day's work was done. Night after night they met after the theater, just as they had done in the old Madison Square days when they went to O'Neil's, on Sixth Avenue, for their frugal repast, dreaming and planning their futures.

CHARLES FROHMAN and DAVID BELASCO

A photograph taken in Boston April 3, 1915, just after the two had renewed their partnership, ending a separation of twenty years.

Now each man had become a great personage. Frohman was the amusement dictator of two worlds; Belasco, the acknowledged stage wizard of his time.

After a week in Boston the all-star cast in "A Celebrated Case" opened at the Empire Theater in New York. History repeated itself Frohman and Belasco sat in the same place in the wings where they sat twenty-two years before at the launching of "The Girl I Left Behind Me," which dedicated the Empire. Now, as then, there were tumultuous calls for the producers. Again David tried to induce Charles to go out, but he said:

"No, you go, David, and speak for me. Stand where you did twenty-two years ago."

In 1915, as in 1893, Belasco went out and spoke Frohman's thanks and his own.

The revival of "A Celebrated Case" not only brought Frohman and Belasco together, but led to an agreement between them to do a production together every year.

There was a tragic hint of the fate which was shaping Charles Frohman's end in his last production on any stage. It was a war play called "The Hyphen," by Justus Miles Forman, the novelist. The scenes were laid in Pennsylvania, and the story dealt with the various attempts to unsettle the loyalty of German-Americans through secret agencies. The whole problem of the hyphenated citizen, which had complicated the American position in the great war, was set forth.

Even in his unconscious stage farewell, Charles was the pioneer, because the acceptance of "The Hyphen" and the prompt organization of the company established a new record in play-producing. Up to a certain

Saturday morning Charles Frohman had never heard of the play. That afternoon the manuscript was put into his hands and he read it. A messenger was sent off post-haste to find the author. In the mean time, Frohman engaged W. H. Thompson, Gail Kane, and a notable group of players for the cast, and gave orders for the construction of the scenery. Late that afternoon Mr. Forman called on Charles, whom he had never met. Without any further ado the manager said to the playwright-author:

"I am going to produce your play. We have nothing to discuss. A manager often discusses at great length the play that he does not intend to produce. Therefore all that I have to tell you is that your play is accepted. I have already engaged the chief actors needed, and the scenery was ordered two hours ago. I am glad to produce a play on this timely subject, but I am especially glad that it is an American who wrote it."

Charles was greatly interested in "The Hyphen." It was American to the core; it flouted treachery to the country of adoption; it appealed to his big sense of patriotism. He felt, with all the large enthusiasm of his nature, that he was doing a distinct national service in producing the piece. He personally supervised every rehearsal. He talked glowingly to his friends about it. At fifty-five he displayed the same bubbling optimism with regard to it that he had shown about his first independent venture.

Now began the last of the chain of dramatic events which ended in death. As soon as "The Hyphen" was announced, Frohman began to get threatening letters warning him that it would be a mistake to produce so sensational a play in the midst of such an acute international situation. Pro-Germans of incendiary tendency especially resented it. To all these intimations Frohman merely shrugged his shoulders and smiled. It made him all the more determined.

"The Hyphen" was produced April 19th at the Knickerbocker Theater before a hostile audience. Unpatriotic pro-Germans had packed the theater. During the progress of the play the dynamite explosions in the Broadway subway construction outside were misinterpreted for bombs, and there was suppressed excitement throughout the whole performance.

The play was a failure. Yet Frohman's confidence in it was unimpaired. He went to see it nearly every night of its short life in New York. He even sent it to Boston for a second verdict, but Boston agreed with New York. Like every production that bore the Charles Frohman stamp, he gave it every chance. Reluctantly he ordered up the notice to close.

Frohman became greatly attached to Forman. With his usual generosity he invited the author to accompany him on his approaching trip to England.

"I want you to come with me and meet Barrie and know some of my other English friends," Charles said, little dreaming that the invitation to a holiday was the beckoning hand of death to both.

XIV

STAR-MAKING AND AUDIENCES

*D*URING all these busy years Frohman had reigned supreme as king of star-makers. Under his persuasive sponsorship more men and women rose to stellar eminence than with all his fellow-managers combined. It was the very instinct of his life to develop talent, and it gave him an extraordinary satisfaction to see the artist emerge from the background into fame.

His attitude in the matter of star-making was never better expressed than in one of his many playful moods with the pencil. Like Caruso, he was a caricaturist. Few things gave him more delight than to make a hasty sketch of one of his friends on any scrap of paper that lay near at hand. He usually made these sketches just as he wrote most of his personal letters, with a heavy blue pencil.

On one occasion he was talking with Pauline Chase about making stars. A smile suddenly burst over his face; he seized pencil and paper and made a sketch of himself walking along at night and pointing to the moon with his stick. Under the picture he wrote, as if addressing the moon:

Watch out, or I'll make a star out of you.

Once he said to Billie Burke, in discussing this familiar star subject:

MARIE TEMPEST

MME. NAZIMOVA

"A star has a unique value in a play. It concentrates interest. In some respects a play is like a dinner. To be a success, no matter how splendidly served, the menu should always have one unique and striking dish that, despite its elaborate gastronomic surroundings, must long be remembered. This is one reason why you need a star in a play."

Despite the fact, as the case of Ann Murdock shows, that Charles could literally lift a girl from the ranks almost overnight, he generally regarded the approach to stardom as a difficult and hard-won path. Just before the great European war, he made this comment to a well-known English journalist, who asked him how he made stars:

"Each of my stars has earned his or her position through honest advancement. If the President of the United States wants to reward a soldier he says to him, 'I will make you a general.' By the same process I say to an actor, 'I will make you a star.'

"All the stars under my management owe their eminence to their own ability and industry, and also to the fact that the American is an individual-loving public. In America we regard the workman first and the work second. Our imaginations are fired not nearly so much by great deeds as by great doers. There are stars in every walk of American life. It has always been so with democracies. Cæsar, Cicero, and the rest were public stars when Rome was at her best, just as in our day Roosevelt and others shine.

"Far from fostering it, the star system as such has simply meant for me that when one of my stars finishes with a play, that play goes permanently on the shelf, no one every hoping to muster together an audience for it without the original actor or actress in the star part.

"Vital acting in plays of consequence is the foundation of theatrical success. You have only to enumerate the plays to realize the drain even one management can make upon what is, after all, a limited supply of capable leading actors. This is because the American stage is short of leaders. There is a world of actors, but too few leading actors."

"What do you mean by leading actor?" he was asked.

"I mean that if in casting a play you can find an actor who looks the part you have in mind for him, be thankful; if you can find an actor who can act the part, be very thankful; and if you can find an actor who can look and act the part, *get down on your knees and thank God!*"

Frohman had a very definite idea about star material. He was once talking with a well-known American publisher who mentioned that a certain very rich woman had announced her determination to go on the stage. The manager made one of his quick and impatient gestures, and said:

"She will never do."

"Why?" asked his friend.

"Because," replied Frohman, "in all my experience with the making of stars I have seldom known of a very rich girl who made a finished success on the stage. The reason is that the daughters of the rich are taught to repress their emotions. In other words, they don't seem to be able to let go their feelings. Give me the common clay, the kind that has suffered and even hungered. It makes the best star material."

There is no doubt that Frohman liked to "make"

careers. He wanted to see people develop under his direction. To indulge in this diversion was often a very costly thing, as this incident shows:

Chauncey Olcott, who had been associated with him in his minstrel days, and become one of the most profitable stars in the country, once sent a message to Frohman saying that he would like to come under his management. To the intermediary Olcott said:

"Tell Mr. Frohman that I make one hundred thousand dollars a year. He can name his own percentage of this income."

Frohman sent back this message:

"I greatly appreciate the offer, but I don't care to manage Olcott. He is *made*. I like to *make* stars."

One reason that lay behind Frohman's success as star-maker was the fact that he wove a great deal of himself into the character of the stars. In other words, the personal element counted a great deal. When somebody once remonstrated with him about giving up so much of his valuable time to what seemed to be inconsequential talks with his women stars, he said:

"It is not a waste of time. I have often helped those young women to take a brighter view of things, and it makes me feel that I am not just their manager, but their friend."

Indeed, as Barrie so well put it, he regarded his women stars as his children. If they were playing in New York they were expected to call on him and talk personalities three or four times a week. On the road they sent him daily telegrams; these were placed on his desk every morning, and were dealt with in person before any other business of the day. He had the names of his stars printed in large type on his business envelopes.

CHARLES FROHMAN

These were so placed on his table that as he sat and wrote or talked he could see their names ranked before him.

When his women stars played in New York he always tried to visit them at night at the theater before the curtain went up. He always said of this that it was like seeing his birds tucked safely in their nests. Then he would go back to his office or his rooms and read manuscripts until late.

One phase of Charles's great success in life was revealed in this attitude toward his women stars. He succeeded because he mixed sentiment with business. He was not all sentiment and he was not all business, but he was an extraordinarily happy blend of each of these qualities, and they endeared him to the people who worked for him.

The attitude of the great star toward Frohman is best explained perhaps by Sir Henry Irving. Once, when the time came for his usual American tour, he said to his long-time manager, Bram Stoker, who was about to start for New York:

"When you get to America just tell Frohman—you need not bother to write him—that I want to come under his management. He always understands. He is always so fair."

One detail will illustrate Frohman's feeling about stars, and it is this: He never wanted them, male or female, to make themselves conspicuous or to do commonplace things. He was sensitive about what they said or did. For example, he did not like to see John Drew walk up and down Broadway. He spent a fortune sheltering Maude Adams from all kinds of intrusion. With her especially he exhausted every resource to keep her aloof and secluded. He preferred that she be known through her work and not through her personal self. It was so with himself.

Frohman was one of the most generous-minded of men in his feeling about his co-workers. On one occasion when he was rehearsing "The Dictator," William Collier suggested a whole new scene. The next night Frohman took a friend to see it. Afterward, accompanied by his guest, he went back on the stage to congratulate his star. He slapped Collier on the back and, turning to his companion, said:

"Wasn't that a bully scene that Willie put into the play?"

He was always willing to admit that his success came from those who worked for him. Once he was asked the question:

"If you had your life to live over again would you be a theatrical manager?"

Quick as a flash Frohman replied:

"If I could be surrounded by the same actors and writers who have made *me*—yes. Otherwise, no."

This feeling led him to say once:

"I believe a manager's success does not come so much from the public as from his players. When they are ready to march with him without regard to results, then he has indeed succeeded. This is my success. My ambition frankly centers in the welfare of the actor. The day's work holds out to me no finer gratification than to see intelligent, earnest, deserving actors go into the fame and fortune of being stars."

Nothing could down his immense pride in his stars. Once he was making his annual visit to England with Dillingham. At that time Olga Nethersole, who had been playing "Carmen," was under his management. She was also on the boat. The passenger-list included many other celebrities, among them Madame Emma Calvé, the-opera-singer, who had just made her great success in the opera "Carmen" at the Metropolitan Opera House. Naturally there was some rivalry between the two *Carmens*.

At the usual ship's concert both Nethersole and Calvé inscribed their names on programs which were auctioned off for the benefit of the disabled sailors' fund. Competition was brisk. The card that Calvé signed fetched nine hundred dollars. When Nethersole's program was put up Frohman led the bidding and drove it up to a thousand dollars, which he paid himself. It was all the money he had with him. Dillingham remonstrated for what seemed a foolish extravagance.

"I wanted my star to get the best of it, and she did," was the reply.

Frohman, as is well known, would never make a contract with his stars. When some one urged him to make written agreements, he said:

"No, I won't do it. I want them to be in a position so that if they ever become dissatisfied they know they are free to leave me."

Like all his other stars, William Collier had no contract with Charles, merely a verbal understanding extending over a period of years. After this agreement expired and another year and a half had gone by, Collier one day asked Frohman if he realized that their original agreement had run out. Frohman looked up with a start and said:

"Is that so? Well, it's all right, Willie, you know."

"Of course," said Collier, and that ended it.

The next Saturday when Collier got his pay-envelope he found inside a very charming letter from Frohman, which said:

> *I'm sorry that I overlooked the expiration of our agreement. I hope that you will find a little increase in your salary satisfactory.*

There was an advance of one hundred dollars a week.

Frohman literally loved the word "star," and he delighted in the so-called "all-star casts." He had great respect for the big names of the profession; for those who had achieved success. He liked to do business with them.

In speaking about "all-star casts," he once said to his brother:

"I have to look after so many enterprises that I have no time to conduct a theatrical kindergarten in developing actors or playwrights save where the play of the unknown author or the exceptional talents of the unknown actor or actress appeal to me strongly. There is an element of safety in considering work by experts, because the theaters I represent need quick results."

In reply to the oft-repeated question as to why he took his American stars to London when they could play to larger audiences and make more money at home, he said:

"In the first place, such exchanges constitute the finest medium for the development of actress or actor and the liberalizing of the public. Face to face with an English audience the American actress finds herself confronted by new tastes, new appreciations, new demands. She must meet them all or fail. What does this result in? Versatility, flexibility, and, in the end, a firmer and more comprehensive hold upon her art."

CHARLES FROHMAN

When Frohman was asked to define success in theatrical management he made this answer:

"The terms of success in the theater seem to me to be the co-operating abilities of playwright and actor with the principal burden on the actor. In other words, the play is not altogether 'the thing.' The right player in the right play is the thing."

The shaping of William Gillette's career is a good example of Frohman's definition of a successful theatrical manager, whose best skill and talents are employed largely in the matter of manipulating a hard-minded person to mutual advantage.

The relationship between stars and audiences is of necessity a very close one. The Frohman philosophy, however, was not the generally accepted theory that audiences make stars.

On one of those very rare occasions in his life when he wrote for publication, he made the following illuminating statement:

> *No star or manager should feel grateful to any audience for the success of a play in which he has figured. A play succeeds because it is a living, vital thing—and that is why it has got upon the stage at all. There is life in it and it does not, and will not, die. It keeps itself alive until the opportunity comes along. Often a kind of instinct makes the opportunity.*
>
> *It is instinct also that prompts an audience to applaud when it is pleased, laugh when it is amused, weep when it is moved, hiss when it is dissatisfied. No actor should feel indebted to an audience for the recognition of good work, be-*

cause that same audience that appears to be so friendly, at another time, when one character or play does not please it, will resent both actor and play. This is as it should be. The loyalty of English audiences to their old favorites is fine, but it is bad for the old favorites. It is stagnating.

The various expressions of approval and disapproval that come from the spectators at a play are involuntary on the part of the spectators. They are hypnotized by the play and the acting. Who ever, on coming out of the theater after seeing a play that has pleased him, has felt a sense of happiness that his pleasure had also pleased the actor, or the author of the play, or the management of the production? Loyalty, generosity, and encouragement, as applied to audiences, are so many empty words. Play-goers who apply them to themselves cheat themselves. Miss Maude Adams is the only stage personage within my experience who has a distinct public following, loyal and encouraging to her in whatever she does.

Audiences interested Frohman immensely. He liked to be a part of them. He had a perfectly definite reason for sitting in the last row of the gallery on the first nights of his productions, which he once explained as follows:

"The best index to the probable career of any play is the back of the head of an auditor who does not know that he is being watched. The play-goer in an orchestra stall is always half-conscious that what he says or does may be observed. But the gallery gods and goddesses have never thought of anything except what is happening on the stage. They may yield the time before the rise of the curtain to watching the audience entering the theater, but once the lights are up and the stage is revealed they have no eyes or thoughts for anything except the life unfolded by the actors. These people in the upper part of the theater represent the masses. They are worth watching, for they are the people who make stage successes."

Frohman had his own theories about audiences, too. Concerning them he declared:

"An American at the theater feels first and thinks afterward. A European at a play thinks first and feels afterward. In conversation a German discusses things sitting down; a Frenchman talks standing up. But the American discusses things walking about. Therefore each must have his play built accordingly."

Once Frohman made this discriminating difference between English and American audiences:

"In England the pit and the gallery of the audience come to the theater, turn in their hard-earned shillings, and demand much. Failing to get what they expect, the theater is filled with boos and cat-calls at the end of the play. This does not mean that the play has failed. It more nearly means that the less a man pays to get into a theater the more he demands of the play.

"An American audience is different, because it has a fine sense of humor. When an American pays his money through the box-office window he feels that it is gone forever. Anything he receives after that—the lights, the pictures on the walls, the music of the orchestra, the sight of a few or many smiling faces—is so much to the good. So keen is the American play-goer's sense of humor that often when a play is wretchedly bad it comes to the rescue, and the applause is terrifically loud. This does not mean that the play has succeeded. It means rather that the play will die, a victim of the deadliest of all possible criticisms—ridicule."

Nor was Frohman often deceived about a first-night verdict. He always said, "Wait for the box-office statement on the second night."

One of his characteristic epigrammatic statements about the failure of plays was this:

"In America the question with a failure is, 'How soon can we get it off the stage?' In London they say, 'How long will the play run even though it is a failure?'"

Indeed, Frohman's whole attitude about openings was characteristic of his deep and generous philosophy about life. He summed up his whole creed as follows:

"A producer of plays, assuming that he is a man of experience, never feels comfortable after a great reception has been given his play on a first night. He knows that the reception in the theater does not always correspond to the feelings of future audiences. Every thinking manager knows that his play, in order to succeed, must send its audience away possessed of some distinct feeling. A successful play is a play that *reflects*, whatever the feeling it reflects.

"The great successes of the stage are plays that are played outside of the theater: over the breakfast-table; in a man's office; to his business associates; in a club, as one member tells the thrilling story of the previous night's experience to another. Great successes upon the stage are plays of such a sort that one audience can play them over to another prospective audience, and so make an endless chain of attendance at the theater.

"I have never in all my experience felt a success on the opening night. I have only felt my failures.

"I invariably leave the theater after a first-night performance knowing full well that neither my friends nor I know anything at all as to the ultimate fortune of the play we have seen."

It is a matter of record that Frohman always viewed his first nights with great nervousness. Although he attached but little importance, save on very rare occasions, to tumultuous applause on first nights, he was sometimes deceived by the reception that was given his productions.

He never tired of telling of one experience. He had left the theater on the first night, as he expressed it, "with the other mourners." He returned to his office immediately to cast a new play for the company. Yet he lived to see this play run successfully for a whole season. This led him to say:

"There's nothing more deluding to the player and the manager than enthusiastic applause. The fine, inspired work of a star actor often makes an audience enthusiastic to such a boisterous extent that one forgets that it is an individual and not the play that has succeeded."

Here, as elsewhere in the Frohman outlook on life and work, one finds clear-headed logic and reason behind the bubbling optimism.

XV

PLAYS AND PLAYERS

ONE day not long before he sailed on the voyage that was to take him to his death, Charles was talking with a celebrated English playwright in his office at the Empire Theater. The conversation suddenly turned to a discussion of life achievement.

"What do you consider the biggest thing that you have done?" asked the visitor.

Frohman rose and pointed with his stick at the rows of book-shelves about him that held the bound copies of the plays he had produced. Then he said with a smile:

"That is what I have done. Don't you think it is a pretty good life's work?"

He was not overstepping the mark when he pointed with pride at that army of plays. This list is the greatest monument, perhaps, to his boundless ambition and energy, for it contains the four hundred original productions he made in America, besides the one hundred and twenty-five plays he put on in London. That Charles should have produced so many plays is not surprising. He adored the theater; it was his very being. To him, in truth, all the world was a stage.

Everything that he saw as he walked the streets or rode in a cab or viewed from a railway train he re-visualized and considered in the terms of the playhouse. If he saw an impressive bit of scenery he would say, "Wouldn't that make a fine background?" If he heard certain murmurs in the country or the tumult of a crowd on the highway, he instinctively said, "How fine it would be to reproduce that sound."

He only read books with a view of their adaptability to plays. Where other men found diversion and recreation in golfing, motoring, or walking, Charles sought entertainment in reading manuscripts. He was never without a play; when he traveled he carried dozens.

In the matter of plays Frohman had what was little less than a contempt for the avowedly academic. He refused to be drawn into discussions of the so-called "high brow" drama. When some one asked him to name the greatest of English dramatists he replied, quick as a flash:

"The one who writes the last great play."

"Whom do you consider the greatest American dramatist?" was the question once put to him. His smiling answer was:

"The one whose play the greatest number of good Americans go to see."

On this same occasion he was asked, "What seat in the theater do you consider the best to view a drama or a musical comedy from?"

"The paid one," he retorted.

Back in Charles's mind was a definite and well-ordered policy about plays. His first production on any stage was a melodrama, and, though in later years he ran the whole range from grave to gay, he was always true to his first love. This is one reason why Sardou's "Diplomacy" was, in many respects, his ideal of a play. It has thrills, suspense, love interests, and emotion. He revived it again and again, and it never failed to give him a certain pleasure.

Once in London Frohman unbosomed himself about play requirements, and this is what he said:

"I start out by asking certain requirements of every piece. If it be a drama, it must have healthfulness and comedy as well as seriousness. We are a young people, but only in the sense of healthy-mindedness. There is no real taste among us for the erotic or the decadent. It is foreign to us because, as a people, we have not felt the corroding touch of decadence. Nor is life here all drab. Hence I expect lights as well as shadows in every play I accept.

"Naturally, I am also influenced by the fitness of the chief parts for my chief stars, but I often purchase the manuscript at once on learning its central idea. I commissioned Clyde Fitch and Cosmo Gordon-Lennox to go to work on "Her Sister" after half an hour's account of the main idea. Ethel Barrymore's work in that play is the best instance that I can give of the artistic growth of that actress. The particular skill she had obtained—and this is the test of an actress worth remembering—is the art of acting scenes essentially melodramatic in an unmelodramatic manner. After all, what is melodrama? Life itself is melodrama, and life put upon the stage only seems untrue when it is acted melodramatically—that is, unnaturally."

The foremost quality that Frohman sought in his plays was human interest. His appraisal of a dramatic product was often influenced by his love for a single character or for certain sentimental or emotional speeches. He would almost invariably discuss these plays with his intimates Often he would act out the whole piece in a vivid and graphic manner and enlarge upon the situations that appealed to his special interest.

Plays thus described by him were found to be extremely entertaining and diverting to his friends, but when presented on the stage to a dispassionate audience they did not always fare so well. A notable example was "The Hyphen." The big, patriotic speech of the old German-American in the third act made an immense impression on Frohman when he read the play. It led him to produce the piece in record time. He recited it to every caller; he almost lost sight of the rest of the play in his admiration for the central effort. But the audience and the critics only saw this speech as part of a long play.

What Charles lacked in his study of plays in manuscript was the analytical quality. He could feel that certain scenes and speeches would have an emotional appeal, but he could not probe down beneath the surface for the why and the wherefore. For analysis, as for details, he had scant time. He accepted plays mainly for their general effect.

He was very susceptible to any charm that a play held out. If he found the characters sympathetic, attractive, and lovable, that would outweigh any objections made on technical grounds. When once he determined to produce a play, only a miracle could prevent him. The more his associates argued to the contrary, the more dogged he became. He had superb confidence in his judgment; yet he invariably accepted failure with serenity and good spirit. He always assumed the responsibility. He listened sometimes to suggestions, but his views were seldom colored by them.

His association with men like J. M. Barrie, Haddon Chambers, Paul Potter, William Gillette, Arthur Wing Pinero, and Augustus Thomas gave him a loftier insight into the workings of the drama. He was quick to absorb ideas, and he had a strong and retentive memory for details.

Frohman loved to present farce. He enjoyed this type of play himself because it appealed to his immense sense of humor. He delighted in rehearsing the many complications and entanglements which arise in such plays. The enthusiasm with which French audiences greeted their native plays often misled him. He felt that American theater-goers would be equally uproarious. But often they failed him.

The same thing frequently happened with English plays. He would be swept off his feet by a British production; he was at once sure that it would be a success in New York. But New York, more than once, upset this belief. The reason was that Frohman saw these plays as an Englishman. He had the cosmopolitan point of view that the average play-goer in America lacked.

This leads to the interesting subject of "locality" in plays. Frohman once summed up this whole question:

"As I go back and forth, crossing and recrossing the Atlantic, the audiences on both sides seem more and more like one. Always, of course, each has his own particular viewpoint, according to the side of the Atlantic I happen to be on. But often they think the same, each from its own angle.

"You bring your English play to America. Nobody is at all disturbed by the mention of Park Lane or Piccadilly Circus. If there is drama in the play, if in itself it interests and holds the audience, nobody pays any attention to its locality or localisms.

"But an English audience sitting before an American play hears mention of West Twenty-third Street or Washington Square, and while it is wondering just where and what these localities are an important incident in the dramatic action slips by unnoticed. Not that English audiences are at all prejudiced against American plays. They take them in the same general way that Americans take English plays. Each public asks, 'What have you got?' As soon as it hears that the play is good it is interested.

"English audiences, for example, were quick to discover the fun in 'The Dictator' when Mr. Collier acted it in London, though it was full of the local color of New York, both in the central character and in the subject. Somehow the type and the speeches seemed to have a sort of universal humor. I tried it first on Barrie. He marked in the manuscript the places that he could understand. The piece never went better in America.

"On the other hand, one reason why 'Brewster's Millions' did not go well in London was because the severely logical British mind took it all as a business proposition. The problem was sedately figured out on the theory that the young man did not spend the inherited millions.

"If the locality of an American play happens to be a mining village, it is better to change its scenes to a similar village in Australia when you take the play to London. Then the audience is sure to understand. The public of London gave 'The Lion and the Mouse' an enthusiastic first night, but it turned out that they had not comprehended the play. It was unthinkable to them that a judge should be disgraced and disbarred by a political 'ring.'"

The ideal play for Charles Frohman was always the one that he had in mind for a particular star. His special desire, however, was for strong and emotional love as the dominant force in the drama. He felt that all humanity was interested in love, and he believed it established a congenial point of contact between the stage and the audience.

Although he did not especially aspire to Shakespearian production, he used the great bard's works as models for appraising other plays. "Shakespeare invented farce comedy," he once said, "and whenever I consider the purchase of such a thing I compare its scenes with the most famous of all farces, 'The Taming of the Shrew.' It goes without saying that when it comes to the stage of the production, my aim is to imbue the performance with a spirit akin to that contained in Shakespeare's humorous masterpiece."

Frohman often "went wrong" on plays. He merely accepted these mistakes as part of the big human hazard and went on to something new. His amazing series of errors of judgment with plays by Augustus Thomas is one of the traditions of the American theater. The reader already knows how he refused "Arizona" and "The Earl of Pawtucket," and how they made fortunes for other managers.

One of the most extraordinary of these Thomas mistakes was with "The Witching Hour." It was about the only time that he permitted his own decision to be swayed by outside influence, and it cost him dearly.

The author read the play to Frohman on a torrid

night in midsummer. Frohman, as usual, sat cross-legged on a divan and sipped orangeade incessantly.

Thomas, who has all the art and eloquence of a finished actor, read his work with magnetic effect. When he finished Frohman sat absolutely still for nearly five minutes. It seemed hours to the playwright, who awaited the decision with tense interest. Finally Frohman said in a whisper:

"That is almost too beautiful to bear."

A pause followed. Then he said, eagerly:

"When shall we do it; whom do you want for star?"

"I'd like to have Gillette," replied Thomas.

"You can't have him," responded Frohman. "He's engaged for something else."

With this the session ended. Frohman seemed strangely under the spell of the play. It made him silent and meditative.

The next day he gave the manuscript to some of his close associates to read. They thought it was too psychological for a concrete dramatic success. To their great surprise he agreed with them.

"The Witching Hour" was produced by another manager and it ran a whole season in New York, and then duplicated its success on the road. This experience made Frohman all the more determined to keep his own counsel and follow his instincts with regard to plays thereafter, and he did.

Charles regarded play-producing just as he regarded life—as a huge adventure. An amusing thing happened during the production of "The Other Girl," a play by Augustus Thomas, in which a pugilist has a prominent rôle.

Lionel Barrymore was playing the part of the prize-fighter, who was generally supposed to be a stage replica of "Kid" McCoy, then in the very height of his fistic powers. In the piece the fighter warns his friends not to bet on a certain fight. The lines, in substance, were:

"You have been pretty loyal to me, but I am giving you a tip not to put any money down on that 'go' in October."

One day Frohman found Barrymore pacing nervously up and down in front of his office.

"What's the matter, Lionel?" he asked.

"Well," was the reply, "I am very much disturbed about something. I made a promise to 'Kid' McCoy, and I don't know how to keep it. You know I have a line in the play in which the prize-fighter warns his friends not to bet on him in a certain fight in October. The 'Kid,' who has been at the play nearly every night since we opened, now has a real fight on for October, and he is afraid it will give people the idea that it is a 'frame-up.'"

"You mean to say that you want me to change Mr. Thomas's lines?" asked Frohman, seriously.

"I can't ask you to do that," answered Barrymore. "But I promised the 'Kid' to speak to you about it, and I have kept my word."

Frohman thought a moment. Then he said, gravely:

"All right, Lionel, I'll postpone the date of the fight in the play until November, even December, but not a day later."

Frohman was not without his sense of imitation. He was quick to follow up a certain type or mood whether it was in the vogue of an actor or the character of a play. This story will illustrate:

One night early in February, 1895, Frohman sat in

his wonted corner at Delmonico's, then on Broadway and Twenty-sixth Street. He had "The Fatal Card," by Chambers and Stephenson, on the boards at Palmer's Theater; he also had A. M. Palmer's Stock Company on the road in Sydney Grundy's play "The New Woman." This naturally gave him a lively interest in Mr. Palmer's productions.

Paul Potter, who was then house dramatist at Palmer's, bustled into the restaurant with the plot of a new novel which had been brought to his attention by the news-stand boy at the Waldorf. Frohman listened to his recital with interest.

"What is the name of the book?" he asked.

"Trilby," replied Potter.

"Well," he continued, "it ought to be called after that conjurer chap, Bengali, or whatever his name is. However, go ahead. Get Lackaye back from 'The District Attorney' company to which Palmer has lent him. Engage young Ditrichstein by all means for one of your Bohemians. Call in Virginia Harned and the rest of the stock company. And there you are."

With uncanny precision he had cast the leading rôles perfectly and on the impulse of the moment.

During the fortnight of the incubation of the play Potter saw Frohman nightly, for they were now fast friends. Frohman was curiously fascinated by "Bengali," as he insisted upon calling Svengali.

"We do it next Monday in Boston," said Potter, "and I count on your coming to see it."

Frohman went to Boston to see the second performance. After the play he and Potter walked silently across the Common to the Thorndyke Hotel. In his room Frohman broke into speech:

"They are roasting it awfully in New York," he began. "Yet Joe Jefferson says it will go around the world." Then he added, "They say you have cut out all the Bohemian stuff."

"Nevertheless," replied Potter, "W. A. Brady has gone to New York to-night to offer Mr. Palmer ten thousand dollars on account for the road rights."

"Well," said Frohman, showing his hand at last, "Jefferson and Brady are right, and if Palmer will let me in I'll go half and half, or, if he prefers, I'll take it all."

At supper after the first performance at the Garden Theater in New York, Frohman advised Sir Herbert Tree to capture the play for London. Henceforth, wherever he traveled, "Trilby" seemed to pursue him.

"I've seen your old 'Bengali,'" he wrote Potter, "in Rome, Vienna, Berlin, everywhere. It haunts me. And, as you cut out the good Bohemian stuff, I'll use it myself at the Empire."

He did so in Clyde Fitch's version of "La Vie de Bohème," which was called "Bohemia."

"How did it go?" Potter wrote him from Switzerland.

"Pretty well," replied Frohman. "Unfortunately we left out 'Bengali.'"

On more than one occasion Frohman produced a play for the mere pleasure of doing it. He put on a certain little dramatic fantasy. It was foredoomed to failure and held the boards only a week.

"Why did you do this play?" asked William H. Crane.

"Because I wanted to see it played," answered Frohman. "I knew it would not be successful, but I simply had to do it. I saw every performance and I liked it better every time I saw it.

Often Frohman would make a contract with a playwright for a play, and long before the first night he would realize that it had no chance. Yet he kept his word with the author, and it was always produced.

The case of "The Heart of a Thief," by the late Paul Armstrong, is typical. Frohman paid him an advance of fifteen hundred dollars. After a week of rehearsals every one connected with the play except Armstrong realized that it was impossible.

Frohman, however, gave it an out-of-town opening and brought it to the Hudson Theater in New York, where it ran for one week. When he decided to close it he called the company together and said:

"You've done the best you could. It's all my fault. I thought it was a good play. I was mistaken."

Frohman took vast pride in the "clean quality" of his plays, as he often phrased it. His whole theatrical career was a rebuke to the salacious. He originally owned Edward Sheldon's dramatization of Suderman's "The Song of Songs." On its production in Philadelphia it was assailed by the press as immoral. Frohman immediately sold it to A. H. Woods, who presented it with enormous financial success in New York.

He was scrupulous to the last degree in his business relations with playwrights. Once a well-known English author, who was in great financial need, cabled to his agent in America that he would sell outright for two thousand dollars all the dramatic rights to a certain play of his that Frohman and an associate had on the road at that time. The associate thought it was a fine opportunity and personally cabled the money through the agent. Then he went to Frohman and said, with great satisfaction:

"I've made some money for us to-day."

"How's that?" asked Frohman.

Then his associate told the story of the author's predicament and what he had done. He stood waiting for commendation. Instead, Frohman's face darkened; he rang a bell, and when his secretary appeared he said:

"Please wire Blank [mentioning the playwright's name] that the money cabled him to-day was an advance on future royalties."

Then he turned to his associate and said:

"Never, so long as you work with me or are associated with me in any enterprise, take advantage of the distress of author or actor. This man's play was good enough for us to produce; it is still good enough to earn money. When it makes money for us it also makes money for him."

By the force of his magnetic personality Charles amiably coerced more than one unwilling playwright into submission to his will. An experience with Margaret Mayo will illustrate.

Miss Mayo returned on the same steamer with him when he made his last trip from London to the United States. As they walked up the gang-plank at Liverpool the manager told the author that he had a play he wished her to adapt.

"But I have decided to adapt no more plays," said Miss Mayo.

"Never mind," replied Frohman "We will see about that."

Needless to say, by the time the ship reached New York the play was in Miss Mayo's trunk and the genial tyrant had exacted a promise for the adaptation.

Miss Mayo immediately went to her country house up the Hudson. For a week she reproached herself for having fallen a victim to the Frohman beguilements. In this state of mind she could do no work on the manuscript.

With his astonishing intuition Frohman divined that the author was making no progress, so he sent her a note asking her to come to town, and adding, "I have something to show you."

Miss Mayo entered the office at the Empire determined to throw herself upon the managerial mercy and beg to be excused from the commission. But before she could say a word Frohman said, cheerily:

"I've found the right title for our play."

Then he rang a bell, and a boy appeared holding a tightly rolled poster in his hand. At a signal he unfolded it, and the astonished playwright beheld these words in large red and white letters:

Charles Frohman

Presents

*I DIDN'T WANT TO DO **IT***

A Farce in Three Acts

By Margaret Mayo

Of course the usual thing happened. No one could resist such an attack. Miss Mayo went back to the country without protest and she finished the play. It was destined, however, to be produced by some other hand than Frohman's.

Frohman always sought seclusion when he wanted to work out the plans for a production. He sometimes went to extreme lengths to achieve aloofness. An incident related by Goodwin will illustrate this.

During the run of "Nathan Hale" in New York Goodwin entered his dressing-room one night, turned on the electric light, and was amazed to see Charles sitting huddled up in a corner.

"What are you doing here, Charley?" asked Goodwin.

"I am casting a new play, and came here to get some inspiration. Good night," was the reply. With that he walked out.

There was one great secret in Charles Frohman's life. It is natural that it should center about the writing of a play; it is natural, too, that this most intimate of incidents in the career of the great manager should be told by his devoted friend and colleague of many years, Paul Potter.

Here it is as set down by Mr. Potter:

We had hired a rickety cab at the Place Saint-François in Lausanne, and had driven along the lake of Geneva to Morges, where, sitting on the terrace of the Hôtel du Mont Blanc, we were watching the shore of Savoy across the lake, and the gray old villages of Thonon and Evian, and the mountains, rising ridge upon ridge, behind them. And Frohman, being in lyric mood, fell to quoting "The Blue Hills Far Away," for Owen Meredith's song was one of the few bits of verse that clung in his memory.

"Odd," said he, relapsing into prose, "that a chap should climb hill after hill, thinking he had reached his goal, and should forever find the blue hills farther and farther away."

While he was ruminating the clouds lifted, and there,

in a gap of the hills, was the crest of Mont Blanc, with its image of Napoleon lying asleep in the snow.

I have seen Frohman in most of the critical moments of his life, but I never saw him utterly awe-stricken till then.

"Gee," said he, at length, "what a mountain to climb!"

"It is sixty miles away," I ventured to suggest.

"Well," he remarked, "I'll climb it some day. As John Russell plastered the Rocky Mountains with 'The City Directory,' so I'll hang a shingle from the top of Mont Blanc: 'Ambition: a comedy in four acts by Charles Frohman.'" And as we went home to Ouchy he told me the secret desire of his heart.

He wanted to write a play.

"Isn't it enough to be a theatrical manager?" I asked.

"No," said he, "a theatrical manager is a joke. The public thinks he spends his days in writing checks and his nights in counting the receipts. Why, when I wanted to become a depositor at the Union Bank in London, the cashier asked me my profession. 'Theatrical manager,' I replied. 'Humph!' said the cashier, taken aback. 'Well, never mind, Mr. Frohman; we'll put you down as 'a gentleman.'"

"But is a playwright," I asked, "more highly reputed than a theatrical manager?"

"Not in America," said Frohman. "Most Americans think that the actors and actresses write their own parts. I was on the Long Branch boat the other day and met a well-known Empire first-nighter. 'What are you going to give us next season, Frohman?' he said.

"'I open with a little thing by Sardou,' I replied.

"'Sardou!' he cried. 'Who in thunder is Sardou?'

"All the same," Frohman continued, "I mean to be a playwright. Didn't Lester Wallack write 'Rosedale' and 'The Veteran'? Didn't Augustin Daly make splendid adaptations of German farces? Doesn't Belasco turn out first-class dramas? Then why not I? I mean to learn the game. Don't give me away, but watch my progress in play-making as we jog along through life."

He got his first tip from Pinero. "When I have sketched out a play," observed the author of "The Second Mrs. Tanqueray," "I go and live among the characters."

Frohman had no characters of his own, but he held in his brain a fabulous store of other people's plays. And whenever they had a historical or a literary origin he ran these origins to their lair. At Ferney, on the Lake of Geneva, he cared nothing about Voltaire; he wanted to see the place where the free-thinkers gathered in A. M. Palmer's production of "Daniel Rochat." At Geneva he was not concerned with Calvin, but with memories of a Union Square melodrama, "The Geneva Cross." At Lyons he expected the ghosts of *Claude Melnotte* and *Pauline* to meet him at the station. In Paris he allowed Napoleon to slumber unnoticed in the Invalides while he hunted the Faubourg Saint-Antoine for traces of "The Tale of Two Cities," and the Place de la Concorde for the site of the guillotine on which *Sidney Carton* died, and the Latin Quarter haunts of *Mimi* and *Musette*, and the Bal Bullier where *Trilby* danced, and the Concert des Ambassadeurs where *Zaza* bade her lover good-by.

Any production was an excuse for these expeditions. Sir Herbert Tree had staged "Colonel Newcome";

we had ourselves plotted a dramatization of "Penden-
nis"; Mrs. Fiske had given "Vanity Fair"; so off we
went, down the Boulevard Saint-Germain, searching for
the place, duly placarded, where Thackeray lunched in
the days of the "Paris Sketch-book" and the "Ballad
of Bouillabaisse."

In the towns of Kent we got on the trail of Dickens
with the enthusiasm of a Hopkinson Smith; in London,
between Drury Lane and Wardour Street, we hunted for
the Old Curiosity Shop; in Yarmouth we discovered the
place where Peggotty's boat-hut might have lain on the
sands. With William Seymour, who knew every street
from his study of "The Rivals," we listened to the
abbey bells of Bath. And when "Romeo and Juliet"
was to be revived with Sothern and Marlowe, Frohman
even proposed that we should visit Verona. He only
abandoned the idea on discovering that the Veronese
had no long-distance telephones, and that, while wandering among the tombs of the Montagus and Capulets,
he would be cut off from his London office.

Having thus steeped himself in the atmosphere of his
work, he set forth to learn the rules of the game. I
met him in Paris on his return from New York. "How
go the rules?" I asked.

"Rotten," said he. "Our American playwrights say
there are no rules; with them it is all inspiration. The
Englishmen say that rules exist, but what the rules are
they either don't know or won't tell."

We went to the Concert Rouge. Those were the
happy days when there were no frills; when the price
of admission was charged with what you drank; when
Saint-Saëns accompanied his "Samson and Delilah"
with an imaginary flute obligato on a walking-stick;

when Massenet, with his librettist, Henri Cain, dozed quietly through the meditation of "Thaïs"; when the students and their girls forgot frivolity under the spell of "L'Arlesienne."

In a smoky corner sat a group of well-known French playwrights, headed by G. A. Caillavet, afterward famous as author of "Le Roi." They were indulging in a heated but whispered discussion. They welcomed Frohman cordially, then returned to the debate.

"What are they talking about?" asked Frohman.

"The rules of the drama," said I.

"Then there are rules!" cried the manager, eagerly.

"Ask Caillavet," said I.

"Rules?" exclaimed Caillavet, who spoke English. "Are there rules of painting, sculpture, music? Why, the drama is a mass of rules! It is nothing but rules."

"And how long," faltered Frohman, thinking of his play—"how long would it take to learn them?"

"A lifetime at the very least," answered Caillavet. Disconsolate, Frohman led me out into the Rue de Tournon. Heartbroken, he convoyed me into Foyot's, and drowned his sorrows in a grenadine.

From that hour he was a changed man. He apparently put aside all thought of the drama whose name was to be stenciled on the summit of Mont Blanc; yet, nevertheless, he applied himself assiduously to learning the principles on which the theater was based.

Another winter had passed before we sat side by side on the terrace of the Café Napolitain.

"I have asked Harry Pettitt, the London melodramatist," Frohman said, "to write me a play. 'I warn you, Frohman,' he replied, 'that I have only one theme—the Persecuted Woman.' Dion Boucicault, who was present, said, 'Add the Persecuted Girl.' Joseph Jefferson was with us, and Jefferson remarked, 'Add the Persecuted Man.' So was Henry Irving, who said: 'Pity is the trump card; but be Aristotelian, my boy; throw in a little Terror; with Pity I can generally go through a season, as with 'Charles the First' or 'Olivia'; with Terror and Pity combined I am liable to have something that will outlast my life." And Irving mentioned "The Bells" and "The Lyons Mail."

"But who will write you your Terror and Pity?" I asked Frohman.

"If Terror means 'thrill,'" said Frohman, "I can count on Belasco and Gillette. If Pity means 'sympathy,' the Englishmen do it pretty well. So does Fitch. So do the French, who used to be masters of the game."

"You don't expect," I said, "to pick up another 'Two Orphans,' a second 'Ticket of Leave Man'?"

"I'm not such a fool," said Frohman. "But I've got hold of something now that will help me to feed my stock company in New York." And off we went with Dillingham to see "The Girl from Maxim's" at the Nouveautés.

When we got home to the Ritz Frohman discussed the play after his manner: "Do you know," he said, "I find the element of pity quite as strongly developed in these French farces as in the Ambigu melodramas. The truant husband leaves home, goes out for a good time, gets buffeted and bastinadoed for his pains, and when the compassionate audience says, 'He has had enough; let up,' he comes humbly home to the bosom of his family and is forgiven. Where can you find a more human theme than that?"

"Then you hold," said I, "that even in a French farce the events should be reasonable?"

"I wouldn't buy one," he replied, "if I didn't consider its basis thoroughly human. Dion Boucicault told me long ago that farce, like tragedy, must be founded on granite. 'Farce, well done,' said he, 'is the most difficult form of dramatic composition. That is why, if successful, it is far the most remunerative.'"

Years went by. The stock company was dead. "Charles Frohman's Comedians" had disappeared. The "stars" had supplanted them. Frohman was at the zenith of his career. American papers called him "the Napoleon of the Drama." Prime Ministers courted him in the grill-room of the London Savoy. The Paris *Figaro* announced the coming of "the celebrated impresario." I heard him call my name in the crowd at the Gare du Nord and we bundled into a cab.

"So you're a great man now," I said.

"Am I?" he remarked. "There's one thing you can bet on. If they put me on a throne to-day they are liable to yank me off to-morrow."

"And how's your own play getting along?"

"Don't!" he winced. "Let us go to the Snail."

In the cozy recesses of the Escargot d'Or, near the Central Markets, he unraveled the mysteries of the "star system" which had made him famous.

"It's the opposite of all we ever believed," he said, while the mussels and shell-fish were being heaped up before him. "Good-by to Caillavet and his rules. Good-by, Terror and Pity. Good-by, dear French farce. Give me a pretty girl with a smile, an actor with charm, and I will defy our old friend Aristotle."

"Is it as easy as that?" I asked, in amazement.

"No," said he, "it's confoundedly difficult to find the girl with the smile and the actor with charm. It is pure accident. There are players of international reputation who can't draw a dollar. There are chits of chorus-girls who can play a night of sixteen hundred dollars in Youngstown, Ohio."

"And the play doesn't matter?" I inquired.

"There you've got me," said Frohman, as the crêpes Suzette arrived in their chafing-dish. "My interest makes me pretend that the play's the thing. I congratulate foreign authors on a week of fourteen thousand dollars in Chicago, and they go away delighted. But I know, all the time, that of this sum the star drew thirteen thousand nine hundred dollars, and the author the rest."

"To what do you attribute such a state of affairs?"

"Feminine curiosity. God bless the women."

"Are there no men in your audiences?" I asked.

"Only those whom the women take," said Frohman. "The others go to musical shows. Have some more crêpes Suzette."

"But what do the critics say?" I persisted.

"My dear Paul," said Frohman, solemnly, "they call me a 'commercial manager' because I won't play Ibsen or Maeterlinck. They didn't help me when I tried for higher game. I had years of poverty, years of privation. To-day I take advantage of a general feminine desire to view Miss Tottie Coughdrop; and, to the critics, I'm a mere Bulgarian, a 'commercial manager.' So was Lester Wallack when he admitted 'The World' to his classic theater. So was Augustin Daly when he banished Shakespeare in favor of 'The Great Ruby.'

If the critics want to reform the stage, let them begin by reforming the public."

In his cabin on the *Lusitania* he showed me a mass of yellow manuscript, scribbled over with hieroglyphics in blue pencil.

"That's my play," he said, very simply.

"Shall I take it home and read it?" I asked.

"No," he replied. "I will try it on Barrie and bring it back in better shape."

So he shook hands and sailed with his cherished drama, which reposes to-day, not on the summit of Mont Blanc, but at the bottom of the Irish Sea.

XVI

"C. F." AT REHEARSALS

*T*HE real Charles Frohman emerged at rehearsals. The shy, sensitive man who shunned the outside world here stood revealed as a dynamic force. Yet he ruled by personality, because he believed in personality. He did every possible thing to bring out the personal element in the men and women in his companies.

In rehearsing he showed one of the most striking of his traits. It was a method of speech that was little short of extraordinary. It grew out of the fact that his vocabulary could not express his enormous imagination. Instead of words he made motions. It was, as Augustus Thomas expressed it, "an exalted pantomime." Those who worked with him interpreted these gestures, for between him and his stars existed the finest kinship.

Frohman seldom finished a sentence, yet those who knew him always understood the unuttered part. Even when he would give a star the first intimation of a new rôle he made it a piece of pantomime interspersed with short, jerky sentences.

William Faversham had complained about having two very bad parts. When he went to see Frohman to hear about the third, this is the way the manager expressed it to him:

"New play—see? . . . Fine part.—First act—*you*

know—romantic—light through the window . . . nice deep tones of your voice, you see? . . . Then, audience say 'Ah!'—then the girl—see?—In the room . . . you . . . one of those big scenes—then, all subdued—light— coming through window.—See?—And then—curtain— audience say 'Great!' . . . Now, second act . . . all that tremolo business—you know?—Then you get down to work . . . a tremendous scene . . . let your voice go . . . Great climax . . . (Oh, a great play this—a great part!) . . . Now, last act—simple—nice—lovable—refined . . . sad tones in your voice—and, well, you know—and then you make a big hit. . . . Well, now we will rehearse this in about a week—and you will be tickled to death. . . . This is a great play—fine part. . . . Now, you see Humphreys—he will arrange everything."

Of course Faversham went away feeling that he was about forty-four feet tall, that he was a great actor, and had a wonderful part.

Like the soldier who thrills at the sound of battle, Frohman became galvanized when he began to work in the theater. He forgot time, space, and all other things save the task at hand. To him it was as the breath of life.

One reason was that the theater was his world; the other that Charles was, first and foremost, a director and producer. His sensibility and force, his feeling and authority, his intelligence and comprehension in matters of dramatic artistry were best, almost solely, known to his players and immediate associates. No stage-director of his day was more admired and desired than he.

At rehearsal the announcement, "C. F. is in front," meant for every one in the cast an eager enthusiasm and a desire to do something unusually good to merit his commendation. His enormous energy, aided by his diplomacy and humor, inspired the player to highest performance.

Such expressions as, "But, Mr. Frohman, this is *my* way of doing it," or "I feel it this way," and like manifestations of actors' conceit or argument would never be met with ridicule or contempt. Sometimes he would say, "Try it my way first," or "Do you like that?" or "Does this give you a better feeling?" He never said, "You *must* do thus and so." He was alert to every suggestion. As a result he got the very best out of his people. It was part of his policy of developing the personal element.

The genial human side of the man always softened his loudest tones, although he was seldom vehement. So gentle was his speech at rehearsals that the actors often came down to the footlights to hear his friendly yet earnest direction.

Frohman had that first essential of a great dramatic director—a psychologic mind in the study of the various human natures of his actors and of the ideas they attempted to portray.

He was an engaging and fascinating figure, too, as he molded speech and shaped the play. An old friend who saw him in action thus describes the picture:

"Here a comedian laughs aloud with the comic quaintness of the director. There a little lady, new to the stage, is made to feel at home and confident. The proud old-timer is sufficiently ameliorated to approve of the change suggested. The leading lady trembles with the shock of realization imparted by the stout little man with chubby smile who, seated alone in the darkened auditorium, conveys his meaning as with invisible wires, quietly, quaintly, simply, and rationally, so as to stir the actors' souls to new sensibilities, awaken thought, and viviby glow of passion, sentiment, or humor."

At rehearsals Frohman usually sat alone about the tenth row back. He rarely rose from his seat, but by voice and gesture indicated the moves on his dramatic chess-board. When it became necessary for him to go on the stage he did so with alacrity. He suggested, by marvelously simple indications and quick transitions, the significance of the scene or the manner of the presentation.

There was a curious similarity, in one respect, between the rehearsing methods of Charles Frohman and Augustin Daly. This comparison is admirably made by Frohman's life-long friend Franklin H. Sargent, Director of the American Academy of Dramatic Arts and the Empire School of Acting, in which Frohman was greatly interested and which he helped in every possible way. He said:

"Like a great painter with a few stray significant lines of drawing, Frohman revealed the spirit and the idea. In this respect he resembled Augustin Daly, who could furnish much dramatic intuition by a grunt and a thumb-joint. Both men used similar methods and possessed equal keenness of intelligence and sense of humor, except that Frohman was rarely sarcastic. Daly usually was. Frohman's demeanor and relationship to his actors was kindly and considerate. Rules, and all strictly enforced, were in Daly's policy of theater management. Frohman did not resort to rules. He regulated his theaters on broad principles, but with firm decision when necessary. In Daly's theater there was obedience; in Frohman's theater there was a willing co-operation. The chief interest of both managers was comedy—comedy of two opposite kinds. Daly's jest was the artificial German farce and Shakespearian refinement. Frohman's tastes ranged between the French school—Sardou's 'Diplomacy' and the modern realities—and the pure sentiments of Barrie's 'The Little Minister.' Frohman was never traditional in an artificial sense, though careful to retain the fundamental original treatment of imported foreign plays.

"The verities, the humanities, the joys of life always existed and grew with him as with a good landscape architect who keeps in nature's ways. His departures into the classicism of Stephen Phillips, the romanticism of Shakespeare, or the exotic French society drama were never as valuable and delightful as his treatment of modern sentiment and comedy."

In this respect a comparison with the workmanship of another genius of the American theater, David Belasco, is inevitable. Belasco, the great designer and painter of theatrical pictures, holds quite a different point of view and possesses different abilities from those of Charles Frohman. Belasco revels in the technique of the actor. Frohman's *métier* was the essentials. The two men were in many ways complements of each other and per force admirers of each other and friends. In brief, Belasco is the technicist; Frohman was the humanitarian.

Charles usually left details of scenery, lighting, and minor matters to his stage-manager. "Look after the little things," he would say, in business as in art, for he himself was interested only in the larger themes.

The lesser people of the play, the early rehearsing of involved business, was shaped by his subordinates. The smaller faults and the mannerisms of the actor did not trouble him, provided the main thought and feeling were there. He would merely laugh at a suggestion to straighten out the legs and walk, to lengthen the drawl, or to heighten the cockney accent of a prominent member of his company, saying:

"The public likes him for these natural things."

Frohman's ear was musically sensitive. The intonations, inflections, the tone colors of voice, orchestral and incidental music, found him an exacting critic.

To plays he gave thought, study, and preparation. The author received much advice and direction from him. He himself possessed the expert knowledge and abilities of a playwright, as is always true of every good stage-director. Each new play was planned, written, cast, and revised completely under his guidance and supervision. His stage-manager had been instructed in advance in the "plotting" of its treatment. The first rehearsals were usually left in charge of this assistant.

At the first rehearsals Frohman made little or no comments. He watched and studied in silence. Thereafter his master-mind would reveal itself in reconstruction of lines and scenes, re-accentuation of the high and low lights of the story involved, and improvement of the acting and representation. Frohman consulted with his authors, artists, and assistants more in his office than in actual rehearsal. In the theater he was sole auditor and judge. His stage-manager would rarely make suggestions during rehearsals unless beckoned to and asked by his manager. When the office-boy came in at rehearsal on some important business errand, he got a curt dismissal, or at most a brief consideration of the despatch, contract, or message.

Here is a vivid view of Frohman at rehearsal by one who often sat under the magic of his direction:

"In the dim theater he sits alone, the stage-manager being at a respectable distance. If by chance there are one or two others present directly concerned in the production, they all sit discreetly in the extreme rear. The company is grouped in the wings, never in the front. The full stage lights throw into prominence the actors in the scene in rehearsal. Occasionally the voice of Mr. Frohman calls from the auditorium, and the direction is sometimes repeated more loudly by the stage-manager. Everybody is listening and watching.

"The wonderfully responsive and painstaking nature of Maude Adams is fully alive, alert, and interested in Mr. Frohman's directions even in the scenes in which she has no personal part, during which, very likely, she will half recline on the floor near the proscenium—all eyes and ears.

"Or perhaps it is a strong emotional scene in which Margaret Anglin is the central character. At the theatrically most effective point in the acting the voice breaks in, Miss Anglin stops, hastens to the footlights, and listens intently to a few simple, quiet words. Over her face pass shadow and storm, and in her eyes tears form. Again she begins the scene, and yet again, with cumulative passion. Each time, with each new incitement from the sympathetic director, new power, deeper feeling, keener thought develop, until a great glow of meaning and of might fills the stage and the theater with its radiance. Mr. Frohman is at last satisfied, and so the play moves on."

Just as Frohman loved humor in life, so did he have a rare gift for comedy rehearsal. William Faversham pays him this tribute:

"I think Charles Frohman was the greatest comedy stage-manager that I have known. I do not think there was a comedy ever written that he could not rehearse and get more out of than any other stage-director I have ever seen—and I have seen a good many. If he had devoted himself, as director, entirely to one company, I think he would have produced the greatest organization of comedians that Europe or America ever saw. I don't suppose there is a comedy scene that he couldn't rehearse and play better than any of the actors who were engaged to play the parts. The subtle touches that he put into 'Lord and Lady Algy' were extraordinary. The same with 'The Counsellor's Wife,' with 'Bohemia,' and again with a play of H. V. Esmond's called 'Imprudence,' which we did. He seemed to love this play, and I never saw a piece grow so in all my life as it did under his direction. All the successes made by the actors and actresses in that play were entirely through the work of Charles Frohman.

"He had a keen sense of sound, a tremendous ear for tones of comedy. He could get ten or twelve inflections out of a speech of about four lines; he had a wonderful method of getting the actors to accept and project these tones over the footlights. He got what he wanted from them in the most extraordinary way. With his disjointed, pantomimic method of instruction he was able to transfer to them, as if by telepathy, what he wanted.

"For instance, he would say: 'Now, you go over there . . . then, just as he is looking at you . . . see?—

say—then . . . that's it! you know?' And simply by this telepathy you *did know*."

His terse summing up of scenes and facts was never better illustrated than when he compressed the instructions of a whole sentimental act into this simple sentence to E. H. Sothern:

"Court—kiss—curtain."

In one detail he differed from all the other great producers of his time. Most managers liked to nurse a play after its production and build it up with new scenes or varied changes. With Frohman it was different. "I am interested in a production until it has been made, and then I don't care for it any more," he said. This is generally true, although some of his productions he could never see often enough.

Frohman's perception about a play was little short of uncanny. An incident that happened during the rehearsal of the Maude Adams all-star revival of "Romeo and Juliet" will illustrate. James K. Hackett was cast for *Mercutio*. He had worked for a month on the Queen Mab speech. He had elaborated and polished it, and thought he had it letter and tone perfect.

Frohman sat down near the front and listened with rapt attention while this fine actor declaimed the speech. When he finished Charles said, in his jerky, epigrammatic way:

"Hackett, that's fine, but just in there somewhere— you know what I mean."

As a matter of fact, Hackett, with all his elaborate preparation, had slipped up on one line, and it was a very essential one. Frohman had never read "Romeo and Juliet" until he cast this production, yet he caught the omission with his extraordinary intuition.

Charles was the most indefatigable of workers. At one time, on arriving in Boston at midnight, he had to stage a new act of "Peter Pan." He worked over it with carpenters, actors, and electricians until three in the morning. Then he made an appointment with the acting manager to take a walk on the Common "in the morning."

The manager took "in the morning" to mean nine o'clock. When he reached the hotel Frohman was just returning from his walk, and handed the man a bunch of cables to send, telegrams to acknowledge, and memoranda of information desired. At ten o'clock Frohman was conducting the rehearsal of a new comedy by Haddon Chambers, which he finished at four. At five he was on a train speeding back to New York, where he probably read manuscripts of plays until two in the morning. This was one of the typical "C. F." days.

Occasionally a single detail would fascinate him in a play. "The Waltz Dream" that he did at the Hicks Theater in London in 1908 was typical. Miss Gertie Millar, who sang the leading part, had an important song. Frohman did not like the way she sang it, so he worked on it for two weeks until it reached the perfection of expression that he desired. But that song made the play and became the most-talked-of feature in it. This led him to say:

"I am willing to give as much time to a single song as to the rehearsal of a whole play."

Frohman had a phrase that he often used with his actors and directors. It was:

"Never get a 'falling curtain.'"

By this he meant a curtain that did not leave interest

or emotion subdued or declining. He wanted the full sweep of rage, terror, pity, suspense, or anger alive with the end of the act.

He always said, "A man who sees a play must feel that he is in the presence of an act." It was his way of putting forth the idea that any acted effort, no matter how humble, must have the ring of sincerity and conviction.

Charles had an almost weird instinct for what was right on the stage. Once at rehearsals he pointed to a heavy candelabrum that stood on a table.

"I want that thing on the mantelpiece," he said.

"You mean the candelabrum?" asked one of his assistants.

"I don't know what it is, but I know that it belongs on the mantelpiece." And it did.

Many of Frohman's rehearsals were held out of town. He was particularly fond of "pointing up" a production in a strange environment. Then the stage-director would ask the local manager for an absolutely empty theater—"a clear auditorium."

"Peter Pan" was to be "finished off" at Washington. The call was issued, the company assembled—everybody was present except Frohman. "Strange," was the thought in all minds, for he was usually so prompt. Ten minutes, fifteen minutes passed until the stage-manager left the theater in search of the manager. He was found at the front entrance of the theater, unsuccessfully arguing with a German door-tender who, not knowing him and immensely amused at the idea that he was pretending to be Charles Frohman, refused to admit him until reassured by the company stage-manager. Later, when the man came to apologize, Frohman's only comment was:

"Oh! I forgot that an hour ago."

Few people knew the Frohman of rehearsals so well as William Seymour, for many years his general stage-director. His illuminating picture of the Little Chief he served so long is as follows:

"At rehearsals Charles Frohman was completely wrapped up in the play and the players. His mind, however, traveled faster than we did. He often stopped me to make a change in a line or in the business which to me was not at all clear. You could not always grasp, at once, just what he was aiming at. But once understood, the idea became illuminative, and extended into the next, or even to succeeding acts of the play. He could detect a weak spot quicker than any one I ever knew, and could remedy or straighten it out just as quickly.

"After the rehearsal of a new play he would think of it probably all the evening and night, and the next morning he had the solutions of the several vague points at his fingers' ends. He was also very positive and firm in what he wanted done, and how he thought it should be done. But what he thought was right, he believed to be right, and he soon made you see it that way.

"I confess to having had many differences of opinion and arguments, sometimes even disagreements, with him. In some instances he came round to my way of thinking, but he often said:

"'I believe you are right—I am sure you are right—but I intend doing it my way.'

"It was his great and wonderful self-confidence, and it was rarely overestimated.

"To his actors in a new play, after a week's 'roughing out' of the lines and business, the announcement that 'C. F. will be here to-morrow' would cause a flutter, some consternation, and to the newer members a great fear. To those who had been with him before he was like a sheet-anchor in a storm. They knew him and trusted and loved him. He was all sympathy, all comfort, all encouragement—if anything, too indulgent and overkind. But he won the confidence and affection of his people at the outset, and I have rarely met a player who would not have done his slightest bidding."

One of Frohman's characteristic hobbies was that he would never allow the leading man or the leading woman of his theater, or anybody in the company, no matter what position he or she held, to presume upon that position and bully the property man, or the assistant stage-manager, or any person in a menial position in the theater. He was invariably on the side of the smaller people.

Very often he would say, "The smallest member of this organization, be he of the staff or in the company, has as much right to his 'say' in an argument as the biggest member has."

On one occasion a certain actor, who was rather fond of issuing his wishes and instructions in a very loud voice, made his exit through a door up the center of the stage which was very difficult to open and shut. It had not worked well, and this had happened, quite by accident, on several occasions during the run of the play. The actor had spoken rather sharply to the carpenter about it instead of going, as he should have done, to the stage-manager. He always called the carpenter

"Charley." The carpenter was a rather dignified person named Charles Heimley.

On the night in question this actor had had the usual trouble with the door. Heimley was not in sight, for he was evidently down in his carpenter-shop under the stage. The actor leaned over the balustrade and called out: "Charley! Charley!"

Frohman, who was just walking through the side door on his way to William Faversham's dressing-room, turned to the star and said:

"Who is calling? Does he want me?"

"Oh no, he is calling the carpenter," replied Faversham.

Frohman tapped the noisy actor on the shoulder with his stick, and said, "You mean *Mr. Heimley*, don't you?" He wanted the carpenter's position to be respected.

XVII

HUMOR AND ANECDOTE

*T*HE most distinctive quality in Charles Frohman's make-up was his sense of humor. He mixed jest with life, and it enabled him to meet crisis and disaster with unflagging spirit and smiling equanimity. Like Lincoln, he often resorted to anecdote and story to illustrate his point. He summed up his whole theory of life one day when he said to Augustus Thomas:

"I am satisfied if the day gives me one good laugh."

He had a brilliancy of retort that suggested Wilde or Whistler. Once he was asked this question:

"What is the difference between metropolitan and out-of-town audiences?"

"Fifty cents," he replied.

Haddon Chambers was writing a note in Frohman's rooms at the Savoy.

"Do you spell high-ball with a hyphen?" he asked.

"No, with a siphon," responded Frohman.

Charles Dillingham, when in Frohman's employ, was ordered to hurry back to New York. From a small town up New York state he wired:

Wash-out on line. Will return as soon as possible.

340

Frohman promptly sent the following reply:

> *Never mind your wash. Buy a new shirt and come along at once.*

That he could also meet failure with a joke is shown by the following incident:

He was producing a play at Atlantic City that seemed doomed from the start. In writing to a member of his family he said:

> *I never saw the waves so high and the receipts so low.*

Frohman and Pinero were dining in the Carleton grill-room one night when a noisy person rushed up to them, slapped each on the shoulder, and said:

"Hello, 'C. F.'! Hello, 'Pin.'! I'm Hopkins."

Frohman looked up gravely and said:

"Ah, Mr. Hopkins, I can't say that I remember your name or your face, but your manner is familiar."

When Edna May married Oscar Lewisohn she gave a reception on her return from the honeymoon. She sent Charles one of the conventional engraved cards that read:

> *" At home Thursday from four to six."*

Frohman immediately sent back the card, on which he had written, "So am I."

Once when Frohman and Dillingham were crossing to Europe on the *Oceanic* they had as fellow-passenger a mutual friend, Henry Dazian, the theatrical costumer, on whom Charles delighted to play pranks. On the first

day out Dillingham came rushing back to Frohman with this exclamation:

"There are a couple of card-sharks on board and Dazian is playing with them. Don't you think we had better warn him?"

"No," replied Frohman. "Warn the sharks."

Some years ago Frohman sent a young actor named John Brennan out on the road in the South in "Too Much Johnson." Brennan was a Southerner, and he believed that he could do a big business in his home country. Frohman then went to London, and, when playing hearts at the Savoy one night with Dillingham, a page brought a cablegram. It was from Brennan, saying:

> *Unless I get two hundred dollars by next Saturday night I can't close.*

Whereupon Frohman wired him:

> *Keep going.*

Frohman delighted to play jokes on his close friends. In 1900, Dillingham opened the New Jersey Academy of Music with Julia Marlowe, and it was a big event. This was before the day of the tubes under the Hudson connecting New Jersey and New York. When Dillingham went down to the ferry to cross over for the opening night he found a basket of flowers from Frohman marked, "Bon voyage."

Nor could Frohman be lacking in the graceful reply. During a return engagement of "The Man from Mexico," in the Garrick Theater, William Collier became

very ill with erysipelas and had to go to a hospital.
The day the engagement was resumed happened to be
Frohman's birthday, and Collier sent him the following
cablegram:

*Many happy returns from all your box
offices.*

He received the following answer from Frohman:

*My happiest return is your return to the
Garrick.*

Behind all of Frohman's jest and humor was a serious
outlook on life. It was mixed with big philosophy, too,
as this incident will show:

He was visiting Sir George Alexander at his country
house in Kent. Alexander, who is a great dog fancier,
asked Frohman to accompany him while he chained up
his animals. Frohman watched the performance with
great interest. Then he turned to the actor-manager
and said:

"I have got a lot of dogs out at my country place in
America, but I never tie them up."

"Why?" asked Alexander.

"Let other people tie up the dogs. You let them
out and they will always like you."

Frohman was known to his friends as a master of
epigram. Some of his distinctive sayings are these:

"The best seat at a theater is the paid one."

"An ounce of imagination is worth a pound of prac-
ticality."

"The man who makes up his mind to corner things
generally gets cornered."

"You cannot monopolize theaters while there are bricks and mortar."

"When I hear of another theater being built I try to build another author."

"No successful theatrical producer ever died rich. He must make money for everybody but himself."

"Great stage successes are the plays that take hold of the masses, not the classes."

Frohman could always reach the heart of a situation with a pithy phrase or reply. On one of the rare occasions when he attended a public dinner he sat at the Metropolitan Club in New York with a group of men representing a variety of interests. He condemned a certain outrageously immodest Oriental dancer, who, at the moment, was shocking New York.

"She must have a nasty mind to dance like that," said Frohman.

"Don't be too hard on her," responded a playwright who sat near by. "Consider how young she is."

"I deny that she is as young as you imply," retorted Frohman. "But I am bound to admit that she is certainly a *stripling*."

Frohman's mind worked with amazing swiftness. Here is an example:

At the formation of a London society called the West End Managers Association, Sir Charles Wyndham gave a luncheon at the Hyde Park Hotel to discuss and arrange preliminaries. Most of the London managers were present, including Frohman. There was a discussion as to what should be the entrance fee for each member. Various sums were discussed from £100 downward. Twenty-five pounds seemed to be the most generally accepted, when one manager said:

"Why should we not each give one night's receipts."

This was discussed for a little while, when Sir Charles said, "What do you say, Frohman?"

· The American replied, "I would sooner give a night's receipts than £25."

There was a short silence, then everybody seemed to remember that he had at that moment a failure at his theater. The humor of it was hailed with a shout of laughter.

Just as he mixed sentiment in business so did Frohman infuse wit into most of his relations. He once instructed W. Lestocq, his London manager, to conduct certain negotiations for a new play with a Scotchwoman whose first play had made an enormous success in America, and whose head had been turned by it. The woman's terms were ten thousand dollars in advance and a fifteen-per-cent. royalty. When Lestocq told Frohman these terms over the telephone, all he said was this:

"Did you tell her not to slam the door?"

Frohman would always have his joke in London, as this incident shows:

He had just arrived in town and went to a bank in Charing Cross with a letter of credit, which he deposited. When he emerged he was smiling all over.

"I got one on that young man behind the counter," he said.

"How's that?" asked Lestocq, who was waiting for him.

"Well," he replied, "the young man bade me good morning and asked me if I have brought over anything good this time. I replied, 'Yes, a letter of credit on your bank, and I am waiting to see if *it* is any good.'"

A manager, who for present purposes must be named Smith, called on Frohman to secure the services of a star at that time under contract to the latter. His plan was to drop in on Frohman at a busy hour, quickly state the case, and, getting an affirmative answer, leave without talking terms at all. Later he knew it would be enough to recall the affirmative answer that had been given without qualification. The transaction took but a moment, just as the manager wished.

"Well, then, I may have him?" said Smith.

"Er-m-ah-er-yes—I will let you have him," replied Frohman, at the same time running over a paper before him. The visitor was already at the door.

"By the way, Smith," called out Frohman, "how much do you want me to pay you for taking him off my hands?"

Frohman was as playful as a child. Once he was riding in a *petit voiture* in Paris. It was a desperately hot night. The old *cocher* took his hat off, hung it on the lamp, and wiped his forehead. Frohman took the hat and hid it under his seat. When the driver looked for his hat it was gone. He stopped the horse and ran back two or three blocks before he could be stopped. Then he went on without it, muttering and cursing, and turning around every few moments. Watching his opportunity, Frohman slipped the hat back on the lamp, and there was the expected climax that he thoroughly enjoyed.

On one of his trips to Paris he was accompanied by Dillingham. Knowing Frohman's fondness for rich food, his friend decided to take him to dine at Durand's famous restaurant opposite the Madeleine. He even went to the café in the afternoon and told the proprietor that he was going to bring the great American manager. Great anticipation prevailed in the establishment.

That night when they got to the restaurant Frohman gave Dillingham the shock of his life by saying:

"I want to be a real American to-night. All I want is an oyster stew."

Dillingham instructed the chef how to make the stew. After long delay there was a commotion. In strode the chef, followed by two assistants, bearing aloft a gigantic silver tureen which was placed on the table and opened with great ceremony. Inside was a huge quantity of consommé with two lonely oysters floating on top.

Frohman regarded it as a great joke, and ever afterward when he met anybody in Paris that he did not like, he would say to them:

"If you want the finest oyster stew in the world, go to Durand's."

Frohman, who was always playing jokes on his friends, was sometimes the victim himself. He was crossing the ocean with Haddon Chambers when the latter was accosted by two enterprising young men who were arranging the ship's concert. Chambers was asked to take part, but declined. Then he had an inspiration.

"We have on board the greatest American singer of coon songs known to the stage."

"Who is that?" asked the men.

"It's Charles Frohman."

The men gasped.

"Of course we knew him as a great manager, but we never knew he could sing."

"Oh yes," said Chambers. "He is a great singer."

He pointed out Frohman and hid behind a lifeboat to await the result. Soon he heard a sputter and a shriek of rage, and the two men came racing down the boat as if pursued by some terror. Up came Frohman, his face livid with rage.

"What do you think?" he said to Chambers, who stood innocently by. "Those men had the nerve to ask me to sing a coon song. I have never been so insulted in all my life."

He was so enraged that he wrote a letter to the steamship line about it and withdrew his patronage from the company for several years in consequence.

Here is another instance when the joke was on Frohman. No one viewed the manager's immense success with keener pride or pleasure than his father, Henry Frohman. As theater after theater came under the son's direction the parent could gratify his great passion for giving people free passes to its fullest extent. He would appear at the offices at the Empire Theater with his pockets bulging with home-made cigars. The men in the office always accepted the cigars, but never smoked them. But they gave him all the passes he wanted.

One day the father stopped in to see Charles. It was a raw spring day. Charles remarked that the overcoat Henry wore was too thin.

"Go to my tailor and get an overcoat," he said.

"Not much," said the father. "Your tailor is too expensive. He robs you. He wouldn't make one under seventy-five dollars, and I never pay more than twenty dollars."

Charles's eye twinkled. He said, quickly:

"You are mistaken. My tailor will make you a coat for twenty dollars. Go down and get one."

Father went down to the fashionable Fifth Avenue tailor. Meanwhile Frohman called him up and gave instructions to make a coat for his father at a very low price and have the difference charged to him.

In an hour Henry Frohman came back all excitement. "I am a real business man," he said. "I persuaded that tailor of yours to make me an overcoat for twenty dollars."

Charles immediately gave him the twenty dollars and sent the tailor a check for the difference between that and the real price, which was ninety-five dollars. He dismissed the matter from his mind.

A few days later Charles had another visit from his father. This time he was in high glee. He could hardly wait to tell the great news.

"You've often said I wasn't a good business man," he told his son. "Well, I can prove to you that I am. The other night one of my friends admired my new overcoat so much that I sold it to him for thirty-five dollars."

Charles said nothing, but had to pay for another one-hundred-and-fifteen-dollar overcoat because he did not want to shatter his father's illusion.

Here is still another. When Frohman got back to New York from a trip few things interested him so much as a good dinner. It always wiped out the memory of hard times or unpleasant experiences. Once he returned from a costly visit to the West. On Broadway he met an old-time comedian who had been in one of his companies. His greeting was cordial.

"And now, 'C. F.,'" said the comedian, "you've got to come to dinner with me. We have a new club, for actors only, and we have the best roast beef in town. We make a specialty of a substantial, homelike dinner. Come right along."

The club rooms were over a saloon on the west side of Broadway, between Thirty-first and Thirty-second streets. The two went up to the room and sat down. The actor ordered dinner for two. The waiter went away and Frohman's spirits began to rise.

"It's the best roast beef in New York, I tell you," said the host, by way of an appetizer.

Then the waiter reappeared, but not with the food. He was visibly embarrassed.

"Sorry, sir," he said to the comedian, "but the steward tells me that you can't have dinner to-night. He says you were posted to-day, and that you can't be served again until everything is settled."

Charles used to tell this story and say that he never had such an appetite for roast beef as he did when he rose from that club table to go out again into Broadway.

Frohman was always interested in mechanical things. When the phonograph was first put on the market he had one in his office at 1127 Broadway. Once in London he found a mechanical tiger that growled, walked, and even clawed. He enjoyed watching it crouch and spring.

He took it with him on the steamer back to New

York, and played with it on the deck. One day Richard Croker, who was a fellow-passenger, came along and became interested in the toy, whereupon Frohman showed him how it worked.

Frohman told of this episode with great satisfaction. He would always end his description by saying:

"Fancy showing the boss of Tammany Hall how to work a tiger!"

The extraordinary affinity that existed between Frohman and a small group of intimates was shown by an incident that occurred on shipboard. He and Dillingham were on their way to Europe. They were playing checkers in the smoking-room when an impertinent, pushing American came up and half hung himself over the table. Frohman said nothing, but made a very ridiculous move. Dillingham followed suit.

"What chumps you are!" said the interloper, and went away.

Frohman wanted to get rid of the man without saying anything. This was his way of doing it, and it succeeded.

Frohman was always having queer adventures out of which he spun the most amazing yarns. This is an experience that he liked to recount:

When Augustus Thomas had an apartment in Paris he received a visit from Frohman. The flat was five flights up, but there was an elevator that worked by pushing a button.

There was a ring at the bell of the Thomas apartment. When the playwright opened the door he found Frohman gasping for breath, and he sank exhausted on a settee.

"I walked up," he managed to say. When he was able to talk Thomas said to him:

"Why in Heaven's name didn't you use the elevator?"

Frohman replied:

"I couldn't make the woman down-stairs understand what I wanted. She made motions and showed me a little door, but I thought she had designs on my life, so I preferred to walk."

That Charles Frohman had the happy faculty of saying the right thing and saying it gracefully is well illustrated by the following:

When the beautiful Scala Theater in London was opened it made such a sensation that Frohman asked Lestocq if he could not inspect it. The proprietor, Dr. Distin Maddick, being an old friend of Lestocq, the latter called informally with Frohman. While they were admiring the white stone and brass interior, Maddick was suddenly called away. He returned in a few minutes to say that a manager friend from Edinburgh, hearing that Frohman was in the theater, had come in and asked to be introduced. Of course Frohman acquiesced. After a little talk the gentleman said:

"We have no beautiful theater like this in Edinburgh."

Quickly Frohman replied, with his fascinating smile, "No, but you have Edinburgh."

Frohman hated exercise. In this he had a great community of interest with Mark Twain.

On Sunday mornings, when he was out at his farm at White Plains, he would read all the dramatic news in the papers, and then he searched them carefully for items

great impression on me. I resolved then never to have
my photograph taken if I could help it."

Once when Frohman and A. L. Erlanger were in London he received the usual request to be photographed
by a newspaper camera man. The two magnates looked
something alike in that they had a more or less Napoleonic cast of face. Frohman, who always saw a joke
in everything, hatched a scheme by which Erlanger was
to be photographed for him. The plan worked admirably, and pictures of Erlanger suddenly began to appear all over London labeled "Charles Frohman."

He could be gracious, however, in his refusal to be
photographed. One bright afternoon he was watching
the races at Henley when he was approached by R. W.
MacFarlane, of New York, who had been on the Frohman staff. MacFarlane asked if he could take a photograph of Frohman and give it to his niece, who was
traveling with him.

"No," said the manager, "but you can take a picture
of your niece and I will pose her for it."

Frohman's shyness led to what is in many respects
the most remarkable of the countless anecdotes about
him. It grew out of his illness. In 1913 he had a
severe attack of neuritis in London. Although his
friends urged him to go and see a doctor, he steadfastly
refused. He dreaded physicians just as he dreaded
photographers.

One day Barrie came to see him at his rooms at the
Savoy. Frohman was in such intense pain that the
Scotch author said:

."Frohman, it is absurd for you not to see a doctor.
You simply must have medical attention. As a matter

of fact, I have already made an engagement for you to see Robson-Roose, the great nerve specialist, at four o'clock to-morrow afternoon."

Frohman, who accepted whatever Barrie said, acquiesced. Next day, when half-past three o'clock came, the manager was almost in a state of panic. He said to Dillingham, who was with him:

"Dillingham, you know how I hate to go to see doctors. You also know what is the matter with me. Why don't you go as my understudy and tell the doctor what is the matter with you? He will give you a nice little prescription or advise you to go to the Riviera or Carlsbad."

"All right," said Dillingham, who adored his friend. "I'll do what you say."

Promptly at four o'clock Dillingham showed up at the great specialist's office and said he was Frohman. He underwent a drastic cross-examination. After which he was asked to remove his clothes, was subjected to the most strenuous massage treatment, and, to cap it all, was given an electric bath that reduced him almost to a wreck. He had entered the doctor's office in the best of health. He emerged from it worn and weary.

When he staggered into Frohman's rooms two hours later and told his tale of woe, Frohman laughed so heartily over the episode that he was a well man the next day.

Frohman had a great fund of pithy sayings, remarkable for their brevity. With these he indicated his wishes to his associates. His charm of manner, his quick insight into a situation, and his influence over the minds of others were great factors in the accomplish-

XVIII

THE MAN FROHMAN

GREAT as producer, star-maker, and conqueror of two stage-worlds, Charles Frohman was greater as a human being. Like Roosevelt, whom he greatly admired, he was more than a man—he was an institution. His quiet courage, his unaffected simplicity, his rare understanding, his ripe philosophy, his uncanny penetration—above all, his abundant humor—made him a figure of fascinating and incessant interest.

No trait of Charles Frohman was more highly developed than his shyness. He was known as "The Great Unphotographed." The only time during the last twenty-five years of his life that he sat for a photograph was when he had to get a picture for his passport, and this picture went to a watery grave with him. Behind his prejudice against being photographed was a perfectly definite reason, which he once explained as follows:

"I once knew a theatrical manager whose prospects were very bright. He became a victim of the camera. Fine pictures of him were made and stuck up on the walls everywhere. He used to spend more time looking at these pictures of himself than he did attending to his business. He made a miserable failure. I was quite a young man when I heard of this, but it made a

358

The thump, thump, thump continued, coming nearer. Just in the middle of the act a German voice spoke up and said:

"Oxkuse me, Meester Dillingham, dere ain't a lam' chop in der house."

It was Max, the butler, who, worried over what seemed the imminent failure of the midnight repast, had come to report to headquarters for further instructions. Fortunately the interruption passed unnoticed and the play made quite a hit.

On one occasion Nat C. Goodwin invited him to the Goodwin residence in West End Avenue, New York. The comedian wanted to place himself under the management of his guest. Goodwin stated the case, and Frohman then asked how remunerative his last season had been. The host produced his books. After a careful examination Frohman remarked, with a smile:

"My dear boy, you don't require a manager. What you need is a lawyer."

ment of his end, often attaining the obviously impossible.

For example, when he would tell his business manager to negotiate a business matter with a man, and it would come to a point where there would be a deadlock, he would say:

"I will see him. Ask him to come down to my hotel."

The next morning he would walk into the office with a smile on his face, and the first thing he would say perhaps would be:

"I fixed it up all right yesterday; it is going your way."

"You are a wonder!" his associates would exclaim.

"Oh no! I just talked to him," was the reply.

Frohman disliked formality. He wanted to go straight to the heart of a thing and have it over with. Somebody once asked him why he did not join the Masonic order. He said:

"I would like to very much if I could just write a check and not bother with all the ceremony."

Although he never spoke of his great power in the profession, occasionally there was a glimpse of how he felt about it as this incident shows:

Once, when Frohman and Paul Potter were coming back from Atlantic City, Potter picked up a theatrical paper and said:

"Shall I read you the theatrical news?"

"No," said Frohman. "I *make* theatrical news."

In that supreme test of a man's character—his attitude toward money—he shone. Though his enterprises involved millions, Frohman had an extraordinary disregard of money. He felt its power, but he never idolized it. To him it was a means to an end. He summed up his whole attitude one day when he said:

"My work is to produce plays that succeed, so that I can produce plays that will not succeed. That is why I must have money.

"What I would really like to do is to produce a wonderful something to which I would only go myself. My pleasure would be in seeing a remarkable performance that nobody else could see. But I can't do that. The next best thing is to produce something for the few critical people. That is what I'm trying for. I have to work through the commercial—it is the white heat through which the artistic in me has to come." It was his answer to the oft-made charge of "commercialism."

No one, perhaps, has summed up this money attitude of Frohman's better than George Bernard Shaw, who said of him:

"There is a prevalent impression that Charles Frohman is a hard-headed American man of business who would not look at anything that is not likely to pay. On the contrary, he is the most wildly romantic and adventurous man of my acquaintance. As Charles XII. became an excellent soldier because of his passion for putting himself in the way of being killed, so Charles Frohman became a famous manager through his passion for putting himself in the way of being ruined."

In many respects Frohman's feeling about money was almost childlike. He left all financial details to his subordinates. All he wanted to do was to produce plays and be let alone. Yet he had an infinite respect for the man to whom he had to pay a large sum. He felt that the actor or author who could command it was invested with peculiar significance. Upon himself he spent little. He once said:

"All I want is a good meal, a good cigar, good clothes, a good bed to sleep in, and freedom to produce whatever plays I like."

He was a magnificent loser. Failure never disturbed him. When he saw that a piece was doomed he indulged in no obituary talk. "Let's go to the next," he said, and on he went.

He lost in the same princely way that he spent. The case of "Thermidor" will illustrate. He spent not less than thirty thousand dollars on this production. Yet the moment the curtain went down he realized it was a failure. He stood at one side of the wings and Miss Marbury, who had induced him to put the play on, was at the other. With the fall of the curtain Frohman moved smilingly among his actors with no trace of disappointment on his face. But when he met Miss Marbury on the other side of the stage he said:

"Well, I suppose we have got a magnificent frost. We'll just write this off and forget it."

Frohman played with the theater as if it were a huge game. Like life itself, it was a great adventure. In the parlance of Wall Street, he was a "bull," for he was always raising salaries and royalties. Somebody once said of him:

"What a shame that Frohman works so hard! He never had a day's fun in his life."

"You are very much mistaken," said one of his friends. "His whole life is full of it. He gets his chief fun out of his work." Indeed, work and humor were in reality the great things with him.

One of the best epigrams ever made about Frohman's extravagance was this:

"Give Charles Frohman a check-book and he will lose money on any production."

To say that his word was his bond is to repeat one of the trite tributes to him. But it was nevertheless very true. Often in discussing a business arrangement with his representatives he would say:

"Did I say that?" On being told that he did, he would invariably reply, "Then it must stand at that."

On one of these occasions he said:

"I have only one thing of value to me, and that is my word. I will keep that until I am broke and then I'll jump overboard."

In starting a new venture his method was first to ascertain not how much it would enrich him, but how much it would cost. Thus fortified, he entered into it with enthusiasm, and if he lost he never murmured. Having settled a thing, for good or ill, he would never refer to the negotiations or anything that might have led up to the culmination of that business, either for or against. If his attention was afterward called to it, he would quietly say, "That's yesterday," and in this way indicate that he did not wish the matter referred to again.

Frohman's great desire was to make money for other people. One of his young authors had had a bad failure in London and was very much depressed. Frohman finally worked out a plan to revive his spirits and recoup his finances. He took Alfred Sutro in his confidence and invited the young man to dine. He was like a child, eager to do something good and pleasing. All through the dinner he chaffed the young man, who visibly grew more despondent. Finally he said:

"I have decided to revive a very good play, and I have booked an American tour for it." Then he told the young man that this play was his first success.

Charles Frohman's ignorance of money matters was proverbial. One day just as he was about to take the train for Washington a friend stopped him and said:

"I've got a great investment for you."

"No," said Frohman, "I never invest in anything except theaters."

"But this is the real thing. The only possible fact that can spoil it is war, and we are widely remote from war."

In order to get rid of the man Frohman consented to a modest investment. When he got to Washington the first thing that greeted him was the announcement that we were on the verge of war with Mexico.

William Harris once gently remonstrated with Frohman for such lavish expenditure of money.

"It's simply awful, Charley, the way you spend money," he said.

Frohman smiled and said:

"It would be awful if I lost a finger or a foot, but spending money on the things that you want to do and enjoy doing is never money wasted."

At one time he owed a great deal of money to actors and printers, but he always scorned all suggestions that he go through bankruptcy and wipe these claims out.

He said he would pay in full some day, and he did, with interest. An actor to whom he owed some four hundred dollars came to him and offered to settle the claim for one hundred dollars. Frohman said he did not believe in taking advantage of a man like that. He advanced the actor one hundred dollars, and eventually paid the other three hundred dollars.

Like every great man, Frohman's tastes were simple. He always wore clothes of one pattern, and the style seldom varied. He wore no jewelry except a Napoleonic ring on his little finger.

Frohman never married. A friend once asked him why he had chosen to be a bachelor.

"My dear fellow," he answered, "had I possessed a wife and family I could never have taken the risks which, as a theatrical manager, I am constantly called upon to do."

He lived, in truth, for and by the theater; it was his world. His heart was in his profession, and no enterprise was too daring, no venture too perilous, to prevent him from boldly facing it if he believed the step was expected of him.

To his intimates Frohman was always known as "C. F." These were the magic initials that opened or shut the doors to theatrical fame and fortune.

Frohman loved sweet things to eat. Pies were his particular fondness, and he never traveled without a box of candy. As he read plays he munched chocolates. He ate with a sort of Johnsonian avidity. When he went to Europe some of his friends, who knew his tastes well, sent him crates of pies instead of flowers or books.

He shared this fondness for sweets with Clyde Fitch. They did not dare to eat as much pastry as they liked before others, so they often retired to Frohman's rooms at Sherry's or to Fitch's house on Fortieth Street, in New York, and had a dessert orgy.

Frohman almost invariably ate as he worked in his office. When people saw sandwiches piled upon his table, he would say:

"A rehearsal accompanied by a sandwich is progress, but a rehearsal interrupted by a meal is delay."

Frohman's letters to his intimates were characteristic. He always wrote them with a blue pencil, and on whatever scrap of paper happened to be at hand. Often it was a sheet of yellow scratch-paper, sometimes the back of an envelope. He wrote as he talked, in quick, epigrammatic sentences. Like Barrie, he wrote one of the most indecipherable of hands. Frequently, instead of a note, he drew a picture to express a sentiment or convey an invitation. One reason for this was that the man saw all life in terms of the theater. It was a series of scenes.

With regard to home life, Frohman had none. He always dwelt in apartments in New York. The only two places where he really relaxed were at Marlow, in England, and at his country place near White Plains in Westchester County, New York. He shared the ownership of this establishment with Dillingham. It entered largely into his plans. Here his few intimates, like Paul Potter, Haddon Chambers, William Gillette, and Augustus Thomas, came and talked over plays and productions. Here, too, he kept vigil on the snowy night when London was to pass judgment on the first production of "Peter Pan" on any stage.

The way he came to acquire an interest in the White Plains house is typical of the man and his methods. Dillingham had bought the place. One day Frohman and Gillette lunched with him there. Frohman was immensely taken with the establishment. He liked the lawn, the garden, the trees, and the aloofness. The three men sat at a round table. Frohman beamed and said:

"This is the place for me. I want to sit at the head of this table." It was his way of saying that he wanted to acquire an ownership in it, and from that time on he was a co-proprietor.

With characteristic generosity he insisted upon paying two-thirds of the expenses. Then, in his usual lavish fashion, he had it remodeled. He wanted a porch built. Instead of engaging the village carpenter, who could have done it very well, he employed the most famous architects in the country and spent thirty thousand dollars. It was the Frohman way.

Out of the Frohman ownership of the White Plains house came one of the many Frohman jests. Its conduct was so expensive that Frohman one day said to Dillingham, "Let's rent a theater and make it pay for the maintenance of the house."

Frohman then leased the Garrick, but instead of making money on it he lost heavily.

The factotum at White Plains was the German Max, whom Dillingham had brought over from the Savoy in

London, where he was a waiter. Max became the center of many amusing incidents. One has already been related.

One night Max secured some fine watermelons. As he came through the door with one of them he slipped and dropped it. He repeated this performance with the second melon. Frohman regarded it as a great joke, and roared with laughter. Just then Gillette was announced.

"Now," said Frohman, quietly, to Dillingham, "we will have Max bring in a watermelon, but I want him to drop it." In order to insure the success of the trick they stretched a string at the door so that Max would be sure to fall. Then they ordered the melon, and Max appeared, bearing it aloft. He fell, however, before he got to the string, and the joke was saved.

All this jest and joke was part of the game of life as Frohman played it. Whatever the cost, there is no doubt that the charming white-and-green cottage up in the Westchester valley gave him hours of relaxation and ease that were among the pleasantest of his life.

This house at White Plains was indirectly the means through which Dillingham branched out as an independent manager. At this time he was in Frohman's employ. One day he said to himself:

"This establishment is costing so much that I will have to send out some companies of my own."

He thereupon got "The Red Mill," acquired Montgomery and Stone, and thus began a new and brilliant managerial career. No one rejoiced over Dillingham's success more than Frohman. When Dillingham opened his Globe Theater in New York Frohman addressed a cable to "Charles Dillingham, Globe Theater, U. S. A."

It is a curious fact about Charles Frohman that though he had millions of dollars at stake, he was never a defendant in litigation. Yet through him foreign authors were enabled to protect their plays from the customary piracy by the memorization of parts. It used to be accepted that if a man went to a play and memorized its speeches he could produce it without paying royalty. N. S. Wood did this with a play called "The World," that Frohman produced. He took the matter to court as a test case and won.

Charles was not good at remembering people's names or their addresses. This is why he was much dependent upon his stenographers. His secretary in England, Miss Frances Slater, was so extraordinary in anticipating his words that he always called her "The Wonder." He used to say:

"Miss Slater, I want to write to the man around the corner," which turned out to be Arthur Bouclier, the manager of the Garrick Theater, which was not really around the corner; but when the subject of the letter came to be dictated, Miss Slater knew whom he meant. He would never express any surprise on these occasions when the letter handed him to sign contained the right name and address. He seemed to take it as a matter of course.

One day Frohman entered his London office and said to Lestocq:

"You would never guess where I have just come from. I have been to your Westminster Abbey."

Lestocq expressed surprise, whereupon Frohman continued:

CHARLES FROHMAN'S OFFICE IN THE EMPIRE THEATER

THE MAN FROHMAN

"Yes, I just walked in and spoke to a man in a gown and said, 'Where is Mr. Irving buried?' He showed me, and I stood there for a few minutes, said a couple of things, and came on here."

Frohman's office at the Empire Theater was characteristic of the man himself. It was a room of considerable proportions, with the atmosphere of a study. It was lined with rather low book-shelves, on which stood the bound copies of the plays he had produced. Interspersed was a complete set of Lincoln's speeches and letters.

On one side was a large stone fireplace; in a corner stood a grand piano; the center was dominated by a simple, flat-topped desk, across which much of the traffic of the American theater passed.

Near at hand was a low and luxurious couch. Here Frohman sat cross-legged and listened to plays. This performance was a sort of sacred rite, and was always observed behind locked doors. No Frohman employee would think of intruding upon his chief at such a time.

Here, as in London, Frohman was surrounded by pictures of his stars. Dominating them was J. W. Alexander's fine painting of Miss Adams in "L'Aiglon." On a shelf stood a bust of John Drew. There were portraits of playwrights, too. A photograph of Clyde Fitch had this inscription:

"To C. F. from c. f."

There was only one real art object in the office, a magnificent marble bust of Napoleon, whom Frohman greatly admired. He was always pleased when he was told that he looked like the Man of Destiny.

His sense of personal modesty was a very genuine thing. Shortly before he sailed on the fatal trip he had a request from a magazine writer who wanted to write the story of his life. He sent back a vigorous refusal to co-operate, saying, among other things:

"It is most obnoxious to me in every way. It is forcing oneself on the public so far as I am concerned, and I don't want that, and, besides, they are not interested. It is only for the great men of our country. It is not for me. It looks like cheek and presumption on my part, because *it is*, and I ask you not to go on with it."

He believed in system. One day he said:

"We must have on file in our office the complete record of every first-class theater in the United States, together with the name of every dramatic editor and bill-poster." Out of this grew the famous "Theatrical Guide" compiled by Julius Cahn.

Charles always provided special sleepers for his company when they had to leave early in the morning. He felt that it was an imposition to make the people go to bed late after a play and rise at five or six to get a train. It not only expressed his kindness, but also his good business sense in keeping his people satisfied and efficient.

One of Frohman's eccentricities was that he never carried a watch. On being asked why he never carried a timepiece, he replied, tersely, "Everybody else carries a watch," meaning that if he wanted to find out the time of day he could do it more quickly by inquiring of his personal or business associates than by looking for a watch that he may have forgotten to wind up.

"Frohman," said a friend, "made it a rule in life not to do anything that he could hire somebody else to do, thus leaving himself all the time possible for those things that he alone could do. He probably figured it out that if he carried a watch he would be obliged to spend a certain amount of time each day winding it.

"And on the same principle he refused to worry as to whether he left his umbrella behind or not, by simply not carrying one. If he couldn't get a cab—a rare occurrence, doubtless, considering the beaten track of his travel—he preferred to walk in the rain."

Some time before his death Frohman said to a distinguished dramatist who is one of his closest friends:

"Whenever I make a rule I never violate it."

A visitor to his place at White Plains came away after spending a night there, and declared that the "real Charles Frohman had three dissipations—he smokes all day, he reads plays all night, and—" He stopped.

"What is it?" was the breathless query.

"He plays croquet."

Frohman had a rare gift for publicity. More than once he turned what seemed to be a complete failure into success. An experience with "Jane" will reveal this side of his versatility.

The bright little comedy hung fire for a while. One reason was that newspaper criticism in New York had been rather unfavorable. Conspicuous among the unfriendly notices was one in the *Herald* which was headed, "Jane Won't Go."

Frohman immediately capitalized this line. He had

thousands of dodgers stuck up all over New York. They contained three sentences, which read:

" Jane won't go."
Of course not.
She's come to stay.

From that time on the piece grew in popularity and receipts and became a success.

In summing up the qualities that made Frohman great, one finds, in the last analysis, that he had two in common with J. P. Morgan and the other dynamic leaders of men. One was an incisive, almost uncanny, ability to probe into the hearts of men, strip away the superficial, and find the real substance.

His experience with Clyde Fitch emphasized this to a remarkable degree. Personally no two men could have been more opposite. One was the product of democracy, buoyant and self-made, while the other represented an intellectual, almost effeminate, aristocracy. Yet nearly from the start Frohman perceived the bigness of vision and the profound understanding that lurked behind Fitch's almost superficial exterior.

In common, too, with Morgan, Roosevelt, and others of the same type, Frohman had an extraordinary quality of unconscious hypnotism. Men who came to him in anger went away in satisfied peace. They succumbed to what was an overwhelming and compelling personality.

He proved this in the handling of his women stars. They combined a group of varied and conflicting temperaments. Each wanted a separate and distinct place in his affections, and each got it. It was part of the

genius of the man to make each of his close associates
feel that he or she had a definite niche apart. His was
the perfecting understanding, and no one better expressed it than Ethel Barrymore, who said, "To try to
explain something to Charles Frohman was to insult
him."

XIX

*A*ND now the final phase.

The last years of Charles Frohman's life were racked with physical pain that strained his courageous philosophy to the utmost. Yet he faced this almost incessant travail just as he had faced all other emergencies—with composure.

One day in 1912 he fell on the porch of the house at White Plains and hurt his right knee. It gave him considerable trouble. At first he believed that it was only a bad bruise. In a few days articular rheumatism developed. It affected all of his joints, and it held him in a thrall of agony until the end of his life.

Shortly after his return to the city (he now lived at the Hotel Knickerbocker) he was compelled to take to his bed. For over six months he was a prisoner in his apartment, suffering tortures. Yet from this pain-racked post he tried to direct his large affairs. There was a telephone at his bedside, and he used it until weakness prevented him from holding the receiver.

He could not go to the theater, so the theater was brought to him. More than one preliminary rehearsal was held in his drawing-room. This was particularly true of musical pieces. The music distracted him from his pain.

376

Though prostrate with pain, his dogged determination to keep on doing things held. Barrie sent him the manuscript of a skit called "A Slice of Life." It was a brilliant satire on the modern play. Frohman picked Ethel Barrymore (who was then playing in "Cousin Kate" at the Empire), John Barrymore, and Hattie Williams to do it, and the rehearsals were held in the manager's rooms at the Knickerbocker.

Frohman was as much interested in this one-act piece as if it had been a five-act drama. His absorption in it helped to divert his mind from the pain that had sadly reduced the once rotund body.

With "A Slice of Life" he introduced another one of the many innovations that he brought to the stage. The play was projected as a surprise. No announcement of title was made. The advertisements simply stated that Charles Frohman would present "A Novelty" at the Empire Theater at eight o'clock on a certain evening.

Frohman was unable to attend the opening performance, so he wrote a little speech which was spoken by William Seymour. The speech was rehearsed as carefully as the play. A dozen times the stage-director delivered it before his chief, who indicated the various phrases to be emphasized.

It was during the era of the New Theater when the so - called "advanced drama" was much exploited. Frohman had little patience with this sort of dramatic thing. The little speech conveys something of his satirical feeling about the millionaire-endowed theatrical project which was then agitating New York.

Here is the speech as Frohman wrote it:

CHARLES FROHMAN

Ladies and Gentlemen:—My appearance here to-night is by way of apology. I am here representing Mr. Charles Frohman—you may have heard of him—the manager of this theater, the Empire.

His idea in announcing a novelty in connection with Miss Barrymore's play, "Cousin Kate," was really for the purpose of getting you here once in time for the ringing up of the curtain. This will be a special performance of a play to be given by a few rising members of the School of Acting connected with this theater, the Empire, of which he is proud—very proud. It is not an old modern play, but what is called to-day "The Advanced Drama," made possible here to-night by the momentary holiday of the New Theater, and it is called "A Slice of Life."

During those desperate days when, like Heinrich Heine, he seemed to be lying in a "mattress grave," his dauntless humor never forsook him, as this little incident will show: Some years previous, Gillette suffered a breakdown from overwork. When the actor-playwright went to his home at Hartford to recuperate his sister remonstrated with him.

"You must stop work for a long while," she said. "That man Frohman is killing you." Gillette afterward told Frohman about it.

Frohman now lay on a bed of agony, and Gillette came to see him. The sick man remembered the episode of the long ago, and said, weakly, to his visitor:

"Gillette, tell your sister that *you* are killing me."

With the martyrdom of incessant pain came a ripen-

378

ing of the man's character. Frohman developed a great admiration for Lincoln. Often he would ask Gillette to read him the famous "Gettysburg Address." Simple, haunting melodies like "The Lost Chord" took hold of him. Marie Doro was frequently summoned to play it for him on the piano. Although his courage did not falter, he looked upon men and events with a larger and deeper philosophy.

During that first critical stage of the rheumatism he sank very low. His two devoted friends, Dillingham and Paul Potter, came to him daily. Each had his regular watch. Dillingham came in the morning and read and talked with the invalid for hours. He managed to bring a new story or a fresh joke every day.

Potter reported at nine in the evening and remained until two o'clock in the morning, or at whatever hour sleep came to the relief of the sick man. One of the compensations of those long vigils was the phonograph. Frohman was very fond of a tune called "Alexander's Rag-Time Band." The nurse would put this record in the machine and then leave. When it ran out, Potter, who never could learn how to renew the instrument, simply turned the crank again. There were many nights when Frohman listened to this famous rag-time song not less than twenty times. But he did not mind it.

In his illness Frohman was like a child. He was afraid of the night. He begged Potter to tell him stories, and the author of so many plays spun and unfolded weird and wonderful tales of travel and adventure. Like a child, too, Frohman kept on saying, "More, more," and often Potter went on talking into the dawn.

Potter, like all his comrades in that small and devoted group of Frohman intimates, did his utmost to shield his friend from hurt. When Frohman launched a new play during those bedridden days Potter would wait until the so-called "bull-dog" editions of the morning papers (the very earliest ones) were out. Then he would go down to the street and get them. If the notice was favorable he would read it to Frohman. If it was unfriendly Potter would say that the paper was not yet out, preferring that the manager read the bad news when it was broad daylight and it could not interfere with his sleep.

The humor and comradeship which always marked Frohman's close personal relations were not lacking in those nights when the life of the valiant little man hung by a thread. When all other means of inducing sleep failed, Potter found a sure cure for insomnia.

"Just as soon as I talked to Frohman about my own dramatic projects," he says, "he would fall asleep. So, when the night grew long and the travel stories failed, and even "Alexander's Rag-Time Band" grew stale, I would start off by saying: 'I have a new play in mind. This is the way the plot goes.' Then Frohman's eyes would close; before long he would be asleep, and I crept noiselessly out."

Occasionally during those long conflicts with pain Frohman saw through the glass darkly. His intense and constant suffering, for the time, put iron into his well-nigh indomitable soul.

"I'm all in," he would say to Potter. "The luck is against me. The star system has killed my judgment. I no longer know a good play from a bad. The sooner they 'scrap' me the better."

His thin fingers tapped on the bedspread, and, like Colonel Newcome, he awaited the Schoolmaster's final call.

"You and I," he would continue, "have seen our period out. What comes next on the American stage? Cheap prices, I suppose. Best seats everywhere for a dollar, or even fifty cents; with musical shows alone excepted. Authors' royalties cut to ribbons; actors' salaries pared to nothing. Popular drama, bloody, murderous, ousting drawing-room comedy. Crook plays, shop-girl plays, slangy American farces, nude women invading the auditorium as in Paris."

"And then?" asked Potter.

"Chaos," said he. "Fortunately you and I won't live to see it. Turn on the phonograph and let 'Alexander's Rag-time Band' cheer us up."

He got well enough to walk around with a stick, and with movement came a return of the old enthusiasm. A man of less indomitable will would have succumbed and become a permanent invalid. Not so with Frohman. He even got humor out of his misfortune, because he called his cane his "wife." He became a familiar sight on that part of Broadway between the Knickerbocker Hotel and the Empire Theater as he walked to and fro. It was about all the walking he could do.

He kept on producing plays, and despite the physical hardships under which he labored he attended and conducted rehearsals. With the pain settling in him more and more, he believed himself incurable. Yet less than four people knew that he felt that the old titanic power was gone, never to return.

The great war, on whose stupendous altar he was to be an innocent victim, affected him strangely. The horror, the tragedy, the wantonness of it all touched him mightily. Indeed, it seemed to be an obsession with him, and he talked about it constantly, unmindful of the fact that the cruel destiny that was shaping its bloody course had also marked him for death.

Early during the war he saw some verses that made a deep impression on him. They were called "In the Ambulance," and related to the experience of a wounded soldier. He learned them by heart, and he never tired of repeating them. They ran like this:

> "*Two rows of cabbages;*
> *Two of curly greens;*
> *Two rows of early peas;*
> *Two of kidney-beans.*"
>
> *That's what he's muttering,*
> *Making such a song,*
> *Keeping all the chaps awake*
> *The whole night long.*
>
> *Both his legs are shot away,*
> *And his head is light,*
> *So he keeps on muttering*
> *All the blessed night:*
>
> "*Two rows of cabbages;*
> *Two of curly greens;*
> *Two rows of early peas,*
> *And two of kidney-beans.*"

It was Frohman's intense feeling about the war that led him to produce "The Hyphen." Its rejection by the public hurt him unspeakably. Yet he regarded the fate of the play as just one more phase of the big game of life. He smiled and went his way.

The rheumatism still oppressed him, but he turned

his face resolutely toward the future. War or peace, pain or relief, he was not to be deprived of his annual trip to England. He was involved in some litigation that required his presence in London. Besides, the city by the Thames called to him, and behind this call was the appeal of old and loved associations. With all his wonted enthusiasm he wrote to his friends at Marlow telling them that he was coming over and that he would soon be in their midst.

Frohman now made ready for this trip. When he announced that he was going on the *Lusitania* his friends and associates made vigorous protest, which he derided with a smile. Thus, in the approach to death, just as in the path to great success, opposition only made him all the more decided. With regard to his sailing on the *Lusitania*, this tenacity of purpose was his doom.

Whether he had a premonition or not, the fact remains that he said and did things during the days before he sailed which uncannily suggested that the end was not unexpected. For one thing, he dictated his whole program for the next season before he started. It was something that he had never done before.

When Marie Doro came to his office to say good-by he pulled out a little red pocket note-book in which he jotted down many things and suddenly said: "Queer, but the little book is full. There is no room for anything else."

Just as he was warned not to produce "The Hyphen," so was he now cautioned by anonymous correspondents (and even by mysterious telephone messages) not to take the *Lusitania*. But all this merely tightened his purpose.

He met the danger with his usual jest. On the day

before he sailed he went up to bid his old friend and colleague, Al Hayman, good-by. Hayman, like all his associates, warned him not to go on the *Lusitania*.

"Do you think there is any danger?" asked Frohman.

"Yes, I do," replied Hayman.

"Well, I am going, anyhow," was the answer.

After he had shaken hands he stopped at the door and said, smilingly:

"Well, Al, if you want to write to me just address the letter care of the German Submarine U 4."

Those last days ashore were filled with a strange mellowness. Ethel Barrymore came down from Boston to see him. They had an intimate talk about the old days. When she left him she saw tears in his eyes. That night, just as she was about to go on in "The Shadow" in Boston, she received this telegram from him:

Nice talk, Ethel. Good-by. C. F.

The *Lusitania* sailed at ten o'clock on Saturday morning, May 1, 1915. Even at the dock Frohman could not resist his little joke. When Paul Potter, who saw him off, said to him:

"Aren't you afraid of the U boats, C. F.?"

"No, I am only afraid of the I O U's," was the reply.

In his farewell steamer letter to Dillingham, written as the huge ship was plowing her way down the bay, he drew a picture of a submarine attacking a transatlantic liner. The last lines he wrote on the boat were prophetic of his fate. Ann Murdock had sent him a large steamer basket in the shape of a ship. The lines to her, brought back by the ship's pilot, were:

"WHY FEAR DEATH?"

*The little ship you sent is more wonderful
than the big one that takes me away from you.*

Like most of his distinguished fellow-voyagers, and
they included Charles Klein, Elbert Hubbard, Justus
Miles Forman, and Alfred G. Vanderbilt, Frohman had
frequently traveled on the *Lusitania*. By a curious
coincidence he had once planned to use her sister ship,
the *Mauretania*, for one of his daring innovations. He
had a transatlantic theater in mind. In other words, he
proposed to produce whole plays on shipboard. He
took over a small company headed by Marie Doro to
try out the experiment. Early on the voyage Miss
Doro succumbed to seasickness and the project was
abandoned.

The last journey of the *Lusitania* was uneventful until
that final fateful day. Frohman had kept to his cabin
during the greater part of the trip. He was still suffering great pain in his right knee, and walked the deck
with difficulty. Occasionally he appeared in the smoking-room, and was present at the ship's concert on the
night before the end.

At 2.33 o'clock on the afternoon of May 7th the great
vessel rode to her death. Eight miles off the Head of
Kinsale, and within sight of the Irish coast, she was
torpedoed by a German submarine. She sank in half
an hour, with frightful loss of life, including more than
a hundred Americans.

Frohman's hour was at hand, and he met it with the
smiling equanimity and unflinching courage with which
he had faced every other crisis in his life. When the
crash came he was on the upper promenade deck. He
had just come from his luncheon and was talking with

George Vernon, the brother-in-law of Rita Jolivet, the actress, who was also on board. They were now joined by Captain Scott, an Englishman on his way from India to enlist. When Miss Jolivet reached them Frohman was smoking a cigar and was calm and apparently undisturbed.

Scott went below to get some life-belts. He returned with only two. He had started up with three, but gave one to a woman on the way. Miss Jolivet had provided herself with a belt.

Scott started to put one of the life-preservers on Frohman, who protested. Finally, with great reluctance, he acquiesced. There was no belt left for Scott. Frohman insisted that he get one, whereupon the soldier said:

"If you must die, it is only for once."

There was a responsive look and a whimsical smile on Frohman's face at this remark. He kept on smoking. Then he started to talk about the Germans. "I didn't think they would do it," he said. He was apparently the most unruffled person on the ship.

The great liner began to lurch. Frohman now said to Miss Jolivet:

"You had better hold on the rail and save your strength."

The ship's list became greater; huge waves rolled up, carrying wreckage and bodies on their crest. Then, with all the terror of destruction about him, Frohman said to his associates, with the serene smile still on his face:

"Why fear death? It is the most beautiful adventure of life."

Instinctively the four people moved closer together, they joined hands by a common impulse, and stood awaiting the end.

The ship gave a sudden lurch; once more a mighty green cliff of water came rushing up, bearing its tide of dead and debris; again Frohman started to say the speech that was to be his valedictory. He had hardly repeated the first three words—"Why fear death?"—when the group was engulfed and all sank beneath the surface of the sea.

No situation of the thousands that he had created in the theater was so vividly or so unaffectedly dramatic as the great manager's own exit from the stage. of life. Smilingly he had made his way through innumerable difficulties; smilingly and with the highest heroism he met his fate.

The only survivor of the quartet that stood hand in hand on those death-cluttered decks was Miss Jolivet, and it was she who told the story of those last thrilling minutes.

Charles Frohman's body was recovered the next day and brought to Queenstown. A fortnight later it reached New York. On the casket was the American flag that the dead man had loved so well. Though princes of capital, famous playwrights, and international authorities on law and art went down with him, the loss of Frohman overshadowed all others. In the eyes of the world, the loss of the *Lusitania* was the loss of Charles Frohman.

His noble and eloquent final words, so rich with courageous philosophy, not only joined the category of the great farewells of all time, but wherever read or uttered will give humanity a fresher faith with which to meet the inevitable. In a supreme moment of the most colossal drama that human passion ever staged, fate literally hurled him into the universal lime-light to enact

a part that gave him an undying glory. The shyest of men became the world's observed.

The last tribute to Charles Frohman was the most remarkable demonstration of sorrow in the history of the theater. The one-time barefoot boy of Sandusky, Ohio, who had projected so many people into eminenc and who had himself hidden behind the rampart of his own activities, was widely mourned.

The principal funeral services were held at the Temple Emanu-El in New York. Here gathered a notable assemblage that took reverent toll of all callings and creeds. It was proud to do honor to the man who had achieved so much and who had died so heroically.

At the bier Augustus Thomas delivered an eloquent address that fittingly summed up the life and purpose of the greatest force that the English-speaking theater has yet known. Among other things he said:

"A wise man counseled, 'Look into your heart and write': 'C. F.' looked into his heart and listened. He had that quoted quality of genius that made him believe his own thought, made him know that what was true for him in his private heart was true for all mankind. That was the secret of his power. It was the golden key to both his understanding and expression.

"He was a fettered and a prisoned poet, often in his finest moments inarticulate. Working in the theater with his companies and stars, with the women and the men who knew and loved him, he accomplished less by word than by a radiating vital force that brought them into his intensity of feeling. In his social intercourse and comradeship, telling a dramatic or a comic story, at a certain pressure of its progress where other men depend on paragraphs and phrases he coined a near-

CHARLES FROHMAN ON BOARD SHIP

Appendix A

*U*NLIKE many men of achievement, Charles Frohman was not a prolific letter-writer. He avoided letter-writing whenever it was possible. When he could not convey his message orally he resorted to the telegraph. Letters were the last resort.

He had a sort of constitutional objection to long letters. The only lengthy epistles that ever came from him were dictated and referred to matters of business. They all have one quality in common. As soon as he had concluded the discussion of the topic in mind he would immediately tell about the fortunes of his plays. He seldom failed to make a reference to the business that Maude Adams was doing (for her immense success was very dear to his heart), and he always commented on his own strenuous activities. He liked to talk about the things he was doing.

The really intimate Frohman letters were always written by hand on scraps of paper, and were short, jerky, and epigrammatic. Most of these were written, or rather scratched, to intimates like James M. Barrie, Paul Potter, and Haddon Chambers.

As indicated in one of the chapters of this book, Frohman delighted in caricature. To a few of his friends he would send a humorous cartoon instead of a letter. He caricatured whatever he saw, whether riding on trains or eating in restaurants. If he wanted a friend to dine with him he would sketch a rough head and mark it "Me"; then he would draw another head and label it "You." Between these heads

26   393

he would make a picture of a table, and under it scrawl, "Knickerbocker, Friday, 7 o'clock."

Frohman seldom used pen and ink. Most of his letters were written with the heavy blue editorial pencil that he liked to use. He wrote an atrocious hand. His only competitor in this way was his close friend Barrie. The general verdict among the people who have read the writing of both men is that Frohman took the palm for illegible chirography.

Frohman could pack a world of meaning into his letters. To a fellow-manager who had written to Boston to ask if he had seen a certain actress play, he replied: "No, I have had the great pleasure of *not* seeing her act."

His letters reflect his moods and throw intimate light on his character. He would always have his joke. To William Collier, who had sent him a box for a play that he was doing in New York, he once wrote: "I do not think I will have any difficulty in finding your theater, although a great many new theaters have gone up. Many old ones have 'gone up' too."

His swift jugglery with words is always manifest. To Alfred Sutro he sent this sentence notifying him that his play was to go into rehearsal: "The die is cast—but not the play."

Through his letters there shines his uncompromising rule of life. Writing to W. Lestocq, his agent in London, in reference to the English failure of "Years of Discretion," he said: "It is a failure, and that is the end of it. You can't get around failure, so we must go on to something else."

The number of available Frohman letters is not large. The following, gathered from various sources, will serve to indicate something of their character:

To an English author whose play, a weak one, was rapidly failing:

No; it is not the war that is affecting your business. It is the play—nothing else.

To Cyril Maude, whose penmanship is notably indecipherable:

I can't read your handwriting very well; but I wonder if you can read my typewriting. Just pretend I typed this myself. . . . Speaking of hits, Granville Barker arrived yesterday, and the city suddenly became terribly cold—awful weather. Barker will do well.

To Haddon Chambers:

Last night we produced "Driven" against your judgment. The press not favorable. But still I'm hoping.

To a colleague:

I announced "Driven" as a comedy. Next day I called it a play. But soon I may call it off.

To W. Lestocq:

The American actors over here are worried about so many English actors in our midst. I employ both kinds—that is, I want good actors only.

To an English author:

As to conditions here being bad for good plays; that is a joke. The distressful business is for the bad plays that I and other managers sometimes produce.

To one of his managers:

Do not use the line "The World-Famous Tri-Star Combination." Just say "The Great Three-Star Combination." It is easier to understand. And all will be well.

To one of his managers who spoke of the superiority of an actress who had replaced another about to retire to private life:

But now that her stage life is over we should remember her years of good work. She had a simple, childish, fairy-like appeal. I write this to you to express my feeling for one who has left our work for good, and I can think now only of pleasant memories. I want you to feel the same.

To an English author, January, 1915:

Over here they say the real heroes of the year are the managers that dare produce new plays.

CHARLES FROHMAN

To a business colleague about a singing comedian who was laid up with a serious illness:

I am sorry he is sick. But that was a rotten thing for him to do—to steal our song. I suppose he is better. Only the good die young.

To Marie Doro:

I saw you in the picture play. It and you were fine. What a lot of money you make! When I return from London I'm going to see if I can earn $10 a day to play in some of the screens. We are all going up to the Atlantic Ocean Island to see them taking you in the "White Pearl" pictures.

Refusing to go to a public banquet:

That's the first free thing that has been offered me this year. But there are three things my physician forbids me from doing—to eat, drink, or talk.

To a manager:

There are no bad towns—only bad plays!

On hearing that an actress in his employ had reflected on his management:

In this message I am charged with neglecting your interests. This is a shock to me, because when one neglects his trust, he is dishonest. This is the first time I have ever been so accused, and I am wondering if you inspired the message. I think it important that you should know.

Being adjured by one of the family to take more exercise:

I drove out to Richmond. Then I walked a mile. Now I hope you'll be satisfied.

To his sisters (he lived then at the Waldorf, but joined the family at a weekly dinner up-town):

I am sending you a cook-book by Oscar of this hotel. You may find some use for it.

396

APPENDIX A

When he came to the next weekly dinner he was offered several choice dishes prepared from Oscar's recipes. "I see my mistake," he said. "I wanted my usual home dinner. You give me what I receive all the time at the hotel."

To Alfred Sutro, in London:

Give us something full of situations, and we will give you a bully time again in America.

To William Seymour, his stage-manager, about a performance of one of his plays:

When you rehearse to-day will you try and get the old woman out of too much crying; get some smiles, and stop her screwing up her face every time she speaks. Of course, it's nervousness, but it looks as if she were ill.

To one of his associates:

Miss Adams's receipts last week in Boston were the largest in the history of Boston theaters or anywhere— $23,000. But I had some others which I won't tell you about.

To an English author in 1913:

At present the taste is "down with light plays, down with literary plays." They want plays with dramatic situations, intrigue, sex conflict. There is no use in giving the public what it does not want and what they ought to have. I am just finding that out, with much cost.

To a French agent:

It seems a little reckless to be asked to pay $2,500 for the privilege of reading a new French play. The author seems to want to get rich quickly. I would be willing to add to his wealth if he has something that can be produced without such a preliminary penalty.

To W. Lestocq:

When one talks to an English author about "Diplomacy," he says, "Oh, that's a theatrical play!" I wish I could get another like it.

CHARLES FROHMAN

To an English manager:

A hundred theaters here are a few too many. Houses have closed on a Saturday night without any warning. Boston, Chicago, and Philadelphia have been better. You see we have this wonderful country to fall back on, which makes it different from London.

To an author in London:

What you say is quite true; a good play is a good play; but the difficulty I find is to ascertain through the public and the box-office what *they* think is a good play. Our opinion is only good for ourselves. But give me a dramatic play and I'll put it at once to the test.

To Hubert Henry Davies, the dramatist, during an interim of that author's activities:

It grieves me when I can't get your material going, especially as I want to come over as soon as I can and get one of those nice lunches in your nice apartment.

To the manager of an up-state New York theater regarding an impending first-night performance:

I hope we shall draw a representative audience the first night. I know audiences with you are sometimes a little reluctant about first nights. I can't understand this myself. In my opinion there is an extra thrill for them in the experience of a first performance, as it is a special event.

To Granville Barker, January, 1913:

I am very jealous of the Barrie plays, and I do want them for my own theater for revivals. . . . I hear such good reports about your Shakespearian work that I am awfully pleased. I have had a Marconi from Shakespeare himself, in which he speaks highly of what you have done for his work. I am sure this will be as gratifying to you as it is to me.

APPENDIX A

Alluding to his painful rheumatism in a letter to George Edwardes, the producer, in England, January, 1913:

I can't run twelve yards, but I can drink a lot of that bottled lemonade of yours when I get over. In fact, at the moment I think that is the best thing running in London.

In February, 1913, Frohman made frequent trips to Baltimore to rehearse and superintend the production of his plays in that city. He has this to say of Baltimore in a letter to Tunis F. Dean, manager of a theater there:

I was glad to have an opportunity of seeing your fine theater, for I have decided on a very important production with one of our leading stars there next season. So that I shall spend a week in Baltimore. I like that. There is no one living in Baltimore that has a greater regard for that fine, dignified city. I have had it for years, and with the beautiful theater and my feeling for Baltimore and you at the head of that theater, I am looking forward with pleasure to coming to you next season.

Frohman was simple, direct, and forcible in his criticism of plays. In rejecting a French play, he wrote to Michael Morton in defense of his judgment, New York, February, 1913:

I was awfully glad you made arrangements for the play, the one I don't like, and I hope the other fellow is right. These three-cornered French plays are going to have a hard time over here in the future unless they contain something that is pretty big, novel, or human. The guilty wife is a joke here now, and they have lots of fun when they play these scenes in these plays. The American and English play is different. They get there quicker in a different manner instead of the old-fashioned scheme. Of course, French plays, as you say, may be laid in England and in America. I understand that. But even then it seems to be about the same as if they were in France.

CHARLES FROHMAN

His brief, epigrammatic style of criticism is evident in a letter to Charles B. Dillingham, wherein he speaks of a certain play under consideration:

I think the end of the play is not good. It is that old-time stand-around-with-a-glass-of-wine-in-your-hand and wish success to the happy people.

Extracts from an interview with Frohman which he wrote for the London papers, March, 1913:

There will be no change in my work of producing for the London stage. I shall continue to do so at my own theaters or with other London managers just as long as I am producing on any stage, and I fear that will be for a long time yet, as I am younger now than I was twenty years ago.

Prior to his departure for England he wrote the following to John Drew in March, 1913:

Thanks for your fine letter. It is like this, John: I hope to get off next week, but I don't seem to be able to get the accommodations I want on either one of the steamers that I should like to travel on, and that sail next week. I need a little special accommodation on account of my leg, which still refuses to answer my call and requires the big stick.

To Alfred Sutro, in January, 1913, on the current taste in plays:

These American plays with thieves, burglars, detectives, and pistols seem to be the real things over here just now. None of them has failed.

Memorandum for his office-boy, Peter, for a week's supply of his favorite drinks:

Get me plenty of orange-juice, lemon soda, ginger ale, sarsaparilla, buttermilk.

To Alfred Sutro, 1913:

Haddon Chambers sails to-day. You may see him before you see this. He leaves behind him what I think

In these great days of the superiority of woman over mere man I don't think it would do.

Referring to a young actress he wished to secure, he writes to Col. Henry W. Savage in January, 1913:

My dear Colonel: I want to enter on your works in this way. You have a girl called ————. I know she is very good, because I have never seen her act, but I understand she is not acting just as you want her to, and therefore not playing, either because she is laying off, or that you have stopped her from playing. I have a part for which I could use this girl. Will you let me have her, and in that way do another great wrong by doing me a favor? If she doesn't, or you do not wish her to play, perhaps it would be as much satisfaction to you if you thought you were doing me a favor and let her play in my company as if she were not playing at all. My best regards, and I hope this letter will not add much to the many pangs of the season to you.

To Sir James M. Barrie, October, 1913:

As I wrote you, I felt we had a good opportunity here under the conditions here, and I produced your "The Dramatists Get What They Want" last night. It went splendidly with the audiences, and has very good press. Of course the class of first-night audience that we had last night understood it. The censor is a new thing over here. The general public don't understand it, and it may on that account not make so strong an impression on further audiences. However, that is all right. I am delighted with the way it went, and you would have been delighted had you been present. I think the press was very good when you consider the subject is so new to us. The three plays have all, I assure you, been nicely done, well produced and cast, and you would be pleased with them as I am pleased in having had them to produce. It helped considerably with plays that would not have made much of an impression without them. It has keep our troupes moving so much that I am compelled to postpone my sailing until April 12th on the *Olympic*, which makes it just a little later when I have the joy of seeing you. My best regards.

To Richard Harding Davis, July, 1913:

All right, we'll fix the title. I am glad they are asking about it. About people, they all seem to want Collier salaries. As you have chiefly character parts, and they are so good, I think it would be a good idea for us to create a few new stars through you, and

Yours truly,
CHARLES FROHMAN.

To George Edwardes, July, 1913:

First, I am glad to hear that you are away giving your heart a chance. I am back here trying to give my pocket-book a chance.

To William Collier, September, 1913:

All right, all arranged, Thursday night in New York; Monday and Tuesday in Springfield, Massachusetts. I shall leave here Monday ready to meet the performance and anything else! I hope all is well.

To Viola Allen, September, 1913:

I was awfully glad to get your letter. First let me say you had better come to see "Much Ado About Nothing" this Saturday, because it is the last week. We withdraw it to-morrow night and produce a new program at once. "Much Ado" wouldn't do for more than two weeks. After that it fell. Of course I find on Broadway it is quite impossible to run Shakespeare to satisfying "star" receipts. So come along to-morrow if you can. It would be fine to have you, and fine to have some of the original members of the Empire company to play in this house, and I should like it beyond words. I don't, however, believe in that sex-against-sex play.

APPENDIX A

will give him many happy returns (box-office) of the season, as Miss Barrymore is doing so well with his "Tante."

To W. Lestocq, concerning one of his leading London actresses:

Miss Titheridge is all right, as I wrote Morton, if her emotions can be kept down, and if she can try to make the audience act more, and act less herself.

To Michael Morton regarding an actress:

She needs to be told that real acting is not to act, but to make the audience feel, and not feel so much herself.

To the editor of a popular monthly magazine upon its first birthday:

I understand that your September issue will be made to mark ⸺'s first birthday. Judging from your paper your birthday plans miss the issue; because ⸺ becomes a year younger every September. I do *not* congratulate you even upon this fact; because you cannot help it. I do *not* congratulate your readers because they get your paper so very cheap. I *do* congratulate myself, however, for calling attention to these wonderful facts.

To W. Lestocq, referring to a statement made by R. C. Carton, the dramatist:

I don't quite understand what he means by "holding up" the play. Over here it is a desperate expression— one that means pistols and murder, and all that. I presume it means something different in London, where Carton lives.

To Mrs. C. C. Cushing, the playwright, declining an invitation:

It is impossible to come and see you because I haven't got Cottage No. 4, but I've got Cell No. 3 on the stage of the Empire Theater, where I am passing the summer months.

CHARLES FROHMAN

*Even Frohman's cablegrams reflected his humor. In 1913
Billie Burke was ill at Carlsbad, so he cabled her some cheering
message nearly every day. Here is a sample:*

> Drove past your house to-day and ran over a dog.
> Your brother glared at me.

*When Blanche Bates's first baby was born (she was at her
country house near Ossining at the time), Frohman sent her
this message:*

> Ossining has now taken its real place among the
> communities of the country. Congratulations.

To Alfred Sutro, January, 1913:

> I was glad to hear from you. First let me strongly
> advise you to take the comedy side for the Alexander
> play. I honestly believe, unless it is something enormous,
> and for big stars and all that, the other side is no good
> any more. For the present, anyway, I speak of my own
> country. The usual serious difficulties between a hus-
> band and wife of that class—really they laugh at here
> now, instead of touching their emotions. They have
> gone along so rapidly. Take my advice in this matter,
> do! I am glad you have dropped that scene from the
> third act of your Du Maurier play.
> Now that I am back to town I intended writing you
> about it. I assure you I had a jolly good time for the
> first two acts of that farce, and I can see Gerald Du
> Maurier all through it. The third act worries me for
> this country, as I wrote you. But the performance may
> change all this. It is so difficult to judge farcical work
> where it is so thoroughly English in its scene that I
> speak of to get any idea from the reading of it for
> this country. Everything is going along splendidly.

To Haddon Chambers, March, 1913:

> I propose, and the troupes dispose! We had a lot
> of floods and things here which keep us on the move, or

APPENDIX A

helped the general business of these plays, which, although it is not great, is good, and makes a fair average every week. It is chiefly what you would call "stall" business. "The Will" has been a fine thing for John Drew, and he is very happy in it. He has made a very deep impression indeed. I think the part with the changes of character as played by him has made it really a star part. If you have any more of them, send them along.

To W. Somerset Maugham, October, 1913:

Regarding the first act of "The Land of Promise," this is what I think, and maybe you will think the same, and, if you do, give me a good speech. Send it as soon as you can. I think that we should have a different ending to the first act, uplifting the ending. After the girl tells about her brother being married, wouldn't it be a good idea for her to say something like this, in your own language, of course: "Canada! Canada! You are right." (Turning to Miss Pringle), "England, why should I stay in England? I'm young, I want gaiety, new life. Then why not go to a young country where all is life and gaiety and sunshine and joy and youth— the land of promise, the land for me?" Remember, in the last act she speaks of all she expected to find and how different the realization. This new idea of the end of the first act will help this speech, I think. And besides uplifting the ending, gives the great contrast we want to show in the play and is driven into the minds of the audience at the end of the first act. Give the girl a good uplifting speech at the end of the first act, instead of a downward one. That is what I mean. Then after that we get the contrast of the countries. I hope this is clear and you will understand what I mean.

To J. E. Dodson, October, 1913:

My greatest regret is that my profession takes me to Baltimore on the day that you are giving the dinner at

the Lotus Club to my friend Cyril Maude. It would give me the greatest pleasure to eat his health with you. I rejoice that you are giving recognition on his first arrival here in New York to such a sincere actor and such a real man. He belongs to all countries.

To Haddon Chambers, June, 1911:

Had a fine trip over. Found it hot here. Started in building your scenery. Am only dropping you a line because I want to ask you, while I think of it, if you will get a copy of that special morning dress that Gerald wears at the beginning of the second act, for Richard Bennett. I think it would be a good idea to bring it over. Bennett is not quite as tall as Du Maurier and just a bit thicker, and as it is a sort of loose dress there will be no difficulty in fitting it here.

Now our cast is in good shape for your play, and I am very pleased with it. We have an asylum full of children awaiting your selection on your arrival.

To Sir Arthur Wing Pinero, August, 1911:

The man I selected to produce your play is Charles Frohman. He is not only good at producing plays that have never been staged before, but he likes your play thoroughly. He has made such a careful study of it that he believes that he knows it in every detail. He feels confident of his ability to handle it and to make the changes you have made just as he thinks you and your public over here would like to have it done.

To Sir James M. Barrie, London, September, 1911:

This will be signed for me, as I am still confined to my bed—fighting rheumatism. I thought I would not write you until you return to London. All goes well here. So far my new productions have met with success. Miss Barrymore began in Mason's play last night in Trenton, New Jersey. The play was well received before a large audience. Miss Adams begins the new season in Buffalo

next Monday night. I am hoping within the next two weeks to be able to get out on crutches. I have been to many rehearsals. They carry me in a Bath chair to and from the theater.

To Somerset Maugham, September, 1911:

Thanks for yours. I am still down with rheumatism —partly on account of the weather, but more especially because you are not doing any work.

To a New York critic, October, 1911:

I hope in two or three weeks to be able to see myself as other good critics, like you, would see me—well and about again in my various theaters.

To Sir James M. Barrie, November, 1911:

Your letter was a delight, and it will be fine news for Miss Adams. I hope you will send the material as soon as you can. Here I am dictating to you from bed; so I will be brief. My foot is now tied to a rope which is tied to the bed with weights. They are trying to stretch the leg. I am hoping that in three or four weeks I may be able to sit around. Five months on one's back is not good for much more than watching aeroplanes.

To Sir James M. Barrie, December, 1911:

I was very glad to get your letter. I am still in bed, so that I am obliged to dictate this letter to you. The manuscript arrived, but found me out of condition to read it. I sent it on at once to Maude Adams. She telegraphed me how delighted she is with it, and I have had a letter from her telling me what a remarkable piece of work it is. When she gets back to town I shall read the manuscript. Any plan you work out for London will be fine. I should judge, without knowing, that your idea for matinées is the best.

I am hoping that in another month I will be out; I am living on that hope. Then I will commence to think about coming over to you. I dare not think of it until I once more get out, I am afraid. All this has naturally disturbed my London season. I am happy in the thought that we will soon have "Peter" on again in London. What a difference your plays made to my London season! I shall write you again soon. "Peter and Wendy" is fine. My most affectionate remembrances.

To Sir James M. Barrie, January, 1912:

I cabled you on receiving your letter because my voice was leaving me rapidly. It was a case of a bad throat, and I wanted to get some reply to you quickly. My throat is better now. I have had about everything, and I fear I shall have to keep to my rooms for some time to come. I hope to see you around the end of March.

I think your Shakespearian play is a most wonderful work. I quite appreciate all you say about its chances. I rather felt that a Shakespearian novelty of this kind would be most striking if produced by Tree on top of his newspaper claim of having lost over 40,000 pounds on Shakespeare.

I am all bungled up here. I don't know quite what to do about London this season. As I understood what you wanted, I replied as I did. You know how I hate to lose any of your work for anybody or anywhere. Now you understand. That is splendid about the Phillpotts play, and I thank you. I am hoping about the Pinero play. I shall be glad to see you.

This is all the voice I have left for dictation; so I end with my best regards.

To David Belasco, February, 1912:

This is written for me. I am still confined to my rooms, and, although able to sit up during the day for work, I do not get out in the evening. I was glad to hear from you, and I hope you will telephone that you will come round any old night that suits you.

I wish you could play "Peter Grimm" up here; I'd like to see it.

APPENDIX A

I haven't written you because lately I have been having a lot of pain. I sent you papers which will tell you how wonderfully your fine play—"A Slice of Life"—has been received. It has caused a tremendous lot of talk; but I just want to tell you that there is absolutely no comparison, in performance, as the play is given here and the way it was given in London. Fine actors, although the London cast had, my people here seem to have a better grasp of what you wanted. They have brought it out with a sincerity and intelligence of stroke that is quite remarkable. Ethel Barrymore never did better work. Her emotional breakdown, tears, her humiliation—when she confesses to her husband that she had been a good woman even before she met him, all this is managed in a keener fashion, and with even a finer display of stage pathos than she showed in her fine performance in "Mid-Channel."

As the husband, Jack Barrymore is every inch a John Drew. He feels, and makes the audience feel, the humiliation of his position. When he confesses, it is a terrible confession. Hattie Williams, in her odd manner, imitated Nazimova—as Nazimova would play a butler.

So these artists step out into the light—before a houseful of great laughter; one feels that they have struck the true note of what you meant your play should have. I think the impossible seriousness of triangle scenes in modern plays has been swept off the stage here—and "A Slice of Life" has done it. . . .

The effect of "A Slice of Life" is even greater and more general than "The Twelve-Pound Look." All agree that each year you have given our stage the real novelty of its theatrical season. And the fine thing about it is that you have given me the opportunity of putting these before the public.

I am getting along very slowly. I am able to do my work in my rooms and go on crutches for a couple of hours at rehearsals. But always I am in great pain.

I hope to see you by the end of March. I don't know whether you will shake my hand or my crutch. But I expect to be there. We can take up the matters of "A Slice of Life," etc., then.

I am so delighted about "Peter Pan" this season. I am wondering if you have done anything about that Shakespeare play, which I believe would be another big novelty.

To Sir Arthur Wing Pinero, March, 1912:

Perhaps this will reach you on your return from the Continent. I hope you have made a good trip and that you are happy.

I hope to give you for the "Mind the Paint Girl" Miss Billie Burke, who is an enormous attraction here. She played in her little piece from the French last week in St. Louis to $15,700. All the way along the line her houses are sold out completely before her appearance. Her play is only a slight thing—an adaptation from the French, but play-goers seem to have gone wild over her. Besides this, she is not only handsome, but every inch the very personification of the "Paint Girl." Moreover, she is a genuinely human actress. It will be a big combination for me to make—the large cast required for the "Paint Girl," together with this valuable star and your great play.

To John Drew, March, 1912:

I am glad to hear from you and to know that you are having freezingly cold weather in the South. The joke is on the people here. They think you are having such nice warm weather.

I am getting along pretty well. I am about the same as when you left me except that there is great excitement among my doctors because I can now move my small toe.

To Sir James M. Barrie, September, 1913:

"Half an Hour" has been going splendidly and had a fine reception the first night. The majority of the press were splendid indeed, one or two felt an awakening to see the change in the work that you have been doing. I am awfully pleased the way it came out. I am delighted to see that you have added another act to the "Adored One." That makes it a splendid program for Miss Adams. Making it a three-act play is fine for this side, as I cabled you. All the Americans coming home who have seen your play are delighted with it in every way. Hope all is going well. I am leaving tomorrow to meet Maude Adams and see the piece that she is now playing called "Peter Pan." I shall be away from New York for perhaps a week, and on my return I will write you again fully.

To Alfred Sutro, September, 1911:

You know how happy your success has made me. You know how I longed for it. You know all that so thoroughly that words were not necessary. My illness prevented me from reading the play. I shall read it in eight or ten days. But it is all understood, and when I get up and out I shall fix up all the business.

John Drew, who is now free of worry concerning his new production, is to read "The Perplexed Husband" next week. I shall write you then. But the main thing is, we have the success and can take care of it. And I am extremely happy over it.

To J. A. E. Malone, the London manager, regarding the American presentation of "The Girl from Utah" and its instantaneous success:

Believe me that the success is due entirely to the *American* members, the *American* work, and, of course, the *American* stars. . . . The English numbers went for nothing. In short, the American numbers caught on.

To Haddon Chambers, in London in 1914:

There have been a number of failures already, but they would have failed if every day was a holiday.

CHARLES FROHMAN

There has been just now a new departure here in play-writing—a great success—"On Trial." This is by a boy twenty-one years of age. The scenes are laid in the court-room, and as the witness gets to the dramatic part of the story the scene changes and the characters are shown to act out the previous incidents of the story that is told in court, and then they go back to the court and work that way through the play. It has been a great sensation and is doing great business.

Concerning one of his English productions in London, he writes Dion Boucicault:

I want on my side to have you understand, however, that as far as I am concerned I am keeping the theater open for the company and the employees, and not for myself. I should have closed positively if I had not my people in mind. That was my only reason. . . .

To Dion Boucicault:

It seems to me that there are too many English actors coming over here, and I fear some of them will be in distress, because there don't seem to be positions enough for all that are coming, and people are wondering why so many are coming instead of enlisting. It might be well for you to inform some of these actors that the chances are not so great now, because there are so many here on the waiting-list. I use a great *many*, but I also use a great *many* Americans, as merit is the chief thing.

To Otis Skinner:

I felt all that you now feel about the vision effect when I saw the dress rehearsal. It looked to me like a magic-lantern scene that would be given in the cellar of a Sunday-school.

To Dion Boucicault, October, 1914:

I am despondent as to what to do in London. I'd rather close. I don't want to put on things at losses, because I do not wish to send money to cover losses to London now. The rates of exchange are something terrific, and therefore I don't want to be burdened with this extra expense. Twelve pounds on every hundred pounds is too much for any business man to handle. Over here we are feeling the effects of the war, but the big things (and I am glad to say I am in some of them) are all right.

To an English actor about to enlist in the army:

I have your letter. I am awfully sorry, but I haven't anything to offer. So therefore I congratulate the army on securing your services.

Declining an invitation for a public dinner:

I thank you very much for your very nice invitation to be present at the dinner, but I regret that, first, I do not speak at dinners, and, next, I do not attend dinners.

One of the lines that Frohman wrote very often, and which came to be somewhat hackneyed, was to to his general manager, Alf Hayman. It was:

Send me a thousand pounds to London.

To W. Lestocq, in 1914, regarding another manager:

I notice that Mr. Z—— has a man who can sign for royalties I send him. I wonder why he can't find some one to sign for royalties that are due me!

Of a production waiting to come to New York:

Broadway may throw things when we play the piece here, still I have failed before on Broadway.

To James B. Fagan, in London, December, 1912, referring to his production of "Bella Donna" in this country:

Mr. Bryant is giving an exceptionally good performance of the part, and is so much taken with my theater and company that I have the newspapers' word that he married my star (Nazimova).

CHARLES FROHMAN

To Alfred Sutro, November, 1914:

It seems to me that a strong human play, with good characters (and clean), is the thing over here; and now, my dear Sutro, I do believe that throughout the United States a play really requires a star artist, man or woman —woman for choice. . . .

To W. Lestocq, in November, 1914:

I have just returned from Chicago, where Miss Adams has a very happy and delightful program in "Leonora" and "The Ladies' Shakespeare." "The Ladies' Shakespeare" is delightful, but very slight. The little scenes that Barrie has written that are spoken before the curtain are awfully well received, but the scenes from Shakespeare's play when they are acted are very short and the whole thing is played in less than an hour. Miss Adams, of course, is delightful in it, and it goes with a sparkle with her; and as it is so slight and so much Shakespeare and so little Barrie, although the Barrie part in front of the curtain is fine, I cannot say how it would go with your audiences [referring to the London public]. I am happy in the thought, however, that Barrie has furnished Miss Adams with a program that will last her all through the season and well into the summer.

To Haddon Chambers:

Hubert Henry Davies's "Outcast" has made a hit, but he really has a wonderful woman—I should say the best young emotional actress on the stage—in Miss Ferguson. So he is in for a good thing.

To Cyril Maude, in Boston, November, 1914:

Yours to Chicago has just reached me here in New York. As soon as I heard that you were going to write me to Chicago I immediately left for New York.

I am glad you are doing so very big in Boston. They say you are going to stay all season. Things are terrible with me in London, and the interests I had outside of

414

APPENDIX A

London have been shocking. I am hoping and believing,
however, that all will be well again on the little island—
the island that I am so devoted to.

In this letter, it is worth adding, Frohman made one of his
very rare confessions of bad business. He only liked to write
about his affairs when they were booming.

To Margaret Mayo Selwyn, New York, November 30, 1914:

I was glad to receive your letter. I have been thinking
about the revival of the play you mentioned. In fact,
the thought has been a long one—three years—but I
haven't reached it yet. I have been thinking more about
the new play you are writing for me. I know you now
have a lot of theaters, a lot of managers, and a lot of
husbands and things like that, but, all the same, I *want*
that play. My best regards.

*Frohman loved sweets. He went to considerable trouble some-
times to get the particular candy he wanted. Here is a letter
that he wrote to William Newman, then manager of the Maude
Adams Company, in care of the Metropolitan Opera House,
St. Paul:*

Will you go to George Smith's Chocolate Works, 6th
and Robert Streets, St. Paul, and get four packages of
Smith's Delicious Cream Patties and send them to me
to the Knickerbocker Hotel, New York?

*Frohman had his own way of acknowledging courtesies. A
London friend, Reginald Nicholson, circulation manager of
the* Times, *sent him some flowers to the Savoy. He received
this reply from the manager, scrawled with blue pencil on a
sheet of hotel paper:*

A lot of thanks from Savoy Court 81.

Frohman's apartment for years at the Savoy Hotel was
Savoy Court 81.

CHARLES FROHMAN

To Paul Potter, written from the Blackstone, Chicago, in February, 1915:

Dear Paul:

I received your telegram, and was glad to get it. The sun is shining here and all is well. I hope to see you Saturday night at the Knickerbocker.

C. F.

This is in every way a typical Charles Frohman personal note. He usually had one thing to say and said it in the fewest possible words.

One day Frohman sent a certain play to his brother Daniel for criticism. On receiving an unfavorable estimate of the work he wrote him the following memorandum:

Who are you and who am I that can decide the financial value of this play? The most extraordinary plays succeed, and many that deserve a better fate fail; so how are we to know until after we test a play before the public?

In reply to Charles Burnham's invitation to attend the Theatrical Managers' dinner, he wrote:

Thank you very much, but my condition is still such that my game leg would require at least four seats, and as we now have at least several managers to every theater, and several theaters in every block, I haven't the heart to accept the needed room, and thus deprive them of any.

Writing to E. H. Sothern and Julia Marlowe, in April, 1915, he said:

I wonder why you don't both sail with me May 1 (*Lusitania*). As far as I am concerned, when you consider all the stars I have managed, mere submarines make me smile. But most affectionate regards to you both.

Appendix B

*A*LTOGETHER Charles Frohman produced more than
five hundred plays—a greater number than any other
manager of his time. The list of his productions,
therefore, is really a large part of the record of the
English-speaking stage during the last quarter of a century.

In the list which follows, the name of the star or stars appear immediately after the title of the piece. Except when
otherwise indicated, the theater mentioned is in New York.

Here is the complete list of Frohman's productions in
chronological order:

I

PRODUCTIONS IN AMERICA

1883

PLAY	DATE	THEATER
The Stranglers of Paris	November 12	New Park

1884

The Pulse of New York	May 10	Star
Caprice (Minnie Maddern)	November 6	Indianapolis

1885

Victor Durand	Road tour with Wallack's Theater Co.	
Moths	" " "	
Lady Clare	" " "	
Diplomacy	" " "	
La Belle Russe	" " "	
The World	" " "	

1886

PLAY	DATE	THEATER
The Golden Giant (McKee Rankin)	April 11	Fifth Avenue
A Toy Pistol (Tony Hart)	February 20	New York Comedy
A Wall Street Bandit	September 20	Standard
A Daughter of Ireland (Georgia Cayvan)	October 18	Standard
The Jilt (Dion Boucicault)	October 29	Standard

1887

| Baron Rudolph | October 24 | Fourteenth Street |
| She | November 29 | Niblo's Garden |

1888

| Held by the Enemy | | Road tour |

1889

| Shenandoah | September 9 | Star |

1890

The Private Secretary	August 26	Grand Opera House
All the Comforts of Home	September 8	Proctor's 23d Street
Men and Women	October 20	Lyceum

1891

Mr. Wilkinson's Widows	March 30	Proctor's 23d Street
Diplomacy	June 12	Los Angeles, Cal.
Jane	August 3	Madison Square
The Solicitor (Henry E. Dixey)	September 8	Hermann's
Thermidor	October 12	Proctor's 23d Street
The Man with a Hundred Heads (Henry E. Dixey)	November 2	Hermann's
Miss Helyett (Mrs. Leslie Carter)	November 3	Star
The Lost Paradise	November 16	Proctor's 23d Street
The Junior Partner	December 8	Hermann's

APPENDIX B

1892

PLAY	DATE	THEATER
Glorianna	February 15	Hermann's
Settled Out of Court	August 8	Hermann's
The Masked Ball (John Drew)	October 3	Palmer's

1893

The Girl I Left Behind Me	January 25	Empire
Ninety Days	February 6	Broadway
Liberty Hall	August 21	Empire
Fanny	September 4	Standard
The Other Man	September 4	Garden
Lady Windermere's Fan	October	Road tour
Charley's Aunt	October 2	Standard
The Younger Son	October 20	Empire
The Councillor's Wife	November 6	Empire
Aristocracy	November 14	Palmer's

1894

Sowing the Wind	January 2	Empire
Poor Girls	January 22	American
The Butterflies (John Drew)	February 5	Palmer's
Gudgeons and The Luck of Roaring Camp	May 14	Empire
The Bauble Shop (John Drew)	September 11	Empire
The New Boy	September 17	Standard
Too Much Johnson	November 26	Standard
The Masqueraders (John Drew)	December 3	Empire
The Fatal Card	December 31	Palmer's

1895

The Foundling	February 25	Hoyt's
John A'Dreams	March 18	Empire
The Importance of Being Earnest	April 22	Empire
The Sporting Duchess	August 29	Academy of Music
The City of Pleasure	September 2	Empire
That Imprudent Young Couple (John Drew)	September 22	Empire
The Gay Parisians	September 23	Hoyt's
Christopher Jr. (John Drew)	October 7	Empire

CHARLES FROHMAN

PLAY	DATE	THEATER
Denise (Olga Nethersole)	December 2	Empire
Frou Frou (Olga Nethersole)	December 5	Empire
Camille (Olga Nethersole)	December 9	Empire
Carmen (Olga Nethersole)	December 24	Empire

1896

Michael and His Lost Angel	January 15	Empire
The Squire of Dames (John Drew)	January 20	Empire
A Woman's Reason	January 27	Empire
A Social Highwayman	February 3	Garrick
(E. M. and Joseph Holland)		
Marriage	February 17	Empire
Bohemia	March 9	Empire
Thoroughbred	April 20	Garrick
Rosemary (John Drew)	August 31	Empire
The Liars	September 7	Hoyt's
Albert Chevalier	September 7	Garrick
Sue (Annie Russell)	September 15	Hoyt's
Secret Service	October 5	Garrick
Honors Are Easy	November 9	Montauk, Brooklyn
Two Little Vagrants	November 23	Academy of Music
Under the Red Robe	December 28	Empire

1897

Heartsease (Henry Miller)	January 11	Garden
Spiritissime	February 22	Knickerbocker
Never Again	March 8	Garrick
Courted Into Court	August 30	Newark, N. J.
The Little Minister	September 27	Empire
(Maude Adams)		
The Proper Caper	October 4	Hoyt's
The First Born and *A Night Session*	October 5	Manhattan
A Marriage of Convenience	November 8	Empire
(John Drew)		
The White Heather	November 22	Academy of Music

1898

Salt of the Earth	January 3	Wallack's
The Conquerors	January 4	Empire
The Circus Girl	January 17	Columbia, Brooklyn

424

APPENDIX B

PLAY	DATE	THEATER
Oh, Susannah	February 7	Hoyt's
One Summer's Day (John Drew)	February 14	Wallack's
The Master (Henry Miller)	February 15	Garden
Little Miss Nobody	September 5	Philadelphia
A Brace of Partridges	September 7	Madison Square
The Countess Valeska	September 26	Troy, N. Y.
(Julia Marlowe)		
On and Off	October 17	Madison Square
Catherine (Annie Russell)	October 24	Garrick
As You Like It (Julia Marlowe)	November 7	Omaha, Nebraska
Phroso	December 26	Empire
Ingomar (Julia Marlowe)	December 26	Indianapolis

1899

Because She Loved Him So	January 16	Madison Square
Her Atonement	February 13	Academy of Music
Lord and Lady Algy	February 14	Empire
The Cuckoo	April 3	Wallack's
Colinette (Julia Marlowe)	April 10	Knickerbocker
Romeo and Juliet	May 8	Empire
(Maude Adams)		
His Excellency the Governor	May 22	Empire
Hamlet (Henry Miller)	August 1	San Francisco
The Girl from Maxim's	August 29	Criterion
Miss Hobbs (Annie Russell)	September 7	Lyceum
The Tyranny of Tears	September 11	Empire
(John Drew)		
The Only Way (Henry Miller)	September 16	Herald Square
Barbara Fritchie	October 23	Criterion
(Julia Marlowe)		
Sherlock Holmes (William Gillette)	November 6	Garrick
Make Way for the Ladies	November 13	Madison Square
My Lady's Lord	December 25	Empire

1900

Brother Officers	January 15	Empire
The Surprises of Love	January 22	Lyceum
Coralie & Co., Dressmakers	February 5	Madison Square
Hearts Are Trumps	February 21	Garden
My Daughter-in-Law	February 26	Lyceum
A Man and His Wife and *The Bugle Call*	April 2	Empire
The Tree of Knowledge	July 2	San Francisco
(Henry Miller)		

28

425

CHARLES FROHMAN

PLAY	DATE	THEATER
A Royal Family (Annie Russell)	September 5	Lyceum
The Rose of Persia	September 6	Daly's
The Husband of Leontine	September 8	Madison Square
Richard Carvel (John Drew)	September 11	Empire
David Harum (W. H. Crane)	October 1	Garrick
Self and Lady	October 8	Madison Square
L'Aiglon (Maude Adams)	October 22	Knickerbocker

1901

Mrs. Dane's Defense	January 7	Empire
The Girl from Up There (Edna May)	January 8	Herald Square
My Lady Dainty (Herbert Kelcey and Effie Shannon)	January 8	Madison Square
Captain Jinks (Ethel Barrymore)	February 4	Garrick
Under Two Flags	February 5	Garden
The Lash of a Whip	February 25	Lyceum
To Have and To Hold	March 4	Knickerbocker
Manon Lescaut (Kelcey and Shannon)	March 19	Wallack's
Are You a Mason?	April 1	Wallack's
A Royal Rival (William Faversham)	August 26	Criterion
The Second in Command (John Drew)	September 2	Empire
A Message from Mars (Charles Hawtrey)	October 7	Garrick
Eben Holden	October 28	Savoy
Quality Street (Maude Adams)	November 11	Knickerbocker
Alice of Old Vincennes (Virginia Harned)	December 2	Garden
The Girl and the Judge (Annie Russell)	December 4	Lyceum
The Wilderness	December 23	Empire
Sweet and Twenty	December 30	Madison Square

1902

Colorado	January 12	Grand Opera House
The Twin Sister	March 3	Empire
Sky Farm	March 17	Garrick
The New Clown	August 25	Garrick
The Mummy and the Humming-Bird (John Drew)	September 4	Empire

426

APPENDIX B

PLAY	DATE	THEATER
There's Many a Slip	September 15 ..	Garrick
Aunt Jeanne	September 16 ..	Garden
(Mrs. Patrick Campbell)		
Iris (Virginia Harned)	September 22 ..	Criterion
Two Schools	September 29 ..	Madison Square
The Second Mrs. Tanqueray	October 6	Garden
(Mrs. Patrick Campbell)		
A Country Mouse and *Carrots*	October 6	Savoy
(Ethel Barrymore)		
Everyman	October 12	Mendelssohn Hall
(Edith Wynne Mathison and Charles Rann Kennedy)		
The Joy of Living	October 23	Garden
(Mrs. Patrick Campbell)		
Imprudence (William Faversham) .	November 7 ...	Lyceum
The Girl with the Green Eyes	December 25 ..	Savoy
(Clara Bloodgood)		

1903

PLAY	DATE	THEATER
A Bird in the Cage	January 12	Bijou
The Unforeseen	January 12	Empire
Mice and Men (Annie Russell) ...	January 19	Garrick
Three Little Maids (G. P. Huntley) .	August 31	Daly's
Ulysses	September 14 ..	Garden
Drink (Charles Warner)	September 14 ..	Academy of Music
The Man from Blankley's	September 14 ..	Criterion
(Charles Hawtrey)		
Captain Dieppe (John Drew)	September 14 ..	Herald Square
Lady Rose's Daughter	September 24 ..	Garrick
(Fay Davis)		
The Spenders (W. H. Crane)	October 5	Savoy
The Best of Friends	October 19	Academy of Music
Cousin Kate (Ethel Barrymore) ..	October 19	Hudson
Charlotte Wiehe (French Players) .	October 21	Vaudeville
The Girl from Kay's	November 2 ...	Herald Square
(Sam Bernard)		
The Pretty Sister of José	November 9 ...	Empire
(Maude Adams)		
The Admirable Crichton	November 16 ..	Lyceum
(William Gillette)		
Elizabeth's Prisoner	November 23 ..	Criterion
(William Faversham)		
Whitewashing Julia	December 2 ...	Garrick
(Fay Davis)		
The Other Girl	December 23 ..	Criterion
Glad of It (Millie James)	December 28 ..	Savoy

CHARLES FROHMAN

1904

PLAY	DATE	THEATER
My Lady Molly (Andrew Mack)	January 4	Daly's
The Light that Lies in Woman's Eyes (Virginia Harned)	January 25	Criterion
The Younger Mrs. Parling (Annie Russell)	January 25	Garrick
Man Proposes (Henry Miller)	March 14	Hudson
The Dictator (William Collier)	April 4	Criterion
Saucy Sally (Charles Hawtrey)	April 4	Lyceum
Camille (Margaret Anglin and Henry Miller)	April 18	Hudson
When Knighthood Was in Flower (Julia Marlowe)	May 2	Empire
Yvette (Hattie Williams)	May 12	Knickerbocker
Ben Greet Players	October 5	
The School Girl (Edna May)	September 1	Daly's
The Duke of Klliecrankie (John Drew)	September 5	Empire
Letty (William Faversham)	September 12	Hudson
Business is Business (W. H. Crane)	September 19	Hudson
The Coronet of the Duchess (Clara Bloodgood)	September 21	Garrick
The Sorceress (Mrs. Patrick Campbell)	October 10	New Amsterdam
Joseph Entangled (Henry Miller)	October 10	Garrick
Shakespearian Repertory (Julia Marlowe and E. H. Sothern)	October 17	Knickerbocker
Granny (Mrs. G. H. Gilbert)	October 24	Lyceum
David Garrick (Charles Wyndham)	November 14	Lyceum
The Rich Mrs. Repton (Fay Davis)	November 14	Criterion
Sunday (Ethel Barrymore)	November 14	Hudson
Brother Jacques (Annie Russell)	December 5	Garrick
Mrs. Goringe's Necklace (Charles Wyndham)	December 12	Lyceum
A Wife Without a Smile (Margaret Illington)	December 19	Criterion

1905

Cousin Billy (Francis Wilson)	January 2	Criterion
The Case of Rebellious Susan (Charles Wyndham)	January 9	Lyceum

428

APPENDIX B

PLAY	DATE	THEATER
Mrs. Leffingwell's Boots	January 11	.... Savoy
Friquet (Marie Doro)	January 30	.... Savoy
'Op o' My Thumb	February 6	.... Empire
(Maude Adams)		
Jinny the Carrier (Annie Russell) .	April 10	...... Criterion
The Freedom of Suzanne	April 17	...... Empire
(Marie Tempest)		
The Rollicking Girl	May 1	.... Herald Square
(Sam Bernard)		
A Doll's House	May 2	.... Lyceum.
(Ethel Barrymore)		
The Catch of the Season	August 28	..... Daly's
(Edna May)		
De Lancey (John Drew)	September 4	... Empire
The Beauty and the Barge	September 6	... Lyceum
(Nat C. Goodwin)		
Just Out of College	September 27	.. Lyceum
(Joseph Wheelock)		
Shakespearian Repertory	October 16	.... Knickerbocker
(Julia Marlowe and E. H. Sothern)		
Wolfville (Nat C. Goodwin)	October 20	.... Philadelphia
Peter Pan (Maude Adams)	November 6	... Empire
On the Quiet (William Collier) ...	November 27	.. Criterion
La Belle Marseillaise	November 27	.. Knickerbocker
(Virginia Harned)		
Alice Sit By the Fire and *Pantaloon* .	December 25	.. Criterion
(Ethel Barrymore)		

1906

Mispah	January 22	.... Baltimore
The Duel (Otis Skinner)	February 12	... Criterion
The Mountain Climber	March 5	...... Criterion
(Francis Wilson)		
The American Lord (W. H. Crane) .	April 16	...... Hudson
The Little Father of the Wilderness .	April 16	...... Criterion
The Little Cherub	August 6	...... Criterion
(Hattie Williams)		
The Price of Money	August 29	..... Garrick
(W. H. Crane)		
The Hypocrites	August 30	..... Hudson
(Doris Keane and Richard Bennett)		
The Judge and Jury	September 1	... Wallack's
His House in Order (John Drew) .	September 3	... Empire
Clarice (William Gillette)	October 15	.... Garrick

CHARLES FROHMAN

PLAY	DATE	THEATER
The House of Mirth (Fay Davis)..October 22....Savoy		
(William Collier)		
The Rich Mr. Hoggenheimer......October 22....Wallack's		
(Sam Bernard)		
Caught in the Rain............December 31..Garrick		

1907

The Truth (Clara Bloodgood)....January 7.....Criterion
Captain Brassbound's Conversion.January 28....Empire
(Ellen Terry)
Good Hope and *Nance Oldfield*....February 11...Empire
(Ellen Terry)
The Silver Box (Ethel Barrymore).March 18.....Empire
When Knights Were Bold........August 20.....Garrick
(Francis Wilson)
The Dairymaids................August 26.....Criterion
(Julia Sanderson and G. P. Huntley)
My Wife (John Drew)..........August 31.....Empire
The Thief.....................September 9...Lyceum
(Margaret Illington and Kyrle Bellew)
The Morals of Marcus..........November 18..Criterion
(Marie Doro)
The Toymaker of Nuremberg......November 25..Garrick
Her Sister (Ethel Barrymore)....December 25..Hudson
Miss Hook of Holland..........December 31..Criterion
(Thomas Wise)

1908

The Jesters (Maude Adams).....January 13....Empire
Twenty Days in the Shade......January 20....Savoy
(Pauline Frederick and Richard Bennett)
The Honor of the Family........February 17...Hudson
(Otis Skinner)
The Irish Players..............February 17...Savoy
Father and the Boys (W. H. Crane).March 2.....Empire
Toddles (John Barrymore)......March 16.....Garrick
Love Watches (Billie Burke)......August 27.....Lyceum
The Mollusc...................September 2...Garrick
(Alexandra Carlisle and Joseph Coyne)
The Girls of Gottenberg.........September 2...Knickerbocker
(Gertie Millar)
Diana of Bobson's.............September 5...Savoy
(Carlotta Nilsson)
Fluffy Ruffles (Hattie Williams)..September 7...Criterion

APPENDIX B

PLAY	DATE	THEATER
Jack Straw (John Drew)........September 14..Empire
Miss Hook of Holland...........October 2.....Albany
(Frank Daniels)
Samson (William Gillette).......October 19....Criterion
Lady Frederick (Ethel Barrymore).November 9...Hudson
The Patriot (William Collier)....November 23..Garrick
The Sicilian Players............November 23..Broadway
What Every Woman Knows......December 23..Empire
(Maude Adams)

1909

Kitty Grey (G. P. Huntley)......January 25....New Amsterdam
The Richest Girl (Marie Doro)...March 1......Criterion
An Englishman's Home..........March 23.....Criterion
The Happy Marriage............April 12.......Garrick
(Doris Keane and Edwin Arden)
The Mollusc....................June 7........Empire
(Sir Charles Wyndham and Mary Moore)
Isadora Duncan in Classical
Dances...................August 18.....Criterion
Detective Sparkes...............August 23.....Garrick
(Hattie Williams)
Arsène Lupin (William Courtnay).August 26.....Lyceum
The Flag Lieutenant.............August 30.....Criterion
(Bruce McRae)
The Dollar Princess............September 6...Knickerbocker
(Donald Brian)
Inconstant George (John Drew)....September 20..Empire
Samson (James K. Hackett).....October 1.....Atlantic City
The Harvest Moon (George Nash).October 15....Garrick
Israel (Constance Collier)......October 25....Criterion
A Builder of Bridges...........October 26....Hudson
(Kyrle Bellew)
Penelope (Marie Tempest).......December 13..Lyceum
The Bachelor's Baby............December 27..Criterion
(Francis Wilson)
Fires of Fate..................December 28..Liberty

1910

Your Humble Servant...........January 3.....Garrick
(Otis Skinner)
The Arcadians (Julia Sanderson)..January 17....Liberty
A Lucky Star (William Collier)..January 18....Hudson
Mrs. Dot (Billie Burke)........January 24....Lyceum

CHARLES FROHMAN

APPENDIX B

CHARLES FROHMAN

1892

PLAY	DATE	THEATER
The Lost Paradise..............December 22..Adelphi

1896

A Night Out..................April 29......Vaudeville

1897

My Friend the Prince...........February 13...Garrick
Secret Service (William Gillette)...May 15.......Adelphi
Never Again...................October 11....Vaudeville

1898

The Heart of Maryland..........April 8.......Adelphi
   (Mrs. Leslie Carter)
Too Much Johnson..............April 19......Garrick
Sue...........................June 10.......Garrick
Adventures of Lady Ursula.......October 11....Duke of York's
On and Off....................December 1...Vaudeville

1899

My Daughter-in-Law............September 27..Criterion
The Christian..................October 16....Duke of York's
Miss Hobbs...................December 18..Duke of York's

1900

The Masked Ball...............January 6.....Criterion
Zaza (Mrs. Leslie Carter).......April 16......Garrick
Madame Butterfly..............April 28......Duke of York's
Kitty Grey....................September 7...Apollo
Self and Lady.................September 19..Vaudeville
The Lackey's Carnival..........September 28..Duke of York's
The Swashbuckler..............November 17..Duke of York's
Alice in Wonderland...........December 19..Vaudeville

436

APPENDIX B

1901

PLAY	DATE	THEATER
The Girl from Up There (Edna May)	April 23	Duke of York's
Sweet and Twenty	April 24	Vaudeville
Sherlock Holmes	September 9	Lyceum
Are You a Mason?	September 12	Shaftesbury
Bluebell in Fairyland	December 8	Vaudeville

1902

The Twin Sister	January 1	Duke of York's
The Girl from Maxim's	March 20	Criterion
All on Account of Eliza	April 3	Shaftesbury
Three Little Maids (Edna May)	May 10	Apollo
The Marriage of Kitty	August 19	Duke of York's
Quality Street	September 17	Vaudeville

1903

The School Girl (Edna May)	May 9	Duke of York's
Billy's Little Love Affair	September 2	Criterion
Little Mary	September 24	Wyndham's
Letty	October 8	Duke of York's
The Cherry Girl	December 21	Vaudeville
Madame Sherry	December 23	Apollo

1904

Love in a Cottage	January 27	Terry's
Captain Dieppe	February 15	Duke of York's
The Duke of Killiecrankie	January 20	Criterion
The Rich Mrs. Repton	April 20	Duke of York's
Cynthia	May 16	Wyndham's
Merely Mary Ann	September 8	Duke of York's
The Catch of the Season	September 9	Vaudeville
The Wife Without a Smile	October 12	Wyndham's
The Freedom of Suzanne	November 15	Criterion
Peter Pan	December 27	Duke of York's

1905

The Lady of Leeds	February 9	Wyndham's
Alice Sit By The Fire	April 5	Duke of York's

CHARLES FROHMAN

PLAY	DATE	THEATER
Widow of Wasdale Head........October 14....Duke of York's
Overruled......................October 14....Duke of York's

1913

The Adored One...............September 4...Duke of York's
The Will.....................September 4...Duke of York's
Years of Discretion............September 8...Globe

1914

The Land of Promise...........February 28...Duke of York's
The Little Minister.............September 3...Duke of York's

1915

Rosy Rapture..................March 22.....Duke of York's
The New Word.................March 22.....Duke of York's

III

Charles Frohman's productions in Paris were these:

Secret Service...................May 25, 1900..Théâter Renaissance
Peter Pan......................June 1, 1909...Vaudeville
Peter Pan......................June 2, 1910...Vaudeville

THE END

100 — bookplates
112 Cuvier